Balaam's Reward

Forty years of desert exile were almost over. The river Jordan, gateway to a lush, fertile region, Israel's to occupy by right of divine edict, was less than ten miles to the east. But before they could cross over and begin occupation, the four tribes inhabiting the west sides of Jordan would have to be dealt with. Otherwise, the Israelites would be vulnerable to attack from all directions. The Amorites, the Bashanites, the Ammonites and the Moabites—these four tribes were all that remained between Israel, and the *promised land*.

The Amorites were the first to be defeated, followed by the Bashanites. Both had been battles in which Israel faced superior forces. Moses was too old for the thrill of these first two victories to affect him. The same could not be said for his men who fought. Confidence was strewn everywhere. There was a sheen to the whole camp, like the deep ruddy glow that emanates from young, oiled muscles. Energy lay tightly coiled, probing for an outlet, insisting to be let loose.

— ♦ —

Balak, king of the Moabites, was too agitated to participate in the festivities. Sihon, the Amorite king, the one who had executed his father, Zippor, in public view, was now dead himself. The heavy tribute extracted from Balak these past years would cease. Perhaps some land could even be reclaimed. Celebrations to mark these changes were spontaneously breaking out everywhere. But what of the peoples who had defeated Sihon? Israelites, they were called, sons of Jacob, a tribe of slaves that had escaped Egypt forty years earlier. And now they were camped within sight of Moabite borders, less than a day's march away. An invisible god was said to protect them. A powerful *barû* led them. His staff held great and terrible power. Dry rock would gush forth water at its touch. They had crossed through a part of the Red Sea on dry ground while their leader held his stick—his *maqqel*—out over the water, commanding it to retreat into two vertical walls. The pursuing Egyptian army had been drowned by the walls' subsequent collapse once the barû had withdrawn his stick. It was said that their god threw down white cakes of grain from his storehouse each morning, enough for the whole people to eat. Their clothes and sandals never wore out. Other stories about these desert nomads circulated. Balak did not know where truth left off and legend began. Nonetheless, the dread he felt would not leave him.

A dozen smaller offshoot clans from the family tribe of Midian lived peacefully within Balak's territory. Each clan was ruled absolutely by a noble elder, and when common concerns required it, they were included in the provisional councils presided over by King Balak. He called such a gathering to consider their new state of affairs.

"Fellow nobles," he began, "the celebrations occurring in our towns are, in my considered judgment, premature. It is true this new tribe, descended, as it were, out of the desert sky, has lifted from our shoulders the chains of Sihon. But is this a moment to be glad? Surely we cannot expect them to leave us unmolested. No, this horde is going to lick up everything around them like an ox licks up the grass in the field. They have already ranged north and returned victors over Og, ruler of Bashan. The Ammonites will sit behind their well-garrisoned chain of border fortresses. Westward, Jericho can withstand a siege of almost any length. Our lands lie open, on their south flank. We are the opportunity of least risk for them. Their gods are strong; their magic is powerful. Chemosh our patron did not help us overly much against the Amorites, and this tribe is even stronger. Our fighting men, even if combined with your kinsmen to the south of us, could never hope to win. And yet, I for one am not willing simply to place my neck meekly under the foot of another tyrant. What is to be done?"

— ♦ —

Balaam[1] was in his sixtieth year when the delegation from the king of Moab petitioned him. He was not overly surprised, but by then there was very little that could do that. Besides, his own private intelligence had already heralded their arrival. To look at him casually there was little to indicate his extraordinary power. He was of average height, with short-cropped hair that was now more grey than black, clean shaven and not yet gone to fat. Stripped of his clothes, his body would have revealed more than the usual number of scars. If asked about them, Balaam would have shrugged them off as a necessary part of his profession. Some of the more complex sorcery required self-mutilation, and if cutting one's own skin was part of summoning up the appropriate daimon from the spirit world, so be it. Balaam was, above everything else, a professional. Besides, drawing one's own blood made an impressive spectacle and Balaam held good showmanship in high regard.

But if his appearance did not advertise his power, certainly the arrival of his visitors did. The fact that they had traveled more than three hundred miles north from their lands, bypassing a dozen men who worked the same trade as Balaam, spoke volumes about the sphere of Balaam's influence. Of all the godkeepers that operated in the fertile crescent, Balaam was the best. Whether it was among the Egyptians, the Kassites of Babylon, the Assyrians, the Hittites, his own Mittani citizens, or the hundreds of tribes and city states that existed within these larger empires, Balaam's reputation was well established.

His home was near Carchemish, a city that lay about seventy miles from the northeast corner of the Mediterranean Sea, in the land of Amaw. He was Mittani by birth, coming from one of the smaller empires lying between the Assyrians and the Hittites. But although small, they ruled their territory without interference from either of their aggressive neighbours. Earlier generations had perfected the horse-drawn war chariot with wheels bound by bronze hoops. On their relatively flat plains these war vehicles made it possible to withstand odds as high as ten attackers for every defender. Beyond their own borders, however, where the terrain changed, the chariots were not of much use, and they therefore did not seek to expand their influence. Instead they reaped the benefits of long years of peace. Their cities were beautified, and artistic endeavours flourished. It had made for a proud and arrogant ethnic group, and not without justification.

Not even Balaam could have told you precisely what he was. In his more indiscreet moments, deep in his cups, he would say that he was more show than substance. Even that self-assessment was not entirely accurate. It was true that he maintained his own private intelligence network, which kept him better informed than the courtiers of most kingdoms. And, if this proprietary information allowed him to speak of the future with greater accuracy, what of it? The clients remained well served, and who cared whether it was from the lips of the gods or from one of his own paid spies that the information came? The gods should not be bothered unnecessarily.

But his retinue of retainers was only a very small contributor to his reputation. Balaam's genius lay in his ability to weave together into a seamless whole, the best of showmanship with genuine communications from the gods.

People sought out Balaam for all kinds of services. Individuals would come with troublesome dreams, wanting an interpretation. They would come to seek the will of their gods in some contemplated adventure. People harbouring grudges against others would come asking for curses. And just as many would come seeking a blessing on some loved one. His was no showy ersatz, although he paid close attention to the staging of his more elaborate performances. People always got what they paid for. His reputation rested on the effectiveness of his blessings, the strength of his curses and the accuracy of his oracles. Balaam delivered.

He had observed, over time, that many people cared less about the specifics of his messages than that the gods had deigned to notice them at all. Poverty, pestilence, wars—these could be endured as part of life. It was the terror of being isolated, an abandoned cosmic orphan, that motivated much of his trade. Even the poorest of the poor needed the patronage of some deity, however humble. And in return, homage was given. Specific directives were often quite secondary. A bit of simple conjuring, perhaps to set the scene (Balaam had several magic maqqels), good use of research when it was appropriate, some general oracles taken from any of the hundreds of *meshalims* he knew by heart and then a somewhat obscure pronouncement in the name of the god being implored—who could determine what the active ingredient was? He was utterly sincere in the powers of the deities, into whose world he would tiptoe like some respectful visitor. It was why he did not venture in if it was not necessary. It was a sincerity that kept him alive. Early in his training, while still apprenticing with an old seer, he had watched the death of a friend and fellow student. His friend, though talented, had exhibited a certain flippancy toward the inhabitants of the underworld. They were called *the Rephaim*, these disembodied souls of the dead, and were accepted as lesser citizens by the assortment of powerful gods who lived there. The two had slipped out once, intent on practising a necromantic ritual without the supervision of their master. A herb mixture had been ingested—a compound that loosened the bonds between body and mind, allowing their minds to float somewhat disconnected from their bodies. His friend had been mocking, calling on the spirits to send up their strongest so that they might have sport. Balaam remembered watching his friend, one minute sitting cross-legged, eyes closed, uttering impetuous demands for someone to come forth, and the next being squeezed violently around the neck, body raised straight up until his feet left the ground altogether. His eyes bulged and his tongue pushed through his teeth, lips curling back on themselves to form a frozen grisly grin. Someone *had* come, and the sport had been swift indeed.

Balaam was the most expert augur of his day, this having been his first training. He knew from memory the thousand-odd minute behaviours of birds that were known to be reliable indicators of future events. Birds eating, birds at rest, in flight, attacking one another or merely congregating—there was very little orniskopia that did not shadow a corollary event within the world of mortals. Augury had first established his reputation, but he had not been content with that skill alone. Balaam was one of those rare individuals whose ego was matched in size only by his exceptional capabilities and as a result Balaam propelled himself both deeper into the magical arts and higher in the eyes of others.

He was a barû—an oracle speaker—obtaining and delivering messages to his clients from any of a number of the gods who lived in the world above, or in the one below. It was a powerful position. Every ruler, no matter how lowly, retained a barû who spoke the voice of the god they served. Kings were circumspect in their treatment of barûs, and as a practical matter, a good barû commanded as much power as the throne. Most barûs established a liaison with only one god. Balaam was singular in that he could speak on behalf of many.

In his early years Balaam had practised blacker powers. Clay miniatures of the intended victims were fashioned and then manipulated through the actions intended for their fleshly equivalents. It was rumoured that once he had stopped an entire army through this technique, carefully fashioning the tiny clay warriors only to sting their eyes with a blinding powder. He tolerated no students. Other practitioners held him in awe and some fear. Twenty years earlier one of his distant colleagues, a man who had shown great promise, was found one morning in his barred bedroom, run through with a large wooden shaft. No one ever took the credit, or the blame, but it was whispered that Balaam was the only one with skill enough to have done it.

Balaam knew the limits of his intercessory role with the gods. If a blessing or curse could not be wheedled, coaxed or bribed out of the god's mouth, Balaam knew better than to fabricate a more favourable response. Nor did he ever taunt the astrals on their own limitations. For in truth he found the gods to be a mixed bag of skills and virtues. Some were immutably rooted in their geographical jurisdictions. Some were slaves to their own appetites, willing to bestow favours in exchange for sacrifices with a compulsion not seen on earth. And some existed only in the minds of their adherents. Did Balaam ever wonder if he, perhaps, could impersonate the voice of the gods from time to time, with greater accuracy and to greater benefit to himself and his clients? It was a tantalizing thought. It would always remain pure speculation.

By the time he was sixty, Balaam had acquired a permanent taste for the creaturely comforts made possible from his rich divination fees. To retire was unthinkable. He spent always up to the limit of his wages and sometimes a little beyond. "It fostered," he told his wife one day, "a most powerful concentration whenever approaching a particularly lucrative assignment." And his ego had grown, lockstep with his fame.

Balaam received the messengers of King Moab with great courtesy. The visitors, once the audience with Balaam began, were formal in their requests.

"Balak our king requires the aid of a great barû. Strong magic prevails against us and can be beaten only by like forces. It is our only salvation from a savage tribe come of late out of Egypt. With ravenous stomachs they consume the kingdoms of Canaan. Their barû is strong. His maqqel can do great things. Only Balaam, whose blessings are as certain as the sun, only Balaam, whose curses are as sure as night, only Balaam can protect us. Come, put a curse on these scavengers."

Balaam in fact knew much more about these "scavengers" than the delegation did. He began carefully.

"These people who are camped beside your lands are indeed powerful. The King of Moab is like a grasshopper in their sight. The princes of Midian, with all their goods, could not satisfy their appetite for even a day."

"If it is too hard a thing for Balaam to do, we ask your leave to depart." A younger prince had spoken. "Our quest is urgent. Perhaps there is another who can help. The fee for the services we seek must be spent somewhere."

"I did not say I *could* not help you," answered Balaam, unruffled. "And if you can find someone else with better access to the heavens, then please, do not let me detain you a minute longer."

"Forgive the excesses of our younger friend," interjected an older delegate. "Balaam is a true servant of the world above. Balaam will do what Balaam will do. *Fee* was a poor choice of words. The gift we have brought is only to show our gratitude for the timely help we seek."

"The point is..." began Balaam in his most conspiratorial tone. Having won the round he could now afford to be familiar. "The point is, there is only one god in all the heavens who can curse these sons of Jacob. It is their own god. Yahweh is his name. This is the god that goes before them, sowing dread into the hearts of their enemies."

"And do you know this god?"

"I know all gods. I know the great Yahweh, who leads these people. I know Mamu of the Akkadians. I knew his rival god Ninhursag, wickedly slain by Mamu. I know Nammur of the Summerians out of whose belly came the lands they occupy. I know Anat, sister to Baal, and I know Mot, whose hands hold the weapons of drought and sterility and who was hacked to pieces by Anat, yet not extinguished. And I also know Tefnut, Shu, Geb and Nepthys. I know Apis, Hathor, Nut and Re. I know all these gods of the Egyptians. And I see them sitting down, still tending their wounds received at the hands of Yahweh when he freed these people forty years ago." Balaam paused to let them digest his list. He had deliberately omitted naming Chemosh, their own god, who also inhabited Sheol, or Baal, whom the Midianites worshipped at Peor. If either of their own deities was of any use, they would not have come to Balaam. He was careful not to insult his clients or shame them unduly. At the same time he wanted to impress on them the difficulty of their request. As yet, Israel's god had prevailed against all others.

"Will you curse these people for us, Balaam?"

"In truth, I cannot answer you yet. Stay the night. I will seek an audience with their god and see how best to persuade him to remove his protection. Perhaps he can be persuaded to return to the top of Mount Horeb from whence he is said to have come. Only if their *El* abandons them, will my curse have any effect."

That night Balaam did seek Yahweh. Though he had not lied to the delegation when he said he knew the Israelite's god, he had been in contact with him only once before and even that had been a peripheral encounter. What he knew, and knew in great detail, was the acts of this god. He had studied the plagues of Egypt that had coincided with the Israelites' departure. He had investigated minutely the migration of the quail that had veered off their usual course to land, literally, into the very cook pots of these people. This was an augur of immense scale and without precedent. All who practised the art were aware of it. None knew precisely what future event it referenced. But all were in agreement that whatever it meant, it would be an action of enormous import. He had attempted to secure some of the white bread that was said to fall out of the sky each night around their campsite, but without success. He had tried to steal the maqqel of their dead high priest, Aaron, and had gotten nowhere. It was said to lie within a great golden box, watched over by winged daimons.

That night Yahweh's voice reached Balaam.

"You have visitors," the voice began.

"Emissaries from the King of Moab," said Balaam. " I am asked to curse the people come out of Egypt, that Moab might prevail against them, and drive them away."

"Those are my people, Balaam. You are not to go back with these men. And you will certainly not utter curses, for these people are blessed." The interview was ended. Balaam had been summarily dismissed. It did not put him in a good humour next morning as he reported on the night's divination.

"Yahweh forbids that I go with you," said Balaam.

"But what of our need for a curse?" asked one of the elders.

"Balaam will do what Balaam will do," replied Balaam, echoing yesterday's words back to them. "And Balaam will not go with you." Balaam walked out of his own reception chamber leaving them as irritated at him as he was at Yahweh. This thing is not over, thought Balaam to himself.

— ◆ —

Balak did not receive the news well.

"He's holding out for a larger fee and in the meantime we have wasted almost two months. He knows our plight, and with the scruples of a snake, he's going to squeeze me until there is nothing left in my treasury. I send you to make a simple request and you come home looking like fools—hill-country simpletons, the whole lot of you. Balaam is probably having the laugh of his life right now at my expense."

The delegation suffered his rage in silence. Finally the eldest of the delegation spoke.

"It is possible that Balaam's refusal is simply a negotiating ruse. But Balak, consider the problem from his perspective. Does a seer get rich by *not* uttering curses? He knew of our willingness to pay. It is no secret that he accepts all colours of money. Is it possible that he was telling the truth?" The heated discourse flowed in its perfectly predictable path retracing all the topics of their first council meeting, coming to rest finally on what was still the only viable option: Balaam would have to be revisited.

Another contingent was assembled and dispatched. They were more senior. They were more numerous. They had more latitude. They carried more gold. But their mission was still the same. Somehow Balaam was to be enticed to return with them and put a curse on the Israelites.

— ◆ —

Balaam was genuinely glad to receive his second set of guests and went out of his way to render the appropriate honours. The journey had not been easy for some of the older nobles—men whose traveling days were long since over. Their obvious sense of duty was worthy of respect. But when their request was finally broached, the same abyss opened up in front of them.

Their leader put their case succinctly.

"All of what we tell you is already known to you. King Balak, son of Zippor, has urgent need of your skills. This pestilence, recently crept in from the desert, must be destroyed. A military operation against them would fail miserably. Only Balaam's words have the strength to turn these people aside. Balak's reward to Balaam will be generous."

Balaam bowed low to the ground.

"You do me great honour, as does Balak, whose promise of wealth and office is humbly acknowledged. Were it in my power, I would accept at once. But if Balaam has had some small success, it is only because Balaam is no more than a humble servant of the heavens. He says neither more, nor less than what the gods direct. And you know already Yahweh's will in this matter."

17

"And is it only Yahweh who can give you leave?" It was the oldest of them who asked, a hawkish man with pointed features. The man looked old enough to have been Balaam's father. Both his voice and gesture were utterly without deference. It was the probing of a man too old to waste time on anything less than the truth. "Yahweh is not a name familiar to me. Has Nut fallen from the sky? Has Dagon drowned in the sea? Has El, the supreme god of the council, become besotted? Has Mot lost the strength of his jaws? Has Marduk, the greatest warrior in all the heavens, laid down his bow? Have all other astrals fled, leaving this Yahweh to reign alone? Does Balaam shift his loyalty to this new god so easily that he forgets how to summon any others? Or perhaps the truth is that other gods no longer pay attention to Balaam?"

The room was suddenly very quiet. The old man had voiced things others had only thought about. Balaam met the old man's gaze squarely.

"Does a servant choose his master? Is it for me to dismiss the dream of Yahweh and demand that some other god appear before me? Does the servant ask of his master which among them has perished? Am I permitted to count the empty seats in El's council chamber? You have not been afraid to challenge me, aged father, and so I will tell you. Unless Yahweh himself curses these people they will not be cursed. He surrounds them like city walls. Yet he moves with them. Surely your own scouts will confirm at least something of what I tell you. Do you deny that a dense white cloud hovers over their camp by day, impervious to wind? Tell me you have not crept out to see the tower of fire that appears at night, so high into the sky that you can see every detail of the great tent over which it sits. Is Yahweh the only living god? No! Is Yahweh the only god in whose name Balaam can utter a curse worthy of Balak's gold? Yes! In the business of Jacob's welfare, Yahweh's will prevails. Let Yahweh be induced to breach his walls, let him be tempted to depart from this tribe and go back to Horeb, then there would be all manner of gods with power to harm. But unless that happens, Balak's gold is useless, and Balaam would be a thief to accept it."

"So there is nothing that you can do for us?" another noble asked.

"Stay the night," replied Balaam. "I will ask Yahweh's mind in this matter again. Perhaps I did not understand him when he approached last time." He ended with a weak smile. "Gods have been known to change their minds."

Yahweh's voice came to Balaam that night. "You have more visitors."

"I have done only what you have ordered," Balaam replied. "They have returned without any encouragement from me. In this matter I am blameless."

"I wonder..." said the voice. "Did you tell them everything I told you at my last visitation? I do not recall you telling your first visitors that the reason you could not go is because these sons of Jacob are blessed."

Balaam was silent. The voice did not seem angry. But one had to be careful. Finally he said, "Blessings can be withdrawn, and in their place, curses. If the Israelites prove unworthy of the protection granted them by Yahweh, perhaps you would consider the petitions of your unworthy servant and depart from this ungrateful tribe whom you rescued out of Egypt."

"Do I need Balak's gold that I can be bought?" the voice asked.

Careful. Be ever so careful, thought Balaam. There is a small opening here. He replied. "Does not Yahweh hear all petitions fairly? Are not his judgments impartial?" Balaam waited, hardly breathing, waiting for a response. He knew the risks he was taking; he might never waken if Yahweh became angry at his impertinence. Still, to bend the will of the deities to the purposes of men—this was his craft! Balaam could not back away from this encounter. And in truth, there was something exhilarating about the confrontation he sensed lay before him.

"Balaam, since Balak, son of Zippor, King of Moab, continues to press you, it pleases me to let you return with this delegation. But Balaam, listen to me very, very carefully. You will do and say only what I tell you. Nothing more. Nothing less." The voice had never once become threatening. Balaam could get no measure of the strength that lay behind it. This would be an interesting contest indeed!

Balaam smiled in his sleep. "Of course."

Next morning Balaam met his guests in the courtyard dressed for travel. Any self-deprecation he might have demonstrated the previous evening was utterly gone. Once more he was the smooth, urbane seer, favourably esteemed by all, a master godkeeper. He exuded control.

"Judging from your cloak, you've decided to journey south with us after all." It was the eldest noble, the one who had so bluntly cross-examined him the night before.

"The omens were favourable," demurred Balaam. "I have at least been permitted to return with you. Beyond that, who knows the mind of Yahweh? But come, let us be off. Balak is not accustomed to waiting, I am sure."

"Balak has been kept waiting for almost four months," snorted the eldest, who was not in the least impressed with Balaam's newly discovered urgency.

"Through no fault of my own, to be sure," said Balaam.

The party left by mid-morning. Balaam rode a she-ass named Emêru, and took the lead. His own two servants mingled with other attendants in the rear, with the baggage. The presumption of leadership was so shockingly absurd that no one thought to challenge him. He carried no weapons, only a maqqel of medium length, richly carved over its entire shaft. It was not his strongest magic stick, but by far and away his most impressive.

Why his mount suddenly veered sharply left into a field, Balaam had no idea. The speed of the action gave him no time to intervene, and his ass was a good fifteen yards into the soft earth, haunches moving rapidly, before Balaam even began to pull the reins. The ass gave no sign of yielding, but only picked up speed. He had owned Emêru for over ten years and always she had proven a quiet, steady, some would say docile mount. It was precisely these qualities that had made him choose her for the long journey. It made her behaviour all the more inexplicable. The delegation had come to a stop, strung out along the field's edge, observing the contest between a determined rider and an equally determined ass. Order was finally restored, ascendancy regained and eventually Balaam rejoined his travelers, but not before he had beat his mount savagely about her head. His handsome cloak, embroidered with symbols related to his profession, now displayed dabs of mud. Both beast and barû were breathing heavily. Balaam, who was rarely at a loss for words, could think of nothing to say which might redeem the scene. He resumed his lead finally, keeping his back rigidly erect.

Within the hour, an even worse disaster befell him. They had been passing through vineyards that grew close on both sides providing only a minimal right of way. Sturdy rock walls, no more than saddle height, edged both sides of the path that allowed for only single file travel. Balaam had slightly more warning this time, not that it did him any good. He had seen Emêru's ears begin to flatten out a split second before his mount flung itself against one of the walls. The flank, neck and head of the beast were pressed into the wall. If ever an animal could be said to cower, Balaam's ass was exemplary. The problem with the stance was, of course, that Balaam's left foot, still lodged in his stirrup was pinned against the wall, held fast by a thousand pounds of frantic horse flesh. Balaam was screaming, cursing—not the high-sounding, mysterious incantations of his craft but the guttural, totally comprehensible cursing of a rude peasant. His maqqel was being used like a common riding crop and still his horse kept him pinned to the wall. The blows that Balaam rained down on her were seemingly preferable to whatever it was that had spooked her.

It seemed like an eternity before Emêru moved back to the centre of the path. Balaam's foot was on fire. His calf stocking was shredded and he was certain that the whole leg had been dislocated from its hip socket. The round ankle bone in particular felt as though it had been reduced to a pouch of small pebbles. He was diffident about what to do next. To dismount might be seen as an act of defeat, and as well, Balaam was not altogether sure that his leg would bear weight. Fortunately, not everyone had been able to see this debacle, and quite illogically, Balaam took comfort that he had been humiliated in front of a smaller number of people this time. In the end he continued. Even had he wanted to, the lead could not be relinquished, although he fell back more on the main party, keeping a shorter distance out in front. There was no accounting for his beast's behaviour.

The section of road on which Emêru chose to give out entirely under Balaam was straight and level, although still quite narrow. She moved methodically. She first bent her head low, then buckled her haunches before lowering her forelegs completely. It was as if she had just quietly decided to end her journey right there. Balaam's rage was without limit. Standing at her neck he began beating her exposed head without stopping. He stood shouting at her.

"Get up! Get back on your feet! I'll serve you to the ravens. Get up, you stupid mother of all darkness." By this time Balaam was kicking her flanks. He made the mistake of using the wrong foot, an error that almost made him pass out from the agony of it. He fell heavily against her side. The rest of the group were by this time tightly bunched a few yards behind him. Several had dismounted and pushed themselves forward. Emêru, who had done her best to avoid his worst blows, finally spoke.

"What have I done to deserve this abuse? Three times now you have beat me without cause."

"Cause!" screamed Balaam. "You call charging headlong into a muddy field and then crushing my foot so that I will probably limp for the rest of my life, being without cause? You have made me look like a village dolt in front of these men. If I were carrying a sword I would kill you here and now."

"For ten years, Balaam, I have carried you willingly. Have I ever given you a moment's concern? Have I ever rejected the bit?"

"No, you have done your job well," said Balaam finally.

"Then why have you beaten my friend, when by your own mouth you agree she is undeserving of it?" It was a young man's voice coming from in front of them. Balaam looked up. A slim figure dressed in a simple blue tunic stood close to them. His skin was pure white, which made his dark red lips stand out prominently. His hair was a black mass of curls which came to rest loosely on his shoulders. His eyes, however, were two brilliant spots of bronze from which seemed to jump short sparks, perpetually refreshed. One hand held a short sword. He was no mortal.

Balaam crouched low to the ground, taking a position not dissimilar to his ass's posture. His head touched the ground. He was aware that this now made it impossible for him to see the face of either Emêru or the apparition in front of him. His traveling companions would wonder at this presentation of his posterior in their faces. It infuriated him that he was literally crouching lower than a donkey, but he dared not risk a more familiar posture. The stranger continued.

"Balaam, you see many things that are not seen. How is it your donkey saw me yet you did not? Three times I have blocked your path, with authority to kill you, and three times Emêru has saved your life by turning away. And what is her reward? You beat her about the head as if she were a savage brute. I would have enjoyed killing you, Balaam, but her I would have spared. She is worthy of carrying Yahweh's messengers on her back, not blind mendicants."

"Truly I have lost my way," said Balaam, "and if Yahweh wills it, I shall not take a single step closer to the land of Moab. You have simply to command it." Balaam was having to address these words to a small pebble that lay an inch from his nose. It irked him wildly. He was sure that both the messenger and Emêru were even now grinning at each other, sharing the humour of listening to Balaam's words emerge up out of his buttocks, which were now the highest part of his body. He was fast losing all interest in proceeding under any circumstances.

"It is Yahweh's wish that you continue," said the blue-decked stranger. "He will have a use for you. But Balaam, it has come to Yahweh's notice your habit of speaking more than just the words you receive from the heavens—of amplifying your oracles somewhat. And while certain deities are no doubt grateful for this skill, Yahweh is not among them. The God whom I serve has instructed me to say to you: 'Listen to me very, very carefully. You will do and say only what I tell you. Nothing more. Nothing less.' Now go and sit upon your ass and consider my words carefully."

Emêru, beside him, started to her feet. Balaam took that as his cue that he could safely rise as well. Turning, he stared for a long time into her eyes, which returned only her usual steady gaze. He did not know whether to mount her. But as a practical matter, he could not walk well at all. He was unsure what the Moabite princes had seen or heard. The noble closest to him finally coughed tentatively and, on speaking, confirmed his worst fears.

"Is Balaam in distress, or has something been dropped in the path?" They had seen nothing except an old man having a conversation with his donkey.

"Balaam has received a visitation." It was all he could think to say. With that he lifted his good foot into the stirrup and settled back into the saddle. Only a close observer would have seen how delicately he settled in his seat and how gently he used the reins. Within the hour, once the road had opened up, he had relinquished the lead.

Emêru had only to breath loudly and Balaam became instantly attentive. There was no stopping himself. He would spend the rest of his life anticipating another conversation with her, which would never come. Riding her normally became impossible. Each time he moved the bridle he could feel the bit crossing over his own tongue. Yet not riding her would have represented a complete loss of face and nerve. Balaam never completely regained either ever again.

Balak himself met the delegation at the north fork of the Arnon river. The princes of Moab had pushed hard and come south in just six days. Balaam's foot was puffy and sent an arrow of pain right up into his lower back every time he walked on it. His precious stick was now a cane and one end of it was fast becoming scraped and disfigured from being pushed into the dirt. Balak was at most half Balaam's age, probably less, and greeted Balaam with all the tact of a charging ox.

"It has taken you long enough to show yourself. Did you doubt my promises of payment or is there some purpose in advertising to the whole world that the king of Moab must beg twice for Balaam's help?"

The normal Balaam would have found the right words to soothe an anxious client and create an ordered calm for which he was famous. The normal Balaam would have made all kinds of allowances for the pressure

Balak was under. But Balaam was anything but normal. He snapped back irritably.

"Well, I am here now, Balak. But you and I may both live to regret it."

That night in the town of Kiriathaim, there was a concerted effort to make amends all round. Balak performed sacrifices and sent the best portions of each animal to where Balaam was lodged. Each member of the delegation was similarly honoured. A healer was sent to attend to Balaam's foot. Balaam's obsession with the quality of care his ass received was politely ignored. It was as if everyone tacitly agreed that nothing would be allowed to distract from tomorrow's task. Balak, his counselors, and Balaam too, breathed deeply. It was the eve of battle.

Next morning the group rode out. It was less than an hour's ride to the top of a hill called Bamoth-baal, an historic religious site. From its height a portion of the Israelite campsite was visible. There was nothing striking about it—dull, tan-coloured tents of a style used everywhere. Nonetheless, Balaam knew beyond doubt that Yahweh was close at hand.

Work began on seven altars as Balaam had asked for. The exorcism of a god followed a specific ritual. To deviate from it was sheer foolishness. Seven altars were constructed, and on each a bull calf and an adult ram were killed. Nothing was salvaged from the animals. Instead, huge stacks of wood were lit around the carcasses. In less than an hour the whole hilltop was erupting oily smoke, visible for miles. The tribe of Jacob would have no doubt what was happening. Heat from the fires made the air dance so that when one looked through it, objects became distorted. It was an extravagant invitation. Around each stone mound, Balaam paced, limping. Seven times he shuffled. Beside one he motioned Balak to stay. To summon a god—any god—was always risky and Balaam always took care to protect everyone involved except himself. If the deity was angry, Balaam would be the foil. Balak would remain protected.

"I will leave you here. Do not move until I return. Perhaps Yahweh will come and give me words to say."

"A curse formula, I trust," said Balak. "That is all I have asked of you. A strong curse exchanged for a fat fee."

Balaam shrugged. He had had no success in convincing Balak that to speak other than what the gods permitted was impossible. Balak remained stubbornly convinced that a curse could be procured with the same ease that anything else could be bought. Whether he needed the world of the gods to be controllable to compensate for the vagaries of his own experience, Balaam did not know. Perhaps Balak was simply naive. In any event he did not present as overly bright.

Balaam moved off to a higher point of land. He stood looking out at the Israelite camp. The wind was taking the smoke from his seven fires toward the campsite. In the distance he could see the white cloud, which remained stationary despite the obvious wind.

He began the customary summons chant. This was familiar magic to him and he entered it like a favourite garment. Closing his eyes, he leaned on his stick. Slowly but steadily the scene around him materialized in his mind. He could see the fires burning, see Balak, now sitting on a rock looking over at where he stood. He saw himself standing fixed against the sky as he allowed another part of himself to drift upward along with the smoke until he surveyed the scene like a great bird. His wings worked the updrafts, enhanced by the fires below. Round, round, round, Balaam flew, breathing in the hot air mingled with the smells of burning meat. Round, round, round. Balaam hovered, his wings stretched wide. Another bird figure joined him, larger than himself, taking a position above. Balaam felt a shiver flow from the back of his head, back down his body and out through his wings. He imagined the talons of the other bird pushing through his exposed feathered back at any minute. He wanted to hide, to fold his wings close into his body and drop. The other bird remained always above him, always out of Balaam's sight so that all he ever really saw was a shadow. Occasionally he would feel a rush of air as the other bird swept close by. Each time that happened, Balaam would brace himself to be pierced. The two birds remained, circling over the scene below. Yahweh had come.

Balaam spoke finally.

"The prescribed oblations have been prepared. See for yourself, there, below us. Smell their burning fat. Warm your wings in the heat of the fire but harm not your servant Balaam, nor Balak on whose behalf I have sought this audience with you."

"You ply your trade persistently. I'll give you that much," said the voice. It was relaxed.

"Yahweh, I am but a poor messenger seeking the intentions of the gods, that men might receive their direction and live in peace. The peace of all tribes is the only thing that concerns me. Jacob's children are newly arrived to our lands. They have upset the natural balance and try to occupy lands that are not theirs. A small thing is all I ask. Send them away from the land of Moab. When, ever, have the sons of Moab harmed the sons of Jacob? Surely the lands of Yahweh stretch beyond the sun. Surely this tribe can inhabit some other corner."

"Come and see my people," was all the voice replied.

Balaam followed the lead of the other bird toward the Israelite camp. Seen from this height, the ordered pattern of the encampment was obvious. There were a dozen discrete sections to it. Three ranged on each side of one huge tent that defined the centre of the camp. Above the tent was the white cloud.

"Is that your home?" wondered Balaam.

Yahweh answered him. "It is one of the places where I meet my people. It is where I receive their offerings. Balak's oxen are not the only incense that reaches up to me. It is also where the ark of promise is kept. Two golden cherubim keep watch."

"Surely you are deserving of a better house than one made of skins. These people show no respect."

"The tabernacle suits me. Notice, Balaam, with what ease it can be moved." Balaam did not know what to make of this last remark. Was Yahweh signaling that he might, given the right incentives, be persuaded to abandon this tribe, or at least move away with them? Or was he warning Balaam that Yahweh could just as easily move into Moabite territory? Balaam did not reply. The two birds hovered. Balaam would not leave.

Finally, the same voice as before: "Balaam, your request is futile. From this very smoke with which you have summoned me, I have prepared my oracle which you will deliver to Balak. Now go."

And with the word "go" Balaam felt a blast of wind that bent his wings, tumbling him downward in a wild freefall. He opened his eyes. The vision had ended and he was in himself again. But the wind had followed him. It raged inside his head, tearing back and forth between his ears. Words marched with heavy feet before his eyes like soldiers in parade. Their feet pounded and pounded until Balaam's whole body shook and shuddered under the vibrations. The wind was building up inside of him. He staggered back to where Balak was. He opened his mouth and it seemed to him like the sound of a waterfall roaring out. Finally, words came:

From the land of Aram was I brought.
The king of Moab summoned me:
"Come curse Jacob and his tribe,
That they might perish, I survive."
But a curse is not within my power
'Tis Yahweh's will controls this hour.
Their tents reside on hallowed ground
And at the core is Yahweh found.

High above their camp I flew,
A people without number.
This desert race of God's creation
Is set apart from other nations.
Rejecting the brotherhood of man,
But bound to God with holy bans,
Even in death they live victorious.
Would that my end is half as glorious.

Balak's reaction to the oracle was perfectly understandable. Up to that very minute not even he had known how invested he was in the outcome. The bitterness he now tasted had all the strength of hope turned sour. He ranted at Balaam publicly, heedless of the damage to his own image. Yet, once committed to so public a solution, it was impossible to retreat into privacy. In truth, neither the emperor nor the hired barû wore clothes.

"I bring you three hundred miles. I pledge you an exorbitant fee. I promise you a public office with great honour. Have I not treated you with the utmost respect? And what is my reward? My barû cannot distinguish between a blessing and a curse!"

Balaam was not about to be drawn into the tirade. He was predictably tired. He had disappointments of his own to contain. "You were warned before I started. Balaam says only what the gods put in his mouth. Your plight has pushed you into strong magic. Strong magic you have received. Is it my fault that the content is not to your liking? Do you think you choose portents as one chooses a pair of sandals?"

A strained silence accompanied the group as they descended and returned to the city. The visible preparations for the anticipated celebration feast were hastily concealed. Supper was a solitary event. Late in the evening a messenger approached Balaam.

"It has come to Balak that his choice of sites was not propitious. The hill we were on—Chemosh has visited it before. This god whose will you seek to bend must have been justifiably offended.

"Balak has an inquiring mind that never rests in seeking the good of the kingdom," replied Balaam. "This conclusion has the ring of verisimilitude." He's had coaching, he thought privately. He continued aloud. "What does the king suggest?"

"The top of Mount Pisgah. There is a meadow close to the summit, and from it another part of Israel's encampment can be seen."

"I am in your king's service," said Balaam. "No doubt Balak has already given orders for the same sacrifices as were made today. I will be ready to leave at first light." Balaam didn't think Balak had given any thought to the sacrifices.

First light was when they did leave, an indication of Balak's anxiety and need for resolution. The summit was reached, the altars built and the animals slaughtered. Black smoke intruded up into the pristine blue. Balaam withdrew and set about his task. The incantation commenced. Balaam drifted upward in the smoke. The other bird was already there above him.

"Come, fly with me," invited the voice. "We did not see this part of the camp yesterday. Tell me, Balaam, are not my people beautiful? See with what order and precision their camp is arranged. Their goodness is as polished brass."

Balaam drifted. Part of his mind was engaged with the task, alert to any opening through which he might advance his request. Another part breathed in the hot, rich smoke, like opium haze that delivered a numbing euphoria. If Yahweh was loquacious, so much the better. His voice was a soothing balm.

"See how the seed of Abraham has flourished—from one man— one man who had faith. What fruit my covenant has born! And the best lies still ahead. They are camped under the very lintel of their own land. Tents will give way to houses, skins replaced by bricks. Moses shall come to his well-deserved rest and Joshua will begin the holy wars of occupancy. They shall drink wine they did not make, and eat corn they did not plant."

Balaam's moment had arrived.

"Truly, you are chief among all gods. And the sons of Jacob do well to have chosen you as their god. For what other god is as just? What other god can be trusted to make his words come to pass? From Yahweh's mouth comes truth. The judgments of God cannot be bought and sold in the streets. But is it justice that Abraham's children eat the corn of their kin? Moab and Ammon are, after all, both the sons of Lot, nephew to Abraham. Lot too, left all and followed with Abraham. What are other nations to think of your justice if you allow cousin to kill cousin?"

The voice that flew beside him was light and bantering." Are all your petitions so coated in honey Balaam? Alas you are not a Levite. I would have enjoyed hearing your prayers. Besides, you are in error. They have not chosen me. I have chosen them."

"Yahweh's words are true. They have not chosen you. Even a poor servant like Balaam has heard how this people made a golden calf image and bowed low to it. More than once has this people grumbled against you—you and your appointed barû, Moses."

"Every babe needs his mother. It is I who teach this tribe to walk in my ways. It is I who teach Ephraim to walk, leading him with the tethers of loving kindness."

"Forty years is a long journey. And do they now follow only you?"

"They know the Ten Words, and of these words, which is the first? *'No gods but me'*."

"Yes, they *know* these words I grant you. But will they *follow* them once they have drunk the wine they did not make and eaten the corn they did not grow and become curious about the gods who inhabit our lands?"

"Balaam." The voice was now stern. Balaam had transgressed the line. "Yahweh will bless whom he chooses to bless. And it pleases me to bless Jacob just as it pleases me to make you my augur. Now fly back. My words are already before you."

The conversation was over. Balaam once more hobbled back to where Balak waited expectantly. He started in.

Rise up O King of Moab,
And hear the oracle you've sought.
Did you think that God, like man,
With double heart and fickle plan,
Might change his blessing into curse
Or let me work their dark inverse?
God's words only can I say;
Your sacrifices hold no sway.

Balak shouted. "Stop. Shut up your mouth. If you cannot curse, then neither should you bless." But Balaam's mouth remained open, as if Balak had said nothing.

> *Twin daimons, Misery and Misfortune. What will*
> *Jacob know of these?*
> *Immune is he to any harm*
> *Invoked through evil incantation.*
> *As lion when his prey's devoured*
> *Roars to augur victory's hour,*
> *Reminding all who've not yet fled,*
> *They'll feel his claws upon their heads.*

Balak's vulnerability was pitiable. And Balaam's sixty-year-old heart wanted to comfort him, but could not. Each generation had to find its own way and live the destiny apportioned it by the gods. Balak was close to tears when he spoke. The obstinacy with which he clung to his idea that success or failure was dependent on geography made Balaam want to weep as well. It was madness to expect a different outcome from a repeated action, but Balaam, nevertheless, could understand it.

"Balaam, come with me to another high place. I have enough sacrifices and the day is not yet spent. Mount Peor is close at hand. Perhaps it will please Yahweh to let you curse them for me there."

"Make the arrangements and I will comply," answered Balaam. It was the least Balaam could do for the young king. And so once more the altars were built, the animals butchered, the fires started and the smoke of appeasement dispatched toward heaven. Balak sat down. Balaam distanced himself as usual.

He could not start the incantation. The words, usually laden with majesty, uttered in slow cadence, threatened to sound like a child's play song. Yahweh came and went irrespective of what Balam might say. The altars, the sacrifices the incantations—it was all so unnecessary.

Instead he simply stood, his stick heavily into the ground, gazing out at the Israelite encampment. He wondered where their own barû was. Moses. A man twice the age of Balaam. Was he too somewhere high up, leaning on a stick, busily petitioning Yahweh's ear? Somehow Balaam did not think so. He imagined the easy friendship that must exist between their god and Moses. Moses would not have to perform tricks as Balaam so frequently was pressed to do. The majesty of Yahweh was not obtained at the expense of his followers' dignity. Yahweh did not know the human curse of insecurity.

Balaam knew one thing for sure. Yahweh was not about to leave the sons of Jacob. Balaam was on a fool's errand. The certainty of this conclusion somehow made Balaam feel lighter. To the victor goes not all the spoils. He continued to stand gazing at the tents, observing the commonplace activities of camp life.

The spirit of Yahweh came upon Balaam.

His first awareness was that he could no longer see the camp below. It was the white cloud come to envelop him. But how it had traveled, or indeed how long Balaam had been inside it before he had become aware, he could not tell. He did not think this was a vision. It lacked the tension that usually accompanied visions. The cloud was not cold. This was not ground fog come suddenly in the late afternoon. It was thicker than a mist, warm, as if somewhere close to him a fire burned and the cloud retained the heat. Never had he felt so soothed. His foot had stopped hurting. The total sense of well-being so filled him that he was not in the least inquisitive about its source. He remained functionally blind, not even able to see himself clearly although he remained delightfully aware of all his fleshy limbs. The noises of the seven sacrifices, their smoke and smells, were nowhere in evidence, even though Balaam knew they had to be still close at hand. He did not care. He kept feeling waves of warmth wash around him like wavelets in a hot bath, rippling back against the edges to lap against his skin. The lapping of the warmth had built up a rhythm. It made Balaam shake and shiver now, like a puppy shakes in the sheer reflex pleasure of being alive and does not even know he's shaking.

Laughter started from somewhere inside. There was no joke, which made the laughter come all the freer. Holy laughter at the joke that could never be told. The holy laugh was a belly chuckle at the absurdity of all that was absurd: Balaam and his ass, kneeling together in the path, braying and praying, and who knew which was doing what; Balak's anxious pomp and incessant demands for a curse, like a child being denied a sweet; the comedy of Balaam trying to manoeuvre Yahweh. Balaam was in the front row of the theatre, close to the stage, watching himself on stage and laughing till tears came at the antics of a conjurer, himself become the entertaining trick in the fingers of Yahweh. It all made Balaam laugh. And the laughter was not his alone. Yahweh would bless Jacob, and that too was a joke of huge proportions. Jacob was going to have the hand of Yahweh rest on him whether he wanted it or not. Balaam threw down his stick. He whirled around, spinning, taking grotesque leaps, deliberating losing his balance so that he could be supported by the cloud and pushed back upright.

Balaam will do what Balaam will do.

What Balaam would do right then was to giggle with the energy of someone who was not quite right in the head but who had, at the same time, never been righter.

Balaam will do what Balaam will do?

Bafflegaff and bird feathers!

Yahweh orders the dance.

And what was more. This was good news. Because if ever Balaam tried to, chaos and darkness once more would choreograph the surface of the deep. Balak had asked such a stupid boon. He should have asked to join the dance, enter into the cosmic joke. Surely there was room enough even for his thick head. Who knew what Yahweh might have said? One thing for certain—however much gold Balak had on hand to pay him, it was nothing more than a heap of lead ballast compared with this experience of being with Yahweh. This was reward enough.

But a cruelty was about to be meted out on Balaam that would have made his death seem merciful. The cloud left. The natural light of everydayness re-emerged to claim his senses. Details of the visitation began to slip through the cracks of his mind like prisoners fleeing through a door set ajar by mistake. Instead, the cruelest joke of all now came to Balaam. Yahweh's presence was not for *him*. He stood outside the circle, the professional voyeur. The lifting of Yahweh's spirit was horrific.

He picked up his stick and walked back toward the King of Moab. The foot hurt once more. Balak braced himself, and Balaam began.

"Three times Balaam has entered the presence of Yahweh on your behalf. Three times have I sought his intentions. And now Balak, son of Zippor, this is the oracle given me to say to you:"

Holy words fill Balaam's mouth.
His eyes see glory, ears hear heaven's voice.
Jacob's tents have been transformed,
And Eden's garden's now reborn.
Her gown, with trailing river train,

Engenders growth of grape and grain.
Wellsprings everywhere will be
Tokens of God's constancy.

Out of Egypt's bondaged box
Did Yahweh lead Jacob.
Into the desert the ox was led,
And from Yahweh's granary was fed.
A raging bull he is now grown
To trod the nations, crush their bones.
A blessing on all on whom Jacob smiles,
A curse on all whom he reviles.

Balak began to shriek. He had started to move forward as if to seize Balaam. Just as quickly, Balaam's stick had come up, one end pointed squarely at Balak's chest. It stopped the man, but not his words.

"Three times have you mocked me. Three times do you sniff at my offer of great reward as if it were a mess of offal. You have betrayed your profession, hiring yourself out for the giving of curses, then playing false. Not one coin will you leave with, Balaam! The fees you would have received I will spend telling the world of your treachery and impotence!"

Balaam charged back. "Played you false, have I? You, still parading about the world with your ears full of wax, unable to hear what I've been saying all along. You could have given me your entire palace and everything in it, and it would have done no good.

"I am leaving you. I should have known better than to come to this brackish backwater. You think I have been callous in not uttering your curse? Has it ever crossed your myopic little mind what Yahweh might have in store for your own tribe? Or perhaps you did not want to spend your gold on such a question. It is a curse you've wanted all along Balak, and so it's a curse I'll leave you with. And, Balak, it's free. Receive it as my farewell present."

Jacob's star is still ascending
High in heavens will it climb.
A royal scepter will emerge
The backs of nations will it scourge.

Edom, Seir, Moab, Sheth,
By its hands will meet their death.
The words of Yahweh fall like hail,
Raining destruction without fail.

Balaam's eyes are finally opened.
He falls prostrate at the glory of Yahweh.
God holds all within his fist
Who can live when God does this?
Kingdoms live subservient,
Their lesser gods in homage bent.
And now must Balaam quit this place,
Shattered by God's iron grace.

And without any more words, Balaam departed.

— ♦ —

Unbeknown to either Balaam or Balak, God had given specific instructions to Moses regarding how he should deal with the Moabites.

Do not harass Moab, or contend with them in battle,
for I will not give you any of their land for a possession,
because I have given it to the descendants of Lot
for a possession.

(Deut. 2: 9)

[1]Balaam's story begins in the book of Numbers, chapter 22.

Balaam's Revenge

Balaam's professional self-confidence remained as shaky as his injured leg. Six months had passed since the disastrous affair on the plain of Moab and still he was in no hurry to seek other assignments. The most accomplished seer in the whole fertile crescent, Balaam's task had been to curse Israel. Instead, the spirit of their god—Yahweh—had accosted Balaam with such force that he had delivered three brilliant oracles of blessing. It had not ended cleanly. True, Balak, the young king of Moab had not carried out his loud threat to publicly discredit Balaam. Balaam's fourfold failure would remain a shared embarrassment. It was impossible to highlight the one man's impotency without also illuminating the other's predicament. For still the tribe of Jacob remained camped on the borders of Moab, showing no signs of moving anywhere. Stalemate. It was an unacceptable conclusion.

Balaam had returned to his spacious home three hundred miles to the north, where he remained in seclusion to reflect on his experience. He had actively sought out encounters with various gods as a consequence of his profession. But in his forty years of practice (he was now in his sixty-first year) he had never encountered a god like Yahweh. The power of this god defied adequate description. Balaam's attempts to subvert this force to his own purposes had been laughable. In comparison, all other god encounters now seemed to resemble tawdry amusements. After Yahweh—well, there was nothing after Yahweh, which was precisely the reason for his professional paralysis. It also explained his intense curiosity. Yahweh became his exclusive area of research. After all, Balaam was, above all else, a professional. Not even to himself would Balaam admit to the possibility of there being a personal score to settle with this strange Hebrew god who had so blatantly subsumed Balaam for his own purposes.

He had confided in no one his preliminary conjecture. The implications of it, if true, would shake the entire world, and he, Balaam, would be at the centre of the new order. Ancient stories told of the one supreme god who ruled above all others—so ancient and so powerful that he had long since ceased to have direct dealings with anything in the mortal realm. The gods whom men worshipped and with whom Balaam consorted were this god's progeny, many sired, or so it was thought, with his chief consort

Asherah. This god was called El and his name was of such ancient origins that no one even knew how it had first been revealed to mortals. In fact, many dialects used the name, in error, as an honorific referent to all gods. This El was the high court of appeal. It was to him that Dagon, the patron god of the Philistines, had petitioned for permission to build a temple in his name. It had been El, so the stories went, who had finally dispatched Shapash, the sun goddess, to mediate the conflict between Mot and Baal. Shapash had established the prescribed rites of their annual combat, when the forces of drought and sterility gave way to springtime fertility, only to repeat the cycle at the next harvest.

The stories of El were fragmentary, but Balaam's forty years of personal experiences had convinced him that El did exist, even if he was unassailable. It was a "sense" rather than any outright confession by any deity he had encountered—a sense that other gods acted with a restraint imposed on them by some superior agent. The God of gods—that was who El was.

The more Balaam reflected on his experience with Yahweh, the more convinced he grew of his hypothesis: El was Yahweh. And what was more, he had appeared to Balaam!

But Yahweh did not appear again to Balaam, despite his best efforts. Balaam's scouts kept him steadily supplied with intelligence. Yahweh's cloud by day and tower of fire by night remained stationary over the tents of Israel, some three hundred miles to the south.

It puzzled him that a god of such power, that El Yahweh—for that was how Balaam now regarded him—would have chosen such an unremarkable band of nomads to watch over. Until forty years earlier, this people had been a slave tribe serving the Egyptian Pharaoh. Their history consisted of four hundred years of servitude. Where had this god Yahweh been for all those years? Sleeping? There was one ancient tale that might support this. But without question, this ragged bunch of tent dwellers were a people in special relationship to Yahweh. Balaam had been told as much by Yahweh himself: "*They have not chosen me; I have chosen them.*" It was counter-intuitive that such a mismatch was meant to endure. Powerful gods resided with powerful nations and barûs.

In time Balaam's patience grew thin. He did not tolerate rejection, in any form, well. Even gods should not ignore ambitious barûs. He thought of Moses, the man who led the Israelite tribe. Though he did not know him, it angered him to think of anyone else enjoying the regular visitations from a god whose presence had *felt* the way El Yahweh's had. It wasn't fair that Balaam should be denied access to such a personality. And so in the end, the seeds of Yahweh's silence yielded the fruits of bitterness and envy. And Balaam searched for a way to retaliate.

— ✦ —

Evi, Rekem, Zur, Reba and Hur were the five senior chiefs of the Midianites who lived within Moab's boundaries. Four of them had traveled north once before as emissaries for King Balak. Balaam greeted them with genuine warmth. Among other things, their visit indicated that his reputation had not suffered overly. Their talk over the evening meal was frank. Neither side was seeking to embarrass or out-manoeuvre the other.

"Our problem is the same as before," said Evi. "This tribe of Israel does not move on. Our gods are unwilling or unable to help us. Even you, the most powerful seer alive, cannot coax the heavenly citizens to our cause. Nevertheless, we cannot sit idly by. The situation is unraveling and our people grow unsettled. The more hot headed and younger among us speak openly of waging war, which we could not hope to win. Those who are closest to the foreigners are the most frantic, farmers mostly. A few have already abandoned their homes and fallen back into the towns. Our own council authority is being sorely tested. Balak, frankly, has lost heart. Time works against us."

"But surely you have not come to ask me for more magic?" interrupted Balaam with a wry smile. "My foot has not yet healed from the last attempt."

"No, we are properly chastened after your last visit," Evi smiled back. "But we have come to ask your advice. Is there nothing we can try to avert the disaster that will necessarily come if we do nothing?"

"I have been making these people the subject of a special study," replied Balaam, "together with their god, Yahweh. And I believe there *is* a way to mitigate their threat."

"We would be grateful to receive your wisdom, and will pay you well for it. Tell us what we should do."

"I can do better than that," said Balaam. " I will return with you. Your problem interests me." He did not elaborate.

"We are in your debt," responded one of the chiefs, genuinely pleased at this offer. It was more than had been hoped for.

"Which you shall settle by way of large gold coins after this affair is over," laughed Balaam, not unkindly. "We have a bargain then? I will devise a strategy for you?"

The five chiefs did not even bother to withdraw for a private deliberation. Glances were exchanged and Evi spoke for them all. "We have a bargain."[1]

— ◆ —

Moses was disturbed by the reports that his administrators kept bringing to him. Ever-increasing numbers of young men were said to be slipping out of camp at night and visiting the nearby towns. It was not hard to imagine what was happening. Having lived in isolation for an entire generation, even the whiff of a new experience would be impossible to resist. The attraction would not necessarily be sexual, although Moses harboured no illusions in that regard. Foods, clothing, permanent buildings, fresh well water, wines—it was an exotic brew that wafted in front of men who were sensorily deprived. No good could possibly come from this social flirting. In the past, Moses had always been able to move the camp on to some other location. But the cloud above the tabernacle stayed stubbornly fixed. A terrible blackness settled into Moses as he deliberated on his options. It was not the depression that comes of age. It was that he knew the inevitable end point to which this behaviour would sweep them all—a destination of bloody judgment and punishment. And for himself, he shrank from the task of being God's agent in the affair.

— ◆ —

Balaam was delighted with his early intelligence reports. The evening festivities hosted by the border towns to "welcome" their new neighbours were attracting even more Israelite men than he had hoped for. Young women from elsewhere were hurriedly recruited. "Don't rush," warned Balaam. "These are a people who have lived in isolation for a whole generation—curious, but also suspicious. And they have strict codes regarding foreign rituals. We will build slowly."

— ◆ —

Moses went to investigate the manna himself. For forty years the crusts of honeyed coriander had appeared each morning to be collected by each family. There was always the right amount. None was ever left on the ground. But now, large patches remained uncollected, degenerating quickly and attracting maggots. People walked through the areas, grinding the bread into the dirt. Where were people getting their food then? Judging from the amount of manna being left, Moses judged that at least a tenth of the camp was no longer gathering their daily quota.

The answer to the puzzle was straightforward. Exotic foods were being brought back from the foreign towns. "Tokens of welcome," it was explained to him. Not since Egypt had there been such variety: vegetables, fruits, spiced meat dishes, fresh olives and wines that had been carefully aged. Forty years of abstinence created considerable appetites.

— ◆ —

"We need to introduce these people to Baal," announced Balaam. "In this we must walk delicately. Our worship rites must not intimidate or threaten. Every action, however common to us, will require explanation to them. Remember, they have never observed any of our fertility customs for they are not farmers. Their god hurls down their bread from his storehouse each day yet they do nothing to induce such gratuitous behaviour. It will seem strange at first that Baal asks the ritual enactment of your own fecundity to aid his own resurrection—strange, but by far the most pleasurable worship rituals they have participated in, I am sure. Their own worship customs are austere. Your invitation will prove a compelling allure. Their young men have no such outlet for their passions. They have tasted of our crops. We have made no secret that we accept them as from the hand of Baal, just as they receive their desert cakes from their god. To be told that the coupling with our young girls is a rite of gratitude will ease whatever qualms they hold. Our women are the warriors in this campaign. They offer their bodies for the preservation of their people. It is the first step in pulling the teeth of these desert interlopers."

The maids of Midian contrasted sharply with their Israelite counterparts. Their clothing was decorative, ornate, and would not have lasted a week on a desert trek. Their skin was soft, hands and feet smooth. Young Israelite girls the same age were not half as attractive. A sultry insolence seemed to hang in the air around these foreign girls. The men of Israel breathed of it deeply. Seduction had never smelled so sweet.

— ♦ —

Balaam was ecstatic when news of the plague reached him. His spies said that it was a sickness of the bowels. The voiding trenches at the camp's edges were overrun. As people grew weaker they could not reach the camp's edges in time and would be found lying in their own liquid stool. The stink caused a reflex gag in any who had to go near. His intelligence confirmed that shallow grave pits were being dug. Bodies were being dumped without ceremony, the workers wearing heavy veils over their mouths and noses. He knew for a certainty that this was not a natural phenomenon. Yahweh could not let idolatry go unchallenged. *"Thou shalt have no other gods but me, for I am a jealous god."* The soft exposed underbelly of their god was that he always kept his word. Balaam wondered how Yahweh was going to respond to his next strategy.

Balaam called for another meeting of the chiefs: Evi, Hur, Reba, Zur and Rekem.

"The young men of Israel have proved most vulnerable to the charms of civilization." Balaam was smiling. "It is unlikely they will want to attack the very towns where they have been made feel so... welcome." He paused slightly over the last word and the smirk that now showed on his face left the chiefs in no doubt what he meant. "The time has come though to move beyond our casual indulgence of their various appetites. We must consolidate our gains."

"What exactly are you proposing that we do?" asked Reba.

"I propose a marriage," replied Balaam. "But a specific marriage— the most noble of ours, with the best of theirs. It will pave the way for others to follow. And it will be no ordinary marriage. Our maid will be given as a gift from the hand of Baal himself. One of his priestesses given as the token of his welcome into his lands. They cannot surely object to a gift, especially considering its shape."

It was Zur who spoke up. "As it happens, my daughter, Cozbi, has been active in the festivities. She has been serving at the shrine for some time now. And her own Israelite friend is not without some status within their tribal hierarchy. His father is Salu, a leader in the tribe of Simeon. The lad seems presentable enough. I would not object to their marriage. His name is Zimri."

"Good," said Balaam. "Arrange the ceremony. And afterwards, she can return with him to his family. It is time we began to visit these people. Zur, your name and that of your daughter's, Cozbi, will be remembered for all generations because of what you have agreed to."

— ◆ —

Moses went to the Tent of Meeting and waited. Yahweh stalked through the camp. And Yahweh was angry. His breath was the breath of contagion. Moses knew Yahweh would have instructions for him. He knew what was coming and waited in defiant silence.

"Kill the ringleaders," said Yahweh. "Find them in the camp. Bind their hands behind their backs and execute them. Force them down on their knees. Hack them down. Do it when the sun stands highest. This is a public spectacle of my punishment on those who would worship other gods. And I will look on while you, my executioner, exact my retribution. Only then will my anger be appeased against this rebellious rabble."

"So it is to be Hebrew against Hebrew is it?" demanded Moses. "Not since Mount Horeb, when we first left Egypt have you ordered the shedding of blood by a kinsman's hand. Not since Aaron made the calf image have my Levite brothers taken up their swords. Am I to go to my grave with the blood of *your* chosen people on my hands?"

"Would you disobey me in this matter, too?" replied Yahweh. "Did you learn nothing at Meribah, where you struck the rock against my orders? Who are you to question me?"

Moses strode out of the tent, shouting for an assembly of the judges. Runners were swift in the dispatch. The senior tribal magistrates gathered quickly. Many had been already close by, anticipating a meeting of some kind. The assembly took place at the entrance to the Tabernacle. Moses stood on a wooden box that a runner had quietly positioned for him.

"The illness spreading among us is not natural. We suffer at the hand of Yahweh. And we will continue to die this wretched death, until we have carried out the instructions he has given me." Moses was shouting, not just to make himself heard. He was a prisoner along with them. It was as if in the shouting he might distance himself from his own words, stand

43

alongside the others and receive them. But he could not avoid the weight of having to utter them.

"Each tribe will discover which of your kinsmen have joined in the worship of the Baal god. And once you have finished your judgments, you will preside over their deaths. The executions are to be in public, carried out by your own hands lest blood feuds start among our tribes. Be careful in your judgments that no one is falsely accused. This is not to be an opportunity to settle old grievances."

A wail went through the gathered men. The Levite leaders in particular were hard struck by the news. The older men started it. They began by stooping down and picking up handfuls of the camp dirt, and, raising their hands high over their heads they released it in a shower onto their heads. Some took their cloaks off and stood on them. Those that had no cloaks tore their tunics. The laments were spontaneous, like a wounded beast with a thousand voices wailing out its pain. The men who would die would be among those that had fought so well in the campaigns against Og and against the Amorites. Somewhere in the group there was a father who would order the execution of his son. It was inevitable. Prayers were offered up. Moses displayed his grief openly. No one left the assembly. Leaving would only force the beginning of their grim duties.

— ♦ —

Phinehas, a priest, grandson to Aaron, could not believe what he was certain he had just seen. The tent of Salu, the leader of a Simeonite family, was within sight of the Tent of Meeting. In broad daylight, while Moses and the elders were still standing at the entrance, wailing out their anguish at the harsh punishment of Yahweh, in broad daylight, Zimri, son of Salu, had come up through the line of tents and disappeared inside *with a Midianite girl on his arm*! His conceited delight at the stir his leisurely parade had caused was visible with every swaggering step. A trophy no one else had—yet. And while others might now go off and make their own arrangements with the Midianites, his bride had been the first.

Phinehas was outraged. A pagan whore, in the service of Baal, flaunted within sight of Yahweh's home. Was there no limit to the brutish indifference that could be meted out toward Yahweh? Yahweh, in whose service

44

Phinehas was pledged for life, would not be besmirched in this way. A holy love for Yahweh filled Phinehas's heart, blotting out all thought. And with the love for Yahweh exploding in his head, he seized a long spear and followed Zimri into the darkness of his tent.

— ◆ —

"Balaam, Balaam," it was Zur shouting hoarsely. "Balaam, come out and see for yourself how your advice has returned to us." Zur stood in the centre of the street. The body of his daughter, Cozbi, lay in a heap at his feet. His chest was heaving. Blood and dirt and sweat coated him from the long walk he had just endured. Cozbi's tunic had a tear by the stomach.

"Do you know where I found her body?" screamed Zur at the door of the house where Balaam lodged. "I found it in a mass grave outside the Israelite camp. I found her body still pinned by a broken spear to her dog husband—the one you said she should marry. Do you know how long it takes to die from a stomach wound, Balaam? Have you ever stood by while they scream for someone to finish them off? Balaam, what advice have you for us now?"

The street stayed empty. Balaam did not appear. Instead he sat inside, grappling with the news that his own scout had brought him. He already knew about Zur's daughter. And for that he was sorry, and would have tried to comfort Zur in his crazed grief. But his scout had brought other news as well. Cozbi and her husband were the *last* two bodies to be delivered to the graves from the camp. The plague had stopped. El Yahweh's anger at his people had been stayed. They were *still* the chosen people. And it would not go well for those who had enticed the sons of Jacob. Something had gone horribly, horribly wrong. *For I am a jealous god.* This God always kept his word. Had Balaam once thought this trait was a soft underbelly to be exploited? It was an awesome strength. And for that Balaam was terrified.

— ◆ —

Moses sat on a stool just inside the Tent of Meeting. Two days had passed since Phinehas had killed Zimri and in so doing had stopped the plague. The hysteria within the camp was subsiding. The mass graves were now covered. The burial detail would remain outside the camp for seven days in compliance with the regulations. He knew he should be glad that the plague was gone, but he lacked the energy for even that response. What he was more aware of was his feeling of failure; failure and humiliation.

Yahweh came.

"My anger has passed. Phinehas and his descendants will be honoured for all time because of his great love for me."

"Yes."

"Those that have worshipped Baal, here at Peor, are now dead. The punishment is complete."

"Yes." Moses, if he said anything more, thought he would begin to sob.

"Moses, you are angry with me." Yahweh was stating a fact.

"Mine is not to question." Moses' voice was flat.

"Nevertheless, you are angry."

"Yahweh, who knows the power of *your* anger? For your wrath is as great as the fear that is due you[2]. Are my last days to end under your wrath? Am I to finish my life with a cry?"

"What is it you desire, Moses?"

Moses started to cry. Tears poured out of his eyes and down the short distance to lose themselves in his beard. His body did not shake; his breathing was even. But the tears kept coming from somewhere deep within him. He spoke through the tears. The voice was quiet but it belonged to a man who was determined to answer the question honestly. He could not have told you why he was weeping. It didn't matter.

"The length of a man's life is three score and ten, and for some, by reason of strength, four score. Yet the best of them is but trouble and sorrow. And you have blessed me with nigh on two score years beyond. I have seen much trouble and sorrow. And now when I am old, you have forbidden me to enter the land you have established for this people."

"We have spoken of this before, Moses." Yahweh's voice was sharp. "Do not speak of it again."

Moses continued. "These people have disgraced themselves and dishonored you before the Midianites. Twenty-four thousand sons of Jacob lie dead yet only *one* Midianite woman. Is this how I am to leave them?

46

You promised me that you would go before us and strike terror into the hearts of the nations we would drive out. But now, what will they say of us? That we were killed at the hand of our own god? What will be the story of the people who escaped Egypt? And how will I be remembered?"

"Moses, never again until the end of time will I reveal myself in my fullness to another man as I have done to you. There will be neither prophet nor king unto whom I will show myself as you have seen me.[3] Is not my presence sufficient?"

Moses had slid down from the stool. For eighty years, since the burning bush, he had conversed with Yahweh, argued with him, received instructions, been supported by his spirit. Pretense and posturing had long dropped away. He knelt, straight-backed, tears still unstaunched.

"Yahweh, you have been my abode. Since before the mountains were born or the earth formed, from everlasting to everlasting, you are Yahweh. But God..." Moses' voice stopped completely. Finally he continued. "May your favour rest on your servant *one* last time. Establish the work of my hands just *once* more. Commission me for a task that displays your splendour to our children."

There was a long, comforting silence. Then, "Moses, go. Go and carry out my vengeance on the Midianites.[4] They are to be wiped out utterly. And after that, Moses, come home to me."

— ◆ —

They fought against Midian, as the LORD commanded Moses, and killed every man. Among their victims were Evi, Rekem, Zur, Hur and Reba—the five kings of Midian. They also killed Balaam with the sword.

(Numbers 31:7ff)

Endnotes

[1] The story of the seduction of Israel may be found in Numbers 25-27. Balaam is specified as a hired strategist in Revelation 2:14.

[2] The basis for this conversation may be found in Psalm 90. The use of it within this story is conjecture.

[3] Deuteronomy 34:10

[4] Numbers 31:1, 2. See also Joshua 13:22.

The Firstborn

Zipporah lay quiet and relaxed. They had finished their love-making with her lying on her back and she had not stirred from that position since. Her husband lay on his side, turned away, but with his back pressing into her. She did not know if he was asleep yet—wedding nights had an energy and an exhaustion that were unique. She could still feel his wetness, and she wondered, if he was still awake, what he was thinking.

How little they really knew of each other for all the sweaty intimacy they had just shared—she the eldest daughter in a Midianite family and he an Israelite who had burst into their quiet obscurity scarcely a year earlier. Even now in the afterglow of their union Zipporah was aware of just how different they were. A Midianite would not have done it the way her husband had taken her. The tip of his member had been cut, exposing the head. She had noticed this even in the gloom of the tent and was curious about its significance. She also wondered if perhaps his turning away like this was out of disappointment. Was there some post-union ritual expected of her of which she was unaware? They differed in so many ways.

They had both worked hard at understanding each other's dialects. Abraham had been their common patriarch, Midian being the offspring of his concubine. At least that much they claimed together. And because of it their speech was not entirely unintelligible. But less than a year was hardly enough time to have command over the subtle nuances required to communicate one's sexual expectations and preferences. And even if that were possible she was sure that the man's shy modesty would have precluded any such conversation. He was so retiring, for all his vigorous energy, so quick to be reduced to inarticulate sounds at the least reference to sexuality. Any one of her six sisters could reduce him instantly to red-faced incoherence at the faintest flirtation or overt physical gesture. Until their father had finally settled her betrothal there had been much competition among them for the interest of this foreigner, this man who walked into their lives from the desert.

It had been late afternoon and Zipporah and her sisters were congregating at the well, each with the small flock she shepherded each day.[1] It

51

was not hot exactly but the dryness was cumulative, permeating everything, even one's thoughts. Speech was an effort. By then the animals' need for water was acute too and as each small cluster of animals broke over the low rim and descended the slopes of the basin-like depression toward the well, they trotted purposefully, packing themselves around the long sluices through which they knew would shortly course water. There was a surliness to their pressing, smaller and younger livestock being quite summarily pushed aside by the stronger animals. The gentle, usually limpid eyes of the sheep had a steely meanness to them as if even their moisture had been sucked dry.

The sisters had not even got their leather water bags prepared before over the ridge rushed another herd in competition for the well. Behind them, driving the herd forward with short whips tied to the ends of their staffs were the men herders, ten in number. The momentum drove their herd straight into the midst of Zipporah and her sisters' flocks. Yelling and cursing, the newly arrived shepherds quickly began to rout the flocks, displacing them from the sluice troughs to make room for their own. Zipporah had run forward to protest, raising her voice in shrill aggrieved protest. She had been unprepared for the whip end that stunned the side of her face, throwing her off balance so that she stumbled. It was then that he had appeared, from nowhere it seemed. But there he was, this man with short-cropped hair, a beard of only a few weeks, in clothes that clearly marked him as a city dweller from a place she did not recognize. There he was leaping in front of her, grabbing the shepherd's staff tip, wrenching it out of his hand and reversing it to flay the owner himself with the lash. He was shouting too, although in what tongue who knew. The shepherd, stung and shocked at this counterattack, turned away, dodging the animals, which were by now in total chaos.

The stranger was everywhere. Another shepherd got a blow to his back making him fall across the trough edge, his cheekbone making first contact. The man's jaw distended sideways. The stranger jumped into the sluice trough and grounded again on the other side into a tightly packed throng of animals, which promptly darted headlong into the legs of yet another of the shepherds. Caught by his own animals, he was hemmed in long enough for the stranger to get within a staff's length. The whip end caught the man's shoulder, making him yelp in surprise, dropping his own stick.

The shepherds had had enough and retreated out of sight, doing their best to regroup their herd and drive them back away from the well along with them. There were other wells. The sisters emerged from the dusty air to push their own animals toward the well. The stranger was busy emptying bags of water into the troughs as quickly as he could work. The smell of open water in the troughs quieted the animals. So full of contrasts, this man from the city with shepherd skills.

Zipporah marveled that the man now lying beside her was one and the same person. That first day he had seemed godlike, oversized and full of fiery energy, emerging from the dusty haze as if from the world of spirits to bring swift justice. Now in the dark of their tent he lay with his face as hidden as his thoughts—a sphinx-like stone. She wondered what she ought to do to bridge the chasm that yawned large between their two touching bodies.

Moses lay with his back to his bride, trying his best to compose his form into a posture of relaxed sleep. She was still obviously awake but had not moved from her back. She seemed so unresponsive, almost resigned. Was he that inept or were the men of her clan possessing of some special prowess or technique that was beyond his ken? It was true that his knowledge was mostly theory but the years spent in Pharaoh's household had included detailed instruction in all the arts, including this one. Surely he was not a complete failure? He wondered just how he might discover if there was something in particular that was expected of him. His face began to redden even as he lay there contemplating the embarrassment of the inquiry. If any of the sisters ever learned of his insecurity, there would be no end to the merriment he would provide.

He thought back to his first encounter with them at the well. He had stopped only to rest. Three weeks earlier he had been living in Egypt, a young man of forty, Egyptian raised, Hebrew born. He had been forced to run because of a small matter of an Egyptian overseer found with his head bashed in—stupid man to have needlessly used force on a Hebrew slave. He had deserved every blow Moses delivered and then some. But not even a member of Pharaoh's court could murder with impunity. Southward and eastward he had fled, crossing out of Egypt at Lake Timsah, which was the beginning of the eastern route to Shur. He had turned south into the wilderness of the Sinai peninsula, keeping to its western shoreline. The long arm of Pharaoh stretched who knew how far. For certain there would be some pursuit.

Moses recalled the silly altercation with the shepherds who had come to run off Zipporah's sheep. Ten ragged little shepherd youths—hardly men—and Moses would not even have intervened were it not for the whips. Seeing the thong connect with Zipporah's face had made him leap to his feet and he found himself venting anger that had been building up since Egypt. The shepherds were a good target to receive his frustrations. The motley gang was quickly pushed back, their herd sent scampering back up the sides of the wadi. It was a game to Moses, who had been trained daily in the gymnasium.

He sighed inwardly to himself. What had happened to his life that less than a year ago he was a prince in Pharaoh's household and now he was sleeping in the tent of a foreigner, married to his daughter, with the prospect of herding sheep for the rest of his life? Better to have died in Egypt—quickly—than to endure the monotony of the future that now stretched out before him. Kind as they were to each other, Moses knew he could not tell Zipporah of his dashed hopes. To do so would render her a consolation prize and Moses was too genuinely kind hearted to be so patronizing. Yet his pain was real and Zipporah, who sensed more than she was aware, turned toward him, drawing his body closer and extending her arms to make a firm embrace. She pressed her breasts firmly into his back—her face and matted hair close to his neck so he could feel her breath. Her one hand had wormed under him, thus encircling his chest and pressing his body against hers. He sighed again but audibly this time and his back relaxed. Her touch needed no translation; she was both happy and accepting of him. She heard the sigh and felt his body relax against hers. They fell asleep in that position. Zipporah, *little bird* (for that was what her name meant), had extended her wing over her man and he was comforted. It was enough for the moment.

Life in the wilderness around Mount Horeb was not as impoverished as one might expect. Jethro, Zipporah's father, was the family clan leader. They were Kenites, a large family within the larger tribe of Midian. Some called them Cushites because of their darker skin. The Kenites had retained their identity more so than other tribal groups because they were coppersmiths—a carefully guarded skill, passed down from father to son. The craft had long and dark roots. Tubal-Cain, the fifth generation after Cain himself, was said to have been the father of all bronze and iron smithing and remained a mythic patron. It was a skill that had made

wanderers out of the Kenite clan. It was not the rapid movement of nomads but a more leisurely mobility as they moved to tend to the various
needs of their customers, some of whom would wait years for their arrival.
It required the special knowledge of where the best malachite ore and tin
deposits could be found within the huge wilderness. Once having found
the base materials they had to mix them in precise ratio at just the right
temperatures. Bronze, a mixture of copper and tin, was never of uniform
quality and the rate at which tools lost their edge or, worse yet, weapons
broke depended on the skill of the smith. These skills came at a price,
however. Respected and appreciated for their services, the Kenites were
never fully trusted lest they forge superior weapons for some other tribe,
and upset the balance of power.

Jethro had been delighted when Moses had been inserted into their
midst. With seven daughters, the prospect of finding husbands for them
all was formidable and Moses seemed a fine solution to at least one such
obligation, perhaps two. As well, Jethro welcomed the companionship of
another adult male. His one and only son, Hobab, was not yet a teenager.
It had become all too clear, however, that Moses would never be a smith.
Try as he would during those early years, Moses could never quite master
even the easiest of alloy mixtures. His bronze was either too soft or too
brittle; his hammering, though energetic, was ineffectual and even his
best efforts at shaping the metal remained grotesque and lumpish. But in
caring for livestock Moses was not only competent but comfortable. And
so to this aspect of Kenite life Moses withdrew.

It seems to fit his personality, thought Jethro, a lonely occupation
requiring little speech and affording much time for contemplation. Moses seemed to need the time alone. He had obviously been on the run
from something when he arrived but although he had stopped outwardly,
inside, the chase continued.

Those early years were the best years for Zipporah. Children did
not come quickly to this union of Hebrew and Kenite. She scoffed at
the dark hints that Moses' seed carried some curse of barrenness and
that she was being punished for uniting with a foreigner. The eldest
daughter, she knew that her most fertile years had come and gone. She
performed what few fertility techniques she knew and remained hopeful. It was enough for her to be married and if children did not come, she
would not complain to the gods. The absence of children gave them other
opportunities. It was Zipporah who became Moses' guide to the wilder-

ness around Horeb. The camp lay in a small cluster of mountains close to the tip of the Sinai peninsula. The two long, protruding fingers of the Red Sea that defined the peninsula were each about fifty miles away. This vast expanse of wilderness, sparsely inhabited, unsettled Moses. How unlike the flat and luxuriant Nile delta and the cities of the Egyptians. It was hard to believe that the two geographies could exist so relatively close together. At the north face of Horeb lay a broad, shallow valley stretching more than three miles in length and up to two miles wide in spots. This was the primary grazing ground for Jethro's flocks, although some distance from their main camp. At the south end of this valley the mountains began abruptly: Horeb, Musa, Katrina and others. The ones further away were higher. Horeb itself was only sixty-five hundred feet. Its base was a mass of ravines, gullies and gulches that afforded at least some vegetation and ample places to hide. The Kenite camp was on the small and irregular valley floor wedged at the base of the mountains.

Under normal conditions the journey between Egypt and Mount Horeb took about twelve days. As Zipporah guided Moses he realized the extent to which even this *desolate wilderness*, for that was what Horeb meant, remained connected to the broader world. To the north, at the end of the three-mile valley was Rephidim, the spring home of the Amalekite tribe, descendants of Jacob's older brother, Esau, who was tricked out of his birth inheritance, or so said the folklore. They certainly had no love for the Hebrews. The mining centre of Dophkah was further north by only fifty miles. Dophkah had long been mined by the Egyptians for malachite and turquoise. The route back to Egypt from this point was therefore well marked. Egypt's long arm had extended into the region for more than two hundred years in its pursuit of copper, and Moses' fear of capture was not without substance. Zipporah and Moses tended to take their flocks to the south and east areas around their home, preferring the more remote canyons and ravines that made up the land surrounding the three mountains.

Here it was quiet. Sometimes Moses would leave Zipporah with the flock and climb to the summit of one of the peaks, climbing in total silence while the hot air shimmered so that one imagined it to be something to be penetrated. The exertion of such a climb under the bright sun more than equaled the intensity of some of Moses' moods, which needed to collide with something of equal strength in order to dissipate. Here the wilderness, which stretched both horizontally and vertically, was a big enough canvas against which Moses could hurl himself, and hurt neither himself nor the land. In fact, against the backdrop of this collection of rock and sun and sweat, Moses himself receded, his problems of a shattered past and uncertain future eroded by the more elemental issues of surviving. He could rail as hard as he wished. At times the land did not even return him an echo as proof of receipt. It simply took his words and consumed them with neither reproof nor retort.

Moses had spent most of his life close to the centre of the universe, for Ramses II, the current reigning Pharaoh, master builder, lord over all the civilized world, commander of the army, not to mention god omnipotent, *was* the centre of the world and Moses, as an adopted son, received his pro rata share of slavish attention. Without being aware, Moses suffered badly from egocentricity. Coming thus into the wilderness over which he had no power and could leave no mark of ascendancy was the very medicine Moses needed. Gradually, but permanently Moses was reduced in size, limping slowly like his ancestor Jacob, to the edge of things. The horizon that had been largely eclipsed by his own shadow now emerged in detail. Humanity focused into individual persons each resplendent in their intricacies. Moses could even see himself with new detachment and acceptance.

Zipporah would watch him return, crusts of salty sweat and grime in the furrows of his forehead but with softer if not sadder eyes—eyes that Zipporah knew were no longer looking past her. It was after such trips that their union was usually the most tender, and sometimes they would not wait for the comfort of their tent but would spread their cloaks in some crevice and give themselves to each other without restraint. She was also a little in awe, for it seemed to her that the more Moses shrank himself, receding into the crevices of the wilderness, the more powerful a person emerged. She loved him all the more for it.

Children came to Zipporah at last and her joy knew no limits. The names Moses gave them,[2] however, bewildered her. She fussed over *Gershom* as is expected at the birth of the first male offspring, keeper of the family name, inheritor of family lands, etc. *Eliezer* was second, born in the dusk of her fertility, and Zipporah loved them both. But Moses did little to acknowledge their progeny and when the times came he did not even bother to hold the circumcision parties, marking their transition to puberty. It was as if they did not exist for Moses. Zipporah, though disappointed, was not one to brood on the deficiencies of her mate, however. It was simply not in her nature to be critical.

The names angered Jethro but he said nothing. The literal meaning of Gershom was *the sojourner*, or as Moses once said publicly, "Because I have become an alien in a foreign land." It was an insult in the face of Jethro's frank and continuing welcome. Eliezer meant *my God is helper.* It at least had the nuance of gratitude if only as an afterthought, for as Moses explained, "My father's God was my helper. He saved me from the sword of Pharaoh."

"Saved from the sword but left to live as an alien wanderer," thought Jethro. "Was this how Moses sees himself, then?" Gradually Jethro came to see, however, that the naming of Gershom was Moses' way of declaring a hard truth. The more attention given to Gershom as firstborn, the more Moses hung back, acutely aware of how little inheritance was available to Gershom, the son of a wandering father who was himself severed from his family roots. The seeds of the father's misfortune were planted in the name of his child.

Perhaps, thought Jethro, Eliezer's naming was Moses' oblique hope that "*my father's god might help again*" and aid the children of Moses as well. Jethro was too wise a father-in-law to inquire pointedly into Moses' gods. He noticed that Moses carried no images, not even an amulet on his neck. He had never asked to have any fashioned, nor expressed any curiosity that Zipporah brought no household gods with her into the marriage. The Kenites were no strangers to cast images. As smiths they routinely fashioned hundreds of household gods for their patrons and in the course of the migrations had an extensive but cursory knowledge of the religious "soup" that made up the Sinai region. But whoever the god was that Moses worshipped, it was, like Jethro's, invisible. Unless, thought Jethro to himself one day, "*my father's god*" was not the god of Moses' Hebrew father, whom Moses had never seen, but of his father-in-law, Jethro. Had Moses encountered the god of Mount Horeb as well?

Jethro accepted his grandchildren into his heart wholeheartedly. They possessed all the healthy exuberances common among children who cared not a fig what their names meant and made their way serenely, unconsciously through the rough and tumble of adolescence and into early manhood. The wilderness was all the home they had ever known or would need to know. Abraham, Isaac and Jacob, Joseph's coloured coat, his eleven brothers, and more latterly Pharaoh's court, the pyramids, and wretched Hebrew enslavement—these were the stuff of evening tales told round the fire. They were not a real history, and certainly not theirs. No, the wilderness was where they lived, a simple existence, illuminated by bright sun heralding an uncluttered future.

Gershom took to metallurgy with an enthusiasm and skill that could not have been more in contrast to his father. Jethro was pleased to receive such a happy apprentice and Gershom, with the help of his uncle Hobab, settled into learning the craft thoroughly. If Gershom was aware of his alien status, he gave no sign; nor would he have reason under the loving tutelage of Jethro. But he took great delight in exploiting his name, *sojourner*, and even used it to persuade his father that he could go on the great trek. The crowning event of his initiation into the guild of the smiths was the four-month journey Hobab and he set out on. It had been presented to Jethro and Moses as an excursion to the rich ore deposits of Arabah for the educating of Gershom. But neither father was fooled. It was a chance for adventure.

Despite a difference of almost ten years, Hobab and Gershom were friends in addition to being kin. They could not have been more unlike kin in appearances. Hobab was taller even than Jethro, lanky with a long reach of arms. He had the build of a person who could walk all day and not get tired. Gershom was short and broad, his upper torso lending itself almost naturally to the hammer, but with legs that could never quite keep up with Hobab's naturally longer stride. Though both were smiths, Hobab's knowledge of the Sinai was a matter of public record and source of pride to Jethro. He held the informal role of scout to Jethro's family and would always go ahead of them whenever circumstances dictated a change of locale. What the two young men did share was a distrust of words and an appreciation for the strength of the wilderness in which they lived. For Hobab this would be the third such trip along the proposed route. For Gershom it would be his first contact with anything outside the tribe.

Their trip went north and a bit east for just over a hundred miles to the tip of the gulf of Aqaba. This was the beginning of the great Arabah depression, a huge valley running about one hundred and twenty miles north to end at the Salt Sea. At the south edge of Arabah was the town of Ezion-geber, and Gershom was round-eyed at the site of urban living—houses of clay brick close together, a crowded market square with hundreds of loud voices all around. This was the gateway to the lands of Edom and Moab, two large and well-established tribes. The route leading north along the east ridge of the valley was relatively well traveled and deep within Moabite and Edomite territory. The *King's Highway* it was called and Hobab took Gershom along this road just far enough to show him the first of a long series of border fortresses defending the route. Directly south of them at that point were the homelands of the Midianites and Hobab provided the sketchiest details of why Jethro had wandered so far from his ancestral soil.

The Midianites had decided views about the world of the gods, and worshipped accordingly. The world above was as crowded and conflicted as the one below. It only made sense that one struck alliances with as many gods as one could. Religious rituals were elaborate, requiring the careful appeasement of the entire pantheon who were represented always by ornate images of various shapes and sizes. Jethro was a senior priest trained in cult ritual, fertility rites for both soil and creatures, sorcery and the utterance of public oracles. One day, quite abruptly he had left, taking with him his family, but not a single idol. Their clan had never made new images, a state of affairs that would not have been tolerated in their homeland. Yet Jethro remained unperturbed and to Hobab's mind, living without the god images seemed to be much less cluttered.

Hobab and Gershom did not visit the land of Midian, preferring to press north into the valley. At the centre point measured from all sides was the old town of Oboth—a mining site for rich veins of malachite and some gold. Here, the earth had opened herself up like a harlot spreading her loins for all and sundry to come and ravage her. The rape would continue for hundreds of years.

Oboth had this sense of excess. There is something about mining towns still in their peak of production that suggests the smell of sweaty sex. The odour of humans was everywhere. There was no effort to conceal the flesh, even flesh that was withered and exhausted. Grit and dirt covered every surface. It was a town that knew that without an accident of geology it would not exist and furthermore knew that its existence would last only one day after the last shovelful of ore had been loaded into a camel's pannier. The knowledge gave the place an air of transience that affected the people and buildings. Everything was for the moment. Permanence and posterity were fool's gold, of interest only to less cosmopolitan and more innocent communities. The buildings reflected this aura of temporality. Most of the homes were of brick and structurally solid but there was nevertheless a squatness and surliness to their shapes which suggested that even this effort had been grudgingly expended.

The people too were an odd assortment of transients and leave-behinds. Slaves had their own part of the town, and lived and died virtually in isolation. Mortality rates were high among those who actually dug the rock. Various tribal groups could be seen in the faces that stared back at Gershom and Hobab making their way through the streets. Some were people sent in clusters to supervise the exporting of metal back to their homelands; others were caravaners who made Oboth their home base.

Hobab and Gershom spent several weeks in the town. There was always work for skilled smiths. To Gershom this extended foray into a completely new world was exhilarating, if exhausting. The sheer force of new foods, languages, customs, scenery, smells and sensations cascaded over him, leaving him quite stunned at times. It was not unpleasant but it required all his energies. This was not just the usual tale of witless wilderness youth colliding with callused frontier urbanity. There was a place here for Gershom though even he could not have put it into words. It did not matter here whose tribe you came from or what your lineage. What mattered here was the skills you carried with you. Everyone was from the tribe of the *here and now*. They were all kin for as long as kinship was significant, all from the tribe of Alien. If Horeb was the wilderness of place, then Oboth was the wilderness of persons. And Gershom, without any self reflection or even awareness, was drawn to the town as a moth is to the night-time oil lamp.

They stayed in the house of Klutil, a huge barrel-shaped man, prematurely bald. He had a large forge with about twenty indentured labourers. Hobab had met him on an earlier visit.

Klutil's shop was somewhat unique. A portion of it was devoted to refinement of the copper before it began its long slow journey via a caravan to some remote customer. Klutil had made a specialty out of smelting bronze, going to the trouble of importing tin from elsewhere, keeping tight control over the process, and charging for it accordingly. Gershom's task was to hammer the metal globs, still hot and soft but no longer molten, into thin sheets about a metre square. Transformed thus, the metal could be easily manipulated by the final user into whatever was required. The sheets were in demand for any kind of overlay work. Large monuments or edifices would usually be shaped first from wood and then overlaid with bronze or even gold sheathing. The big users were the god-makers and priestmen whose job included creating the icons, sometimes on a huge scale, to represent the deities. To Gershom, who had been schooled only in cast images, this method of idol manufacture was novel.

Klutil's only god seemed to reside somewhere in the inner recesses of his coin purse. The man was openly contemptuous of the image trade, never weary of remarking that half the gods in Sinai had been sired by his shop—bastards all of them! He took a cynic's satisfaction in taking a profit from a custom for which he had no use. Indeed Gershom himself felt an illicit thrill as he hammered away at the dull metal, knowing that it might end up somewhere as a god image. The act of bringing the hammer down again and again literally on the head of a god gave him a sense of superiority tinged with fear. Some of Klutil's cynicism rubbed off as well.

They decided to return home via the trade route leading through the Shur wilderness. It meant going a fair bit more north before turning west, touching Egypt at Lake Timsah, not far from Goshen. From there they turned south, retracing, unbeknown to Gershom, the path his own father had so hurriedly taken years earlier. South, down to Dophkah, which in comparison to Oboth looked worn and bleached—lying as if with her legs wrenched open, a discarded whore close to exhaustion. Her copper would not last much longer and Gershom realized that Oboth too would someday share this kind of fate. South they went, down to Rephidim until finally the broad valley to the north of Horeb stretched out in front like a lush carpet to welcome the weary feet of the returning sons!

Gershom was quite unprepared when Zipporah took him aside one evening and said, "We're leaving shortly, our family—your father, Eliezer, you and I. We're going back to Egypt. Jethro has given us his blessing on the trip."

"Egypt!" Gershom replied in a way that asked all the obvious questions that such news generated. "It's been forty years since Father came from there. Why?"

Zipporah was slow in her response, choosing her words carefully like someone would search for a footpath in the darkness. "Your father has been given a job, a big job, not one he sought. Dangerous for him certainly. While you were gone your father has...met the Hebrew God here on Horeb. He came in a fire, settling on a small bush but not consuming it. I am not sure exactly what your father saw, or how the God spoke to him, but he has received a commissioning. The Hebrews are to leave Egypt now and go to their own land. Your father says...this God..." Her voice kept trailing off into uncertainty. This was her first time repeating anything of what Moses had confided in her. Converting her thoughts to audible sounds gave the story a substance it did not have before—solidifying the future by clothing it with guttural sound, confirming its certainty. She continued.

"Your father's people are a kind of eldest son to this God... He made a solemn promise to Abraham that has not been forgotten. There is land waiting for these Hebrews—this firstborn people. Moses is going back to lead them out of Egypt and travel to this land."

"How is all this to happen?" asked Gershom. He was comprehending only in part.

"Your father has been given... help." She could find no other word to describe what she was about to tell. "His brother Aaron is still alive and something of a leader in Goshen. He is to be his spokesman. There will be a great conflict between Pharaoh and this Hebrew God. But Moses' shepherd stick is now... alive. It's connected to this God somehow. It can turn into a snake." Her voice broke again, but was now threatening an hysterical laugh. If she started, she might not stop.

"The snake will win in the end. Moses is to say to Pharaoh, 'This is what the Yahweh God says to you: Israel is my firstborn son; not your forced labourer. I have told you to relinquish him back to me that he may worship me. But you have refused. So it will be firstborn for firstborn. You keep mine captive? I will kill yours!'" She had said all she could. Gershom and she clung to each other in the dark, not frontally as if giving mutual comfort or love but huddled side by side, cringing together at the enormity of the story which confronted them.

"And what about me, mother?" Gershom finally whispered. "Am I not a firstborn, too?"

She continued, not having heard his question. "Moses cannot escape this job. He has tried. Oh how he has tried. But as for us, who knows if we have been seen by this God. We are not Hebrew. It was we Midianites who purchased Joseph from his brothers and resold him in Egypt. Perhaps neither Moses nor his God has any further use for us." Gershom realized at last what lay at the root of Zipporah's distress. How desperately Zipporah loved her man, this distant, driven, mysterious man whom Gershom hardly knew but who was loved zealously by his *little bird*. Losing him would break her heart. "But how can I compete with a God, and Gershom with his firstborn?"

— ◆ —

They had stopped near Dophkah for the night and were using an old broken down hovel as shelter. Gershom was wakened by the rough shaking from Zipporah.[3]

"Quickly! Turn toward me. Your phallus—let me see it." Her voice was hoarse, guttural. Her eyes were quite crazed and her hair, still matted from sleep, had stuck across her forehead from new sweat. She looked quite wild. Gershom turned slightly toward her and in an instant felt her urgent fumbling beneath his robe. Then sharp pain made him cry out. Then sticky wet. Blood on his clothes. He turned fully now into the room, sitting up, fighting off the reflex dry retching that his bloodied groin had induced. Moses lay on his back close to the opening that had once been the doorway. His eyes were open but he lay rigid. The room was cold, far colder than desert night air. They were not alone in the room. A terror , or something worse, was visiting them. Cold, methodical Anger was stalking Moses, holding him rigid but wakeful. There was a foul smell. It was as if the cold air had taken on a mass that one had to fight through to move, even to breath. It slowed everything down, even thinking. There was an eternity before what the eyes saw got translated to meaning. The room was claustrophobic as when a nightmare threatens to smother the sleeper and he thrashes about, racing to wake up before the air runs out.

Gershom watched his mother bending over Eliezer and by his reactions knew that Eliezer too had been cut. Zipporah was now back in the centre of the room with two small scraps of foreskin in one hand, an ancient flint knife in the other. Where she had found the ceremonial weapon he had no idea. Blood was on her hands. She tore the covering from Moses, exposing his feet, and began to savagely rub the bits of flesh against their soles.

"Husband of blood!" she shouted. "You'll walk now forever on the blood of your firstborn and on your children. Your blood, my blood, all the blood that is demanded by this God of yours from every one of his Hebrew males. This is your firstborn seed, Moses!" Zipporah was shrieking now, hunched over Moses' feet, grinding the foreskins as if to graft them onto his feet. He lay still and rigid, a corpse.

"Would you actually abandon your own while going to save the firstborn of God? God himself will not let you. See now how He has come to kill you?" She had dropped the flint and skins, now bending forward to cover as much of Moses' body with hers as she could. "Moses, Moses, he will not get you. Moses, he will not get you." It was not to Moses she was really speaking. Could she see something in the room Gershom could not see? Her cries settled into a softer cadence. "Moses, Moses, he will not get you." It was the voice of a mother who was herself frantic, reassuring a child. Gradually even this ceased and Gershom saw them lying together, Moses' head pulled tight into her breasts and her thigh draped across to envelop as much of him as possible. Little bird protecting her own. The room was warmer. Zipporah had stayed the executioner.

Moses never mentioned the incident. Gershom found himself feeding on his own anger mingled with scorn. Moses on a mission, the man who carried a holy staff, almost killed for not performing the minimal obligations required of a Hebrew father. The obvious failure gave Gershom a kind of power against his father. The holy man walked now with bloodied feet of clay. The power was sweet in his mouth.

The months in Egypt were a jumbled blur of events to Gershom. Aaron, Moses' brother, met them in the desert and Gershom took an instant dislike to him. Shorter than Moses, he had that constant market-huckster smile, with eyes that missed nothing. His hair was thin and straggly. It was the hair of an old woman and he wore it shoulder length. Permanent beads of sweat dotted his upper lip and he kept dabbing at them with a rag only for them to reform moments later.

An oily opportunist, thought Gershom. It was painful to watch him fawning all over Moses: a lavish kiss and embrace, tears, head bobbing and rapid speech. Then, rag to his lips, and the whole thing repeated. Moses his younger brother (by all of three years) was returning, a holy man, come from out of the desert. Aaron made much of greeting Zipporah although Gershom noted the way his hard little eyes took in her dress, her much darker skin and "foreign" accent. She is a liability, his eyes said. He was polite to Gershom and Eliezer but neither of them were of any use, and therefore of no interest, to Aaron. Aaron's sons were large, lumpish men with big feet and hands, broad foreheads: Nadab, Abihu, Eleazar and Ithamar. Gershom was not in the least intimidated by their size. Nadab in particular was fat. Across the front of his tunic horizontal bands of sweat had soaked through where the rolls of fat overlapped and squeezed together. His chest sank in the middle between two mounds of fat that hung like mutant breasts. When he ran, his whole body would jiggle, the fatty overlay heaving up and down independently of his frame, an involuntary, grotesque shimmery dance of flesh.

They stayed in Aaron's house and Zipporah tolerated with great grace the ever-so-subtle insults received from Elisheba, wife of Aaron but "sister to the leader of Judah," as Elisheba never tired of inserting into conversation. Political manoeuvring for tribal leadership was totally new to Gershom but despite the gap in his vocabulary it was odious for him to observe it just the same. Moses was rarely with them, always in meetings or gone to the Egyptian court; Aaron always with him. Gershom was glad to have learned at least some of his father's dialect from his father and he quickly built on it. Zipporah had learned the tongue decades earlier but would always speak it with an accent. They lived in the north end of Egypt, in Goshen, a huge ghetto of forced labourers for Ramses II's building projects. Squalour was everywhere. Fatigue filled the spaces between the huts. Gershom longed for the clean emptiness of Mount Horeb.

Gershom only half understood what was happening. Moses, Aaron by his side, had begun a great conflict with Pharaoh. The staff was as powerful as God had promised. The serpent was loose in Egypt and would not be contained. The confrontation was dramatic and intense. Disasters fell on Egyptians but stopped at the borders of Goshen. As the months went by and the conflict escalated, Gershom sensed that Zipporah, Eliezer and he were being isolated. They were the family of Moses, this holy man from the desert who had burst into the Hebrews' dull existence with stories of freedom and a great trek to their own land. It was the promise to Abraham made good at last. The ancient stories stirred, leaving the sentimental confines of the night fires to stride brazenly through their midst in the bright sun, catching them up, conscripting them as actors in the play. Gershom felt their apprehension mixed with hope, and sympathized with their fear of anyone who had close ties with Moses. It was all too fantastical. This was magic on a grand scale.

Details of the great conflict swirled around Goshen, which, like the centre of a hurricane, remained untouched. Frogs had overrun the Nile banks, flies and gnats had appeared in huge numbers, ravenous locusts had descended, hail storms erupted from nowhere, it was dark when it should have been daylight, and boils erupted on everyone that no ointment could soothe. Pharaoh would let them leave. Get ready! Pharaoh had changed his mind. Unpack. Pharaoh would let them go but only for three days. Pharaoh had changed his mind again. Not even three days.

And then the final punishment: every firstborn in Egypt dead. It was the visitation at Dophkah re-enacted over an entire nation. This time the executioner completed his mission. Gershom remembered the night it happened. Together with Aaron's family, they had been eating a dinner of roasted lamb. They ate it standing up, with their coats and footwear on, waiting for the new beginning. Outside the blood of the dead lamb was smeared on the three sides of their door. Each Hebrew family followed the same instructions given by Moses for this night. Each Hebrew family listened to the mounting wails that moved like waves through Egyptian quarters. Each Hebrew firstborn wondered whether the smears of blood at the door would be seen; each Hebrew father wished he had put more on. All were finally silenced by the enormity of what was happening.

If the night's events reminded Moses of Dophkah, he did not mention it. But sometimes Gershom would look up to find his father staring fixedly at him. Gershom found himself filled with an intense wish that he and his father could find a way to begin again. The strength of Gershom's longing was uncontrollable. His chest contracted, his breathing became shallow but louder.

But before either Moses or Gershom could act, the moment passed, stillborn, shattered by shouts outside. It was a squad of Pharaoh's palace guards escorting Pharaoh's first advisor, requesting them to attend an audience with Pharaoh that instant. Capitulation! Pharaoh's firstborn had not escaped. Gershom watched Moses and Aaron hurry out into the night. He finished his meal in silence: lamb, unleavened bread and bitter herbs.

That was their last night in Egypt. By dawn the march out of Egypt had begun, with thousands of people shoving their livestock before them, carrying bundles. Carts had been prepared for those who could not walk: the very old, the very young and mothers who were near term. It had all been quite carefully planned. People said that a man called Joshua was to be credited. Young and energetic, he had attached himself to Moses early on his coming. Gershom and he were cautious acquaintances. While Gershom did not like the obvious rapport he had with Moses, he could not blame Joshua. The young man was too transparent and took on the details of the march with tireless energy. He was everywhere and his barely restrained glee at leaving was contagious. Even the bones of Joseph had been retrieved from the Egyptian cave where they had lain for more than four hundred years. Joseph had extracted a promise from his sons that he would not be abandoned to Egyptian soil. Gershom pictured the skull wrapped up in the cloth, grinning idiotically at all the Egyptians.

Gershom found a position near a cart reserved for pregnant women, on which had been constructed a rude shelter to give the pretense of privacy during delivery. A young girl had seated herself on the very back, legs dangling. One hand above her head gripped the top edge of the walls, trying to soften the cart's lurching. Her other hand was holding her stomach, distended and ripe. She was in obvious pain but nothing would prevent her from gazing at the passing scenes. Gershom wondered what kind of stories she would croon to her yet unborn child about this day. The child would be among the first generation of freeborn after four hundred years of servitude.

Their exit route took them through the south of Egypt. Daylight came quickly and it seemed to Gershom as if the morning light thawed out the frozen Egyptian figures, releasing them instantly back into action. But there was a woodenness to their movements as if they had lost their coordination. Around him he could see Egyptian families dealing with the carnage of the night before. Everywhere there were silent groups standing around the carcasses of animals or beginning to dig graves for firstborn children—a people still in shock. The serpentine wave of Hebrews threading its way through was showered with gifts: gold and silver jewelry, nose rings, ankle bracelets, clothing—desperate gifts given without ceremony and quickly thrust into the hands of anyone who was close. Most were exchanges between the women, mothers paying to protect their wombs. The woman in the cart had been given something, a gold chain on which hung a large flat medallion. She clutched it with the hand cradling her stomach. Egyptian gold pressed close to kicking Hebrew. They were free. The serpent had won.

Moses talked with his wife and sons that night. It was to Zipporah that he spoke. "Your father should know of what's happened," he said without preamble. "I need you to go ahead of us. Tell him..." Moses' voice slowed. What exactly should the message be? "Tell him that the unseen Hebrew God has indeed won over Pharaoh and that there is to be a great celebration at Horeb. God will meet us there and prepare us for the journey to our own lands. Tell him that the invisible God of the mountain has showed his arms. Tell him that it would be good to see him." Moses' voice trailed off again. It was left to Zipporah to fill in the unspoken message she was being asked to carry. Her heart melted at Moses' vulnerability.

"Yes, certainly he should be told and we are the logical messengers," she said including Gershom and Eliezer with her hands. "And yes, certainly we will tell him everything," including, she added to herself, that you are lonely and already frightened and that you know you are just at the start of your task and already these people threaten to consume you with their overwhelming needs. I will tell him all of that, too.

They left early next day and it was not until weeks later, when they met again at Horeb, that they learned of the further adventures they had missed. It was Nadab, Aaron's eldest who told Gershom and had Gershom not been in Egypt he would not have believed Nadab. But Nadab had no motive to stretch the details of the march through the Great Sea, the annihilation of Pharaoh's army, the column of fire that hovered over the camp each night and the food that kept appearing each morning. Gershom sensed Nadab's satisfaction at describing to Gershom all the details of the Amalekites' attack.[4] They had struck at Rephidim, not far north of Horeb, and Joshua had been the hero of the day, leading a volunteer mob of young men equipped with the few weapons brought from Egypt out to meet this new threat.

"Your father," Nadab said, "stood on top of a hill with his snake/staff held high above his head. My father Aaron and our uncle Hur, Miriam's husband, stood with him and as the day got hotter they each supported an arm so that Moses' hands remained stretched high all day. We could see their silhouettes whenever we looked up. It was a magnificent spectacle—Joshua leaping and shouting, everywhere at once urging us on and the three men high up standing tall against the sky as if bestowing on us below the blessing of immortality. Afterwards your father ordered a huge heap of stones to be piled up and my father, I and my brothers, Abihu, Ithamar and Eleazar, we slaughtered a cow in front of all the people. It was exhilarating," finished Nadab. Whether it was the battle or the sacrifice to which his last comment referred was unclear. "A shame that you missed it." Both his face and tone were inscrutable.

The meeting of Jethro and Moses was rich.[5] Though Moses greeted Zipporah and his sons kindly enough, the strain of the journey from Egypt showed plainly. Hobab had come as well, always glad for any excuse to travel and to see Gershom, his favourite nephew. Moses had actually run toward Jethro, eyes shining with the pleasure of the reunion. Zipporah watched her husband visibly absorb the strength of Jethro's presence. She had never much thought of her father in his role of clan leader and priest but seeing the two men together gave her new appreciation for the skills needed to lead. Jethro entered into Moses' accomplishments and adventures with uncompromised enthusiasm, listening to all the details of the journey. They had set up a makeshift camp at the base of Horeb, some distance outside the main Hebrew encampment. It was night by the time Moses had finished telling Jethro everything that had happened. The fire kept catching Jethro's face, illuminating a ruddy glow of vicarious delight that remained even after Moses had finished talking.

"Truly the God of the mountain has rescued you from the hands of Pharaoh. Now I know that he is mightier and more powerful than all other gods," said Jethro. "I will pay homage to this God who has chosen your people."

Next day, true to his word, Jethro prepared sacrifices with portions enough left over for Aaron and other leaders to eat together.

Zipporah watched from the edges.

Jethro stood upright in the brilliant sun, carrying out the rites of sacrifice over a large central fire with a steady dignity. And the Hebrew elders, about seventy-five of them squatting in the desert dirt, received their portions of meat and bread, eating solemnly in silence, looking for all the world to be what they were—old men of the tribe in tattered clothing, still uncertain if their parole was genuine. The meal of thanksgiving and praise was consumed in the very presence of the unseen God. That the presiding priest and initiator of the sacred feast was a Cushite went unremarked.

The day after the feast found Moses back inside the main camp, heavily immersed in the affairs of camp management. It was the appointed day of petitions, and a disorderly throng had remained clustered around Moses since early morning. These were the days that grievances and disputes were aired, some so trivial as to be comical, some severe: a woman who was alleged to have cracked the cookpot of another by deliberately kicking it and refused to make good; the theft of a knife; what to do with the young man found returning to camp in disheveled state with an even younger and more disheveled girl. On and on through the day the questions, petitions and arguments came before Moses. Jethro had quietly joined the throng about midday and watched quietly until finally it was over at dusk. He caught up with Moses walking back to his tent.

"You will exhaust yourself if you persist," Jethro said quietly.

"But the people insist on hearing God's will in these matters," replied Moses.

"God's will is that women should not ruin each other's cookpots, thieves must be sought out and punished, and young men held responsible for their sexual behaviour. It is unlikely he will change his mind on such matters." The kindly jibe was obvious. Jethro went on, "Listen and I will give you some advice. Write down the instructions God has given you. Teach these people their duties, what God expects of them, and what is required for orderly camp governance. Lord knows they are used to taking orders; in fact they love the security it gives. Appoint capable men over tens, hundreds, thousands and so on. Save yourself as the high court of appeal and for cases that are complex or new."

"Will this satisfy the people?" asked Moses.

"Justice delayed is justice denied," replied Jethro. "And a burden split among many is lighter for all," he continued.

"Yes, yes," rejoined Moses, his voice a little lighter. "I know a few Kenite proverbs myself Jethro. But what you say is right. I will do it."

It was a more settled, resolute Moses who finally kissed Jethro on his departure. "You have been generous in your counsel," said Moses.

"The same God counsels us both," responded Jethro. "But he has chosen very different journeys for us." He paused, trying to make up his mind whether to say the next thing. He finally continued, "For over sixty years I have been waiting here at this mountain, waiting with never a clear sense of what I was waiting for but certain I could not leave, wondering if ever the God of this mountain would show himself. He is about to, Moses, and in a great and terrible way, not just in signs but his actual self. It will not be repeated ever again. But he is not coming to me. Moses, he is coming to you. You are the one he has chosen. My lot is to leave now that you have arrived. I am returning to my father's homelands east of Aqaba. That is my land; yours is in front of you still."

— ◆ —

And it was true—this prescience of Jethro's. Thick clouds of smoke enveloping the top of Horeb marked the beginning of the "giving of the Ten Words" as the story tellers would later call it. Moses kept ascending and descending into the cloud. The whole people were ceremonially cleansed and led in solemn march toward the base where on the third day the mountain erupted in noise, fire and whirling clouds of black smoke, heralding the presence of God himself and sending the people back in all directions, carried on a wave of holy terror. Never before and never again would God come this close to his people. They could not bear it and told Moses so.[6]

From then on it was Moses who went alone up into the smoke to receive the words of God. Once though, Aaron, accompanied by his sons Nadab and Abihu, and Joshua, and seventy of the elders went with him.[7] Gershom heard the details of what he had missed from cousin Nadab.

"Moses took us about two thirds up the mountain. It was quite a climb," began Nadab. Gershom smiled to himself at the thought of Nadab's fatty bulk making the climb.

"I'm sure it was," he replied politely.

"We were sitting, resting. Higher up, it seemed that the smoke cloud started to move down toward us, but the air around us stayed bright no matter how close it came. We could see each other but for some reason we could not see other things. Below, the camp was gone. Above was the smoke. Yet we ourselves were visible. We just sort of hung there in a kind of space. I was afraid to move, I tell you. Despite its being clear light, I could see nothing of the mountain itself. We could see each other, but everything else was just gone. And then out of the smoke above us a blue path formed—like a long blue cloth being unrolled—stretching out right through the centre of where we all crouched. But it wasn't thin like cloth even though it was pliable. This carpet was transparent; a brilliant blue quartz that sparkled with a light of its own. And then HE appeared, walking out from the smoke along the blue pavement. It was terrible. I thought I was going to die just from the sight of him. But none of us did. Afterwards we shared our water skins and passed around what food had been brought. Nobody spoke really or asked about the figure we had seen. I was glad just to be alive. We all were."

Nadab, Aaron and the others had returned. Moses had remained alone except for his aide, Joshua. The affairs of the camp were left to Aaron and Hur, Miriam's husband. The top of the mountain remained hidden in the smoke, now tinged with red as if the centre had caught fire and was glowing. It was not inviting and Moses did not return quickly.

The trouble started soon after. "Who could blame them?" as Aaron would plead afterwards to Moses. "You were slow in returning to us."

Hysteria began to surge through the camp like a low, long swell, a wave that started far far out from shore, not high and white crested but deep and mean. It surged finally toward Aaron, demanding assurances that they had not been abandoned. Aaron, sweat dripping from his upper lip, came finally to Gershom for help.

"They need an image, Gershom, something they can see and touch and pay homage to. Help me with it. You have the skills and the tools. Look, they have given me more than enough gold jewelry. Just something to focus people's attention."

Gershom stared back at Aaron, making no effort to hide his disgust. Aaron tried again, his voice taking on a faint menace. "Gershom, a mob's an ugly thing. It won't just stop at me you know. Do you think they won't take it out on the son of Moses as well as his brother?" It was a fatal error, this appeal to Gershom's personal safety, and Aaron, just by watching Gershom's face, realized his mistake.

He tried again; this time his voice betrayed both his real anxiety and his fear. "I can't hold them together any other way Gershom. They'll run amok or worse, run back to Egypt. Your father—we both know he's coming back—he'll be the joke of Sinai. Help me hold them together just until Moses returns. I don't know any other way to keep control, Gershom. Gershom, for the honour of your father, help me. At least lend me your tools!" Aaron had found the nerve he needed. Gershom turned toward his tent in search of his tools. Aaron began to organize a fire. For some reason Klutil's smirking face kept drifting through Gershom's head.

The golden calf[8] image did its job. The people rallied, paid ceremonial homage for their freedom and then quickly degenerated into debauchery. Aaron had badly miscalculated everything except that Moses would return. When he did, it was with a hot rage so visible that it was obvious even through people's drunken haze. The camp was cleansed. The Levite clan rallied around their kin and restored order with a brutality like nothing seen in Egypt. Hebrew killed Hebrew for the first time. Aaron offered excuses to Moses. Gershom avoided his father.

Not long after, the work on the Tent of the Promises began, and not just the portable tent itself but on all the ceremonial artifacts of worship: a huge tent, an outer perimeter wall that formed a courtyard around the tent, furniture for the interior, lampstands, gold rings, frames for the tent poles, skins and fabrics as coverings, clothing for the priests, Aaron's special symbols of high office, including the breastplate of divination, and lesser costumes for his sons, heirs to the position. The God of the mountain was coming to live among them and was particular about his dwelling.

The scope of the project was enormous and yet Moses' detailing of each and every item was explicit. Moses had received the instructions on the mountain top. It fell to Bezalel, Miriam's son, and another man, Oholiab, a Danite tribesman, to be the chief artisans. Gershom watched them from time to time as they personally shaped the more intricate pieces of furniture. Some said that the Spirit of God himself rested on them, so advanced was their workmanship, and Gershom, watching them, knew it to be true.

The chest of God's Law was perfection itself, made of acacia wood overlaid with gold. The gold used was quite pure, giving a soft deep lustre to the entire piece. The lid of the chest was a work unlike anything Gershom had ever seen. At each end rising up out of the lid itself was a human-like form, kneeling. They looked toward each other but with heads bowed slightly downward. They had wings and Bezalel had managed to scribe the details of each individual feather along their broad edges. These were the servants of God, keeping perpetual watch over the empty space between them until he would come. Both figures had been created without severing them from the gold used to overlay the lid. Gershom knew the almost impossible job of trying to heat one section of gold malleable enough to work on while not disturbing the designs already complete. But Bezalel had done it. In the soft indeterminate light that comes just at dusk the creatures looked alive—feathers twitching ever so slightly in the air. Waiting.

Gershom stood one night staring fixedly at the chest when it was almost done. There was a fullness inside of him that he could not explain. Up until now this God of the mountain had been a God of grand gestures and spectacular entrances, holy presence writ large. Gershom, for reasons he did not know, had remained unmoved. But here before him was such a lavish attention to detail, and to delicate beauty. He remembered his father's story.

He took his shoes off, bowed himself low to the ground and crept away quietly into the darkening night.

The inauguration of the temple overwhelmed even Moses. The erection of the outer perimeter wall came first creating a huge courtyard with only one entrance. Then the Tent of Meeting was raised at one end, leaving about two thirds of the enclosure free for Aaron and his sons to make the sacrifices on the big altar. Into the tent went the furniture: the Ark of Testimony, the candlesticks, table, lamps and incense altar. The courtyard held the large bowl of water for the purification of the priests. Moses himself washed Aaron first and then dressed him in the robes of office. Gershom watched as Moses consecrated Aaron, installing him in the position of priest, chief servant of their God. Aaron's sons were installed as well into their lesser offices—Nadab, Abihu, Eleazar and Ithamar.

"Their anointing will be to a priesthood that will continue for all generations to come." Moses' voice when he spoke slowly had a majestic cadence to it without the least trace of his customary stammer. The firstborn male would succeed his father as chief priest. What was Moses thinking of by this outlandish devolving of power to Aaron and his sons? Gershom marveled at his father's serenity that he could so resolutely reduce himself by elevating his older brother.

The ceremonies continued, Aaron seeming to grow into his role and robes and even Gershom, for all he did not like the man, was impressed with the change. The sacrifices began with Aaron's own sin offering, a bull calf not yet weaned. Gershom could see his legs buckle and then kick spasmodically as the blood spurted from his neck; a strong stream at first, splashing into the desert sand but subsiding as the calf's heart grew weaker. The blooding of the altar! Aaron dipped his fingers in some of the blood, turning to smear the altar horns. Then the fire was started. Nadab and his brothers began butchering the bull calf, cutting off chunks to be handed to Aaron who then placed each piece carefully into the fire. The rituals of slaughter continued. Fire and blood and fatty flesh merged together into a savoury appeasement.

Other animals followed. Nadab killed a goat next. Eleazar held a basin to catch some of the blood which Aaron then took and threw against all four sides of the altar. The ground immediately around the altar was dark as if it was the altar itself that bled. Aaron stepped forward, away from the altar area raising his hands—the hands of God—to pronounce a blessing on the people. Moses and Aaron then slowly entered the Tent of Meeting. Gershom watched their retreating backs. Aaron, with his ornate headgear seemed the taller, but it was his hand that reached out at the last moment to grab Moses' before they disappeared behind the curtain. Gershom thought about the two winged creatures who waited within.

He watched the two men emerge from the tent a short while later, raising their arms in a salutatory blessing over the people. Aaron's installation was complete. God had accepted him into the office. The fire on the altar leaped higher. The spirit of God had come down to eat.

What happened next would remain an issue of whispered controversy for years. Nadab and Abihu collapsed in the sand in front of the altar. Their bronze incense pots, which they had been waving in front of the altar, were still clutched in their hands smoldering. Dead.[9]

Some said later that they had reached out and taken hot coals from the altar fire for their own incense pots—improvised ritual outside the prescriptions laid down. It was right after they had taken the fire that the two fell down. The fire must have killed them somehow. The theories raged: judgment for having added their own spontaneous act of worship outside the ritual rites; judgment for wanting to attract attention to themselves; judgment for having been drunk on this of all days. It fell to their cousins to haul the bodies away outside the camp. Aaron, still consecrated, could not leave the altar courtyard.

Aaron was silent. He stood not moving just at the edge of the circle of the dark stain around the altar's base, which itself still smoldered. He kept looking at the spot where his sons had fallen. The blooding of the altar indeed! Who was this God in whose service he was bound? He, who made the golden calf, spared, while his two sons consumed for much lesser improvisation. The sins of the father resting horribly on the bodies of his children.

— ◆ —

The departure of Gershom, Eliezer and their mother Zipporah happened in this way.[10]

While they were still camped at Zion, Miriam and Aaron launched a campaign to become co-leaders along with Moses. It was a clever stratagem designed for broad appeal. The safety of the tribe required it. What if Moses misheard the instruction of God? There was no need to elaborate on what could happen. Aaron played the part of grieving father with all sincerity. Had not God also spoken to Aaron and Miriam? Three wise heads were better than one. Was not Aaron the high priest of God? Had he not gone into the Tent of Meeting *along* with Moses and emerged unscathed? And was not Miriam a wise and elder sister, whose leadership had been obvious since Egypt?

Gershom watched in frank amazement at the orchestration of the campaign. Miriam's telling thrust though was her appeal to the people on the basis of tribal purity. "His wife is wonderfully supportive. Moses is lucky to have met her. It's hard to think of her as a Cushite and not one of our own. She fits in so well. Still is it safe to have an outsider so close to the ear of our leader? If she ever led him astray, unintentionally of course, we'd all be destroyed. Moses needs our protection and we need the safety of a tribunal leadership." It was the elder sister reluctantly stepping into leadership for the good of others and the love for her younger brother. It made Gershom nauseous. Political intrigue has a special stench all its own.

Gershom did not know exactly how Moses deflected the leadership challenge. What he did know was that the three of them had gone to the Tent of Meeting and that only Aaron and Moses had returned to camp, with Aaron subdued and silent. Miriam had been hustled away to a small tent on the edge of camp but the cloak under which she cringed could not keep her secret. Leprosy. Her skin was a layer of large white flakes like a dried fish whose scales flake off. For seven days it would last. Divine punishment.

Moses sought out Gershom. "Your mother is returning to her father," he said. "I would like you to escort her safely."

"Of course," Gershom responded instantly.

Uncomfortable silence hung between them. Finally, "She feels it's the best for what I have to do...doesn't want to be the cause of any more trouble for me although I've told her that it's impossible... She'll join up again once we've reached the land and get settled. My job will be over then."

"I'll see her personally to Jethro's very tent flap," promised Gershom. There was another pause, this time broken by Gershom.

"I'm not sure that I'll be back soon either. Might do some more smith work. Thinking about going back to Oboth for a while." His voice was low and his hands worked furiously at the ends of his belt, eyes downward. "You'll need good smiths in the new land." He suddenly looked up straight into Moses' face. "You'll be all right, Father. Uncle Hobab has accepted your offer and will be a good scout.[11] He knows the whole Sinai better than any of us. And Joshua's a good choice for your primary aide. He has the respect of the people and he'll not betray you ever." His voice had become rushed, pleading for agreement that his own departure was not desertion nor rejection, that it wasn't the fault of either. It just was.

Moses' stammer was pronounced. "I've tried my best. There have been so many demands."

"It's all right."

And so they left, without ceremony, early next day. They went out through the tents and finally past Miriam's little shelter. She sat in the entrance, white skin watching black skin, watching white skin. Gershom delivered his mother to Jethro and then turned east. To Oboth. Home.

— ◆ —

Years passed. Gershom remained in Oboth. He and Klutil, his head shinier than ever, slowly became friends. Gershom grew to love his vocation. And then came news of a huge encampment of nomads thirty miles eastward at a site called Punon, wanderers who had come out of Egypt some thirty-five odd years earlier.

"It's my people," said Gershom to Klutil when he heard the news. "No doubt about it. But what they are doing this far south and still not settled in the land is anybody's guess. My uncle is their scout. You remember him—Hobab. He introduced me to you." He added more quietly, "My father leads them."

"You should visit him," Klutil said.

The camp was not hard to find. But as he approached, Gershom sensed something radically wrong.[12] He smelled rotting flesh—corpses not properly buried. And a veteran tribe of nomads would never let a stranger walk through a camp unchallenged. Yet everywhere people were indifferent to him. Some sat in obvious pain. A plague of some kind was among them. Gershom looked more closely. He saw desert snakes, six inches long and the colour of the rock itself. The bite was deadly. What had happened? And why had they infested the camp in such numbers?

Gershom found his father easily enough—at the centre of camp close to where the Tent of Meeting was pitched. Moses was bent over a rock. There was a hot fire nearby. The clunk of metal hitting metal coincided with Moses' arm movements. The rhythm was irregular, awkward. Gershom knew the sound but could not digest what his ear was telling him. Moses was never any good at smithing. What was the head of the clan doing? He coughed loudly behind Moses' back so as to announce his presence. He was suddenly quite nervous. Thirty-five years! Better not to have come.

"Hello, father," he said. His voice sounded foolish even to himself.

Moses' arm stopped mid-stroke. He swung half around, not moving his feet but only the top half of his body. Sweat was everywhere on his face. Slowly he put the hammer and tongs down. This time his feet moved as he turned more fully.

"Gershom?" the voice was strained, and thickened with age. The face was deeply etched, each line a story. But his eyes were clear and strong. And sad. Neither knew what to say. Gershom looked for an opening.

"The metal will cool if you don't keep up the work," he said, pointing to the elongated lump of bronze Moses had been hammering. "I didn't think you ever really took to smithing," continued Gershom. The tone was light, feeling its way.

"I haven't," replied Moses, wiping his forehead with the back of his arm, and giving a small laugh. "That should be self evident." Gershom stepped toward his father, his right hand open in front of him and without more words Moses put the hammer into it. Stepping aside he watched Gershom pick up the bronze with the tongs and thrust it back into the fire, stooping to blow at the base and pile on more wood.

"What are we making?" asked Gershom.

"A snake," said Moses

"I've seen a few of them around. A god image then ?"

"An antidote. There are snakes in the camp. This will prevent people from dying. Those who look at it will live"

"Oh," was all Gershom said. The explanation made no sense, but then what else was new? Moses must have sensed the strangeness of his abridged story so, as Gershom began to hammer , he resumed speaking.

"The people were complaining about the manna—and anything else they could think of to complain about. Everything was my fault again. God drove snakes in out of the desert as punishment. They are asps, I think. We had them in Egypt. But I interceded finally once the dying started. They became frightened, and sorry. And pitiful. I always intercede for them it seems." Moses made this last comment more to himself than to Gershom. Gershom said nothing. His arm and hammer settling into a steady clunk, clunk, clunk—the bar of bronze becoming longer and thinner. This story was as weird as all the rest. Nothing had changed.

"So I am to make this talisman and walk through the camp. Those that humble themselves and look at it will live. Those that remain stubborn will die."

"Your God's care for his people has always been original," Gershom said dryly. "I'd best hurry."

More silence. Then, "You still haven't made it to your lands." Gershom did not know how else to put the obvious question. The obvious question was what his people were doing thirty-five years later still in the wilderness when the original journey should have taken them at most a few months.

"We got to the border years ago. Sent scouts. It's good land. But the people got frightened. Didn't want to go forward. The younger ones did. I expect we'll get there shortly. Almost a whole generation has died off."

"Where is Hobab?"

"Out scouting. We need better water."

"And Aaron?"

"Dead. Eleazar is the high priest. Doing a good job."

"Oh...Miriam?"

"Died too. I miss them both. They were good helpers with me through these years."

It was Moses' turn to start questioning. "You stayed in Oboth all this time?"

"Yes, they needed smiths."

"Your mother?"

"Last I heard, still alive. Lives with Jethro's family. Eliezer too."

"Jethro?"

"Gone."

"It will be my turn soon."

The work of hammering did not encourage long bursts of speech. Gershom's mind was in hopeless disarray. Thirty-five years and yet some memories of the past rushing in from who knew where. Frankly he was glad for the work at hand. He asked finally: "Is the ark still with you? The one with the two winged creatures?"

"Yes."

"It was beautiful work. I was always sorry that I could not do something. But the calf image...Lucky I wasn't killed I suppose."

"We were all killed. Some just died sooner than others."

Gershom chose not to respond. More silence. Then Moses spoke again. "I'll go and find a long pole heavy enough to support the snake.

Can you form it around?"

"Yes."

The job was finally finished. Gershom had hurried. The camp noises had increased since he had arrived. The bronze icon was not pretty work. But it was a snake and Moses could carry it easily on the tall pole.

"Thank you, Gershom."

They stood facing each other. The snake between them. Awkward silence.

"You'd best start through the camp," said Gershom.

"You'll be here when I get back?"

Gershom did not answer. He watched his father disappear behind the first tent. The top of the pole could be seen moving slowly, bobbing along as if riding the crests of the waves formed by the tips of the tents. The bronze snake occasionally caught the light.

Gershom laid the tools neatly on the rock.

Endnotes:
[1] Exodus 2:16ff
[2] Exodus 18:3f
[3] Exodus 4:24ff
[4] Exodus 17:8
[5] Exodus 18:1-12
[6] Exodus 20:19
[7] Exodus 24:9
[8] Exodus 32
[9] Numbers 3:4
[10] Numbers 12:1
[11] Numbers 10:29
[12] Numbers 21:4-9

The Woman With No Name

It was the hot time of the day, early in the afternoon, when the woman slipped silently from the shadow of her door into the dirty heat. The town lane ways were empty for the most part. Morning market session had ended hours ago. The noon meal had been eaten indoors and there would be little activity of any kind until the advancing evening breezes and retreating sun made movement more comfortable. It was, for the woman, her favourite time of the day—a time that was hers alone. She had left her husband in conversation with his friend Eshilem, who served with him on the council of town elders. She would not be needed until the evening meal and the two would not miss her. This coming together to discuss town business was more ritual companionship than necessity for the two men. Neither was gifted with great charisma, the problems of their small town were of no real consequence; nor were their ideas overly innovative or much listened to. They were what they appeared to be: small merchants living in the small town of Zorah, content to be occupied with the daily routines of living, having come to an easy and early acceptance of their place within the universe, for which they cared not a fig, and of their place within their town, about which they cared greatly.

The woman continued to watch the two men in her mind's eye as she walked purposefully toward the town gate. She was aware and envious of how easily her husband seemed to fit into life. Everything about their lives seemed so comfortably away from any edges. The house that was neither too grand lest it attract envy nor too rude lest it cause shame; their market stall positioned in neither the best nor worst place; their modest barn, more of a shed, with an adjoining fenced pen in which their small flock of goats was housed each night; their three fields, property handed down from her husband's father, a field of winter wheat, a field of barley and a field left fallow in which their ten olive trees grew. They were neither the best of lands, which were at the bottom of the wadi, enriched by centuries of flood runoff, nor the worst, which were at the top of the ridges that marked the end of the valley sides and the beginning of the rough hill country. They were the epitome of quiet living. It was all so ordinary and her husband seemed to thrive on it all, revel almost in the security of the mundane and the predictable.

85

She wondered if perhaps their marriage hadn't been his one attempt to break the pattern. She had brought little with her that enhanced their staid stability. Rather, as his father had said, her wild flirtatious beauty was something to be reckoned with. If his son must have her, then best to begin a family immediately. Children would be sure to calm the sultry wildness that was so evident in her youthful form. Her good looks had not deserted her. By this time she was outside the town wall and following the path leading to their furthest field, the highest of the three on the north side of the valley. A breeze kept her tunic flat against her smooth taut stomach and her nipples, not yet stretched from years of suck, protruded outward against the rough material.

Even if you asked her she could not have told you wherein lay the root of her inability to fit in. Perhaps she was simply a reflection of the times in which she lived. Perhaps she was in fact the only one who understood how turbulent life really was beneath the thin veneer of market hours and town council assemblies. For her, life was as vibrant and in flux as the heat waves that made the whole horizon dance at midday. There they all lived—a small cluster of people of the tribe of Dan—perched in a town, itself perched on the northeast side of a valley that ended further north and west, losing itself in the fertile coastal lowland. It was all so precarious. Their tribe's claim to this region did not go unchallenged, and the foreign, coastal people still held sway over the other end of the valley—*People of the Sea*, the Philistines, as they were called in her tongue, said to have come latterly from Egypt but before that from across the great sea. They were a rough lot, these coastal people that shared their valley, with a tradition of stocky resiliency and bravery every bit as rich in folklore and story as their own. Between them lay what was a kind of stage in which stratagems for supremacy were played out. Some were no more than harmless harassments with little loss of life or property, but other assaults were more earnest. Still, despite the ongoing friction there had been no general war. Neither the Danites nor their tribal cousins had any stomach for what would have resulted in their wholesale genocide. And from the Philistines' perspective, waging traditional war on the flat lands of the coast where their chariots could manoeuvre was a far different thing than mounting an expedition into the hill country, trying to dislodge the Danites from the mountain strongholds.

The proximity of the foreigners only seemed to heighten the feeling that the land itself was still growing, shifting underfoot, like a child going through puberty. Boundaries were still movable, domination was constantly shifting and though the sun would set in a blaze of tranquillity, illuminating the settled coastal plain, it cast long shadows over the purple-black hill country that lay to the east. The Danites were a small tribe, one of twelve small tribes newly arrived, trying to wedge themselves into a land and to find a toehold in the hill country that seemed reluctant to open up to these people. The woman saw her own life as a pond, mirroring the times, energetic but uncertain in its application, for the reflection was always distorted when the waters moved.

How unlike her husband, who saw life in the minutia of ordered convention. He held dear to each routine as if by claiming these, the larger uncertainties of life could be kept at bay and ignored. The confines of Zorah's daily routine with its market gossip, the exchange of the news of the day, were more than the woman could tolerate and she looked forward to this afternoon escape eagerly. Though ostensibly there was always some purpose to each trip—the hens to be checked on, weeds to be dug out, olive trees pruned, crops inspected for infestations of pestilence—she and her husband had long ago tacitly agreed not to discuss this need to escape the confines of the town.

The woman touched her stomach again through the tunic and as the path veered upward she frowned and across her face flashed an unspoken pain. Flat, smooth stomach, wide hips, breasts that were firm and pleasingly obvious regardless of the clothes she wore. In the early years of their marriage she had been glad of the open and frank admiration her body generated. Her husband in his own stiff way was pleased at the envious glances other men gave him as they imagined the pleasure she gave him. And it was true, the nights were everything one could wish for.

But there had been no children. The town women's advice had become more pointed over time; the concoctions of roots, nuts and herbs became more outrageous as the woman had resorted to more and more fanciful cures. But still the children would not come. Her stomach remained flat and taut.

In the end the town folk did what town folk of every time and place do with the oddities of life. Open consolation became silent pity, turning to speculation on the reason for her barrenness. And following the human obsession with needing a reason for everything, they had finally found one for her. The barrenness was a punishment from Yahweh himself. She was getting only what she deserved and it was not the job of the community to lift the stigma of her sterility. Theirs was not to question the punishment of another. And though they never meant to be unkind, somehow to be *too* accepting of someone so obviously out of favour with the supreme unseen God was perhaps to court some kind of awful disaster for oneself. To be sure, her husband never chided her, and he loved her insofar as it is possible for a man who is caught between his vow of fidelity and the need to retain his position within the town. But she knew his heart ached for the gift of normality—to be in all respects like others. How could they hope to settle in the land without the strength of family? Indeed the obligation to their tribe required offspring. What other hope was there to push the Philistines back to the coast and secure some little land to the tribe of Dan? And because she loved him, her heart ached too.

She had reached the field of olive trees and walked along the northern most edge, as she always did, to the jumble of rocks that offered a seat. From here she could see almost the whole valley. Valley was perhaps too grand a word for the large indentation—a wadi was more accurate. The small river bed at the bottom was dried up for at least two months of each year but in the springtime the valley channeled the runoff from the higher, interior hills. The hills on the south side were much lower, for on the north side the hills and ridges marked the beginning of the hill country, rugged terrain that, when retreated into, made it possible to withstand even the most concerted attack. Zorah did not have the wadi to itself. At the bottom and some scant four miles distant was the village of Timnah, the furthest advance of the Philistine tribe. As a town it did not really compare to the hill fortress of Zorah, with not even a wall for demarcation. She wondered if this casual, careless attitude to its construction and security stemmed from the people's relaxed, arrogant confidence that the Danites posed no threat to them, or if the residents relied on the safety of the larger city built further west and on the opposing high land that formed the southern border of the wadi. Beth-Shemesh was its name—*The House of the Sun*—and from her lookout about seven miles away and higher up, with the sun still high, the name seemed apt. Its white buildings were clean and pure from this distance and she could make out the taller, irregular roof line of their largest building—a temple to the sun god himself! Rumour abounded as to what transpired within its walls. No Danite had ever been inside.

Their gods were different from the one God of the Danites. Yahweh, the invisible God was supreme above all others. She knew only a few of the stories told about their God dealing with her people: a great trek across the desert with Yahweh at their head, who had gone before in a tower of fire striking fear into all their enemies; the leader Moses, who was said to have been the only man ever actually to have seen the Yahweh God and lived, albeit with a face so brilliantly illumined by the encounter that he wore a veil for months afterwards; the man Joshua, who had led the first and by far the most successful foray into this their promised land; a city called Jericho, whose walls had been pulled down by the invisible hand of Yahweh and which still lay as a rubble heap. Yahweh was mighty. But there was a price to be paid for such protection. One worshipped him and no other god or family of gods. He would not share his people with other gods. Was this not the first and most important of the Ten Words given to Moses and written by the very finger of Yahweh? And images too were forbidden. This Yahweh was not to be subjected to artistic speculation.

So different was Yahweh from the earthy exuberance of the Philistines' gods. To begin with, there seemed so many of them. *Baals* they were called: gods in charge of the rains, gods in charge of the harvests, gods in charge of most every aspect of life. The god Dagon was thought to be half fish and half man. He was worshipped far to the south in an elaborately built temple at Gaza, a city close to the sea. He was one of their chief gods.

The rumours about their worship seemed to the woman to be as wild as the land. There was dancing of a kind that made the blood run hot, sweat running in rivulets off the dancers' skin, fortified wines drunk to excess, spiced brews made from grains, foods of all kinds consumed at feasts that lasted for days. Their worship was a state of wild ecstasy where no desires were taboo. Some even said there were blood sacrifices ("of humans," it was whispered) laid out in front of strange images. There was something enchanting about the sensual invitation of these gods, to be nothing other than oneself, released at some primordial level to follow one's passions without thought or reflection. The gods themselves seemed subject to these very same passions. One never quite knew what they might do next. The stories of their gods were full of uncertain struggle mixed with excess. Stories circulated about ritual copulation that caused the fertility of the land each year and which needed mimicking on earth as if to remind the gods to do their part. They spilled each other's blood in fits of anger or jealousy. Creatures of the earth were made by trial and error with the early, lesser formed attempts hurled down to earth to live as dwarfs, cripples or foreign tribes. Such an approach to one's religion seemed more faithful to the way life was in this country—always a little out of control and uncertain, and, because of this always full of the adrenaline that comes from living on the edge.

In contrast, the way of Yahweh seemed austere and stern. And aloof. There had been no visitation of his spirit among the tribes for more than forty years now. Instead, the lure of the foreign gods had proved too powerful and among most of the tribes worship of others gods had taken hold. Zorah, perhaps by being so remote and inaccessible seemed to have escaped the more obvious inroads of these foreign gods. But Yahweh still seemed remote, and the stories about his past exploits of salvation seemed tepid and anemic against the fleshy, vibrant rituals that were enacted within the towns she gazed at.

The woman had no word for this longing of an experience that would transcend her predictable life of isolation and loneliness. A sterile woman in a land crying out to be inhabited. She had found some comfort in her drink. It was the best way she knew of making things seem different, if only for a time. On the nights she took more drink than usual, their lovemaking seemed to hold the promise of children. On those nights the awful silence of her fellow townspeople, made all the more cruel because of the continuous prattle which encased it, was rendered bearable. On those nights the thickness of the air seemed ripe with mystery, fully pregnant, on the verge of birthing something that would shatter the drudgery of her days.

She would never be quite sure when she first was aware of his presence.[1] Whether he had walked quietly out from the trees, had been hiding among the stones or had materialized out of air itself she would never know, nor in the end did it matter. His dress was of material that showed no signs of wear, nor was it readily apparent whether it was cloth or hide. The broad girdle around his middle was devoid of any ornamentation or design; his hands carried neither weapon nor purse, and his head was bare. His frame was perfect in every way. Although the woman was at once aware both of his physical perfection and her own vulnerability she felt neither fear nor desire. The face gave no clue as to his tribe or lineage. Certainly the Philistines or Danites could never lay claim to him. It was his eyes that she would remember for the rest of her life. She stared, rooted to her stone, transfixed by his gaze.

"You are sterile and childless," he said without preamble. As the woman continued staring into his eyes, she knew that he had said the only words that were true, the only words that mattered.

"How can eyes be both totally black and yet filled with all consuming fire at once?" her husband asked later that night when she tried to describe what she had seen. Yet it was true. As she looked straight finally into those eyes she saw all the fires that had ever been. She saw the tower that had led their ancestors through the desert, saw the brilliance that must have radiated from Moses' face, saw the terrible fire that rained down on her people the day they worshipped the golden calf image. Yes, against this fire she and her whole people were sterile. It was not just her own life that had remained barren. The past forty years in which Yahweh's spirit had not rested on any man were barren, as circular in their significance as the forty years of desert wanderings so long ago. The man had spoken right. "You are sterile and childless." And in an instant she realized that she was not the outcast oddity of her time. Rather she was the symbol of all that was. Sterile. Childless.

That the man had uttered the most intimate details of the woman's life seemed to dispense with any of the normal conversational exchanges. She realized afterward that she had asked him neither his name nor his lineage. He would remain forever and always simply the man who had come to her in the field. She listened as he continued.

"You are sterile now, but you are going to conceive and bear a son. The man will be special—set apart his whole life to the service of Yahweh. And on him will come to rest Yahweh's spirit. He will take the vows of a Nazarite. His hair will remain uncut, he will drink no wine nor eat unclean meat. He will be a Nazarite until the day of his death. And he will begin the deliverance of Israel from the domination of the Philistines. As for you, his mother, you too will take the vow of one set apart to the service of Yahweh. You are to stop drinking your wines and other fortified drinks. Eat nothing unclean. Yahweh has claimed you for his service too."

It was a fantastical message and Manoah, on listening to the tale that night did not know what to think of it. True, it was obvious that his wife had witnessed something disturbing and powerful earlier in the day. True, she had no tendency toward fanciful tales or even exaggeration. But all the same, he knew her better than she thought. Perhaps this tale of a man who offered so much was the projection of what she longed for—a place, a purpose and a promise. Yet, "... a man child who would begin the deliverance of Israel from the Philistines!" There had been no such hope for more than forty years. And from his loins no less! Manoah could not suppress the excitement that came from such a thought.

In the end he believed her. In retrospect it was perhaps this moment of fidelity that was preparation for all that was to come. It made no sense that the deliverance of their tribes would start with such a visitation—a man, whose name and lineage were not even known, appearing to his wife while alone in a field. But Manoah knew the old stories better than his wife. Was this any more fantastical than the birth of other heroes? Had not Sarah been ninety years barren when the two visitors came to Abraham to announce her pregnancy? Had not Rebekah been barren until the birth of the twins Esau and Jacob? And Rachel, Jacob's wife after her, was her womb not closed until Yahweh relented and brought about deliverance of his people through her son Joseph?

They lay closer together that night than usual. Their lovemaking had been intense but serious, both aware that their bodies were no longer theirs in the way they had been that morning. The seed leaving Manoah was now part of a larger plan. The womb which opened to receive it was the womb of salvation for their people. The knowledge made them self conscious. Yahweh it seemed was everywhere, and not even their private coupling here in the dark inner room of an obscure home in a wilderness town was exempt from his eye and purposes. Distant and historic transcendence had suddenly become disconcerting immanence. Thay were lost in their own thoughts. The woman lay contemplating life in the service of Yahweh—a woman Nazarite no less—what would it feel like? But she knew she would keep the vows. The memory of those eyes that seemed to hold the fires of the true God held also a promise of hope that the future was not just the senseless repetition of the past and that the intensity of that flame would survive long after the fires that burned on the altars of other gods had been extinguished. The offer she had seen in those eyes had been as sensual and mysterious as any she had felt from any other source.

Manoah's thoughts were more indulgent. He could see some distant band of boys sitting in a circle around a teacher reciting the names of the great men of the past. First there had been Abraham with his barren wife, Isaac with his barren wife, Jacob with his barren wife, Manoah with his barren wife! A nonsense dream, of course, but just at that moment to be forgiven. It was the perfect dream for someone who was deeply nurtured by the well-ordered approbation of his fellow tribesmen. And for some-one who in his waking moments was at best a junior member of an irrelevant town council, this was his chance at immortality. The waking Manoah was also a more prudent practical man. And next day he prayed himself.

"Oh LORD, I beg of you, hear the prayers of a man who is neither a priest, prophet nor leader. Hear the prayer of a man whose wife has no experience in the raising of children, much less one set apart for such a mighty task as the beginning of the deliverance of your people against the Philistines. Send your messenger again to us that we might know how to bring the boy up to be equipped for his mission. What is to be the rule for the boy's life and work?" The words rolled off his tongue with a laborious ponderousness. He had rarely prayed anything original, and could only guess as to the correct form for addressing the supreme God, maker of the whole world. In the end he sought for the tone and words of supplication that would have appealed to him. He chose the voice of one clearly of much lesser rank but not slavish or obsequious, a petition of substance from a distant but loyal serf. He had even kneeled facing in the direction of Shiloh, the town wherein the holy ark of promises resided, having heard this helped the prayer. Still, beneath his veneer of convention the man was deeply troubled. They were not equipped for the task of parenting the deliverance of Israel. They needed more instruction: rules, guidelines and observances for their job. One did not simply raise up God's salvation according to one's fancy. The stakes were too great and the possibility of failure, exposing him to public shame and ridicule, were immense.

"God, oh God, how I need the comfort of rules to live by for this task," he muttered in the end, unaware that he had at last uttered an honest prayer that sped its way immediately to God and was answered immediately.

It was not a week later that he appeared again, the man with the eyes of fire. And although in answer to Manoah's prayer, it was to the woman alone that he came while she was in the olive orchard. It was as if to reassure the woman that the first visitation had been sufficient and that whatever drama was now about to happen was not because she needed more signs and wonders to stiffen her resolve or belief. No, this second appearance was all for the reassurance of Manoah with his penchant for logical order and fear of public censure and humiliation. The woman ran back toward the town gate to fetch her husband. And in the moment of running she forgave Manoah with a tenderness not of her own creation. She would not despise his timidity. He had been loyal, though uncomprehending, during her own troubled days. Who had made her

93

judge of how God should deal with another? She could not tell him that already the hardest rule had been established and accepted. The contract was with her, and had already been sealed.

They returned together and Manoah, having had at least some little time to collect his thoughts, approached, and asked, "Are you the one who talked to my wife?"

"I am," the man said.

"When the boy, our son...my son," Manoah began, "is born, how are we to raise him so that he will fulfill the tasks ordained for him?" Try as he might Manoah could not stop his speech from becoming stilted and affected. It made the woman smile to herself and she wondered how the man was responding. She thought she could just see the hint of a twitch around his mouth.

"Your wife has received all the necessary instructions and must obey them," the man replied. "They are not many and I am sure you can remember them since they are part of the vows of a Nazarite. She is to drink nothing from the grapevine, no wine or other fermented drink, and she is to eat nothing unclean. And the boy likewise is to be a Nazarite from birth."

Either Manoah seemed not to realize that nothing new had been added to the details his wife had already told him or he had not even taken in the substance of the man's words. The important thing was that he had asked his question and received an answer. For the moment he was satisfied and would deal with its implications later. He found himself fixating on the form of the interview as if by focusing on the details he might recover his orientation. But try as he might he could find nothing in his past that gave him a clue as to the appropriate protocol. An open field certainly seemed no place to receive a distinguished visitor. Had not Abraham (or so went the story) prepared a meal for the people who visited him? Yes. He latched on to the idea like a long-lost friend. Yes, a meal, in the privacy and security of their home, where Manoah would be in charge as host and all the time-honoured conventions falling on host and guest alike would modulate the pace of the encounter. There, within the sanctity of a meal, he could cross examine his guest more completely. He visualized how he would talk of this meal afterward to others in the town. "Yes, the man sat there in that chair, facing just so," he would demonstrate. "And I sat here," he would demonstrate again.

"Good sir, please, I ask of you to stay until we can prepare a suitable meal for you. A young goat perhaps." To his credit Manoah did not know whether it was guile or sheer fright that prompted his invitation. The man's response contained the mildest of reproofs.

"Though you would detain me, I will not eat. But if you prepare a burnt offering, offer it to Yahweh." To the woman listening, the man's response was reminiscent of some older story she had heard, but it remained just beyond her recall. Who else had sought to detain a divine messenger through manipulation? Manoah continued:

"If not food then, what is your name that we might honour you when your word comes true?" A name at least to show as proof of the encounter, thought Manoah. Besides, most names contained at least the vestiges of one's lineage. It would be a clue he could follow up most thoroughly in the weeks ahead. The man replied:

"Why do you ask my name? It is beyond your understanding." The words were said in such a way that even Manoah did not dare to continue the conversation. A sacrifice had been suggested, and without speech the man and wife hurried to their barn, returning with a goat and a basket of ground meal. Even in the choice of sacrifices Manoah still sought to make some kind of connection with the visitor. The goat was a fellowship offering in which the priests partook of the flesh and only the fat was burned as a kind of pleasing aroma for the nose of Yahweh. The grain offering too required that only a portion of the flour be consumed in the fire, with the rest to be baked into cakes and eaten by the priest.

The goat's throat was slit efficiently and without ceremony. Blood started to pool among the rocks—the same rocks on which the woman had sat when the man first appeared. The warmth of the day only heightened the smells attending the slaughter. The goat's belly was slit. The entrails were removed and dumped into one of the deeper crevices while fatty portions of the carcass were heaped up into a small pile. Over these pieces were sprinkled several handfuls of the grain meal. The remainder of both grain and goat were pushed to one side to be dealt with later. Just now both Manoah and his wife searched the field for wood and began laying the sticks around the mound of flesh and meal. Their visitor stood to one side, saying nothing and making no effort to help. It was not until all was ready and Manoah was about the start the fire that their visitor stepped forward, bending his head close to the heap of wood and meat.

Manoah would never quite be sure of exactly what happened next. Although he held his spark stones in his hands there was just no possible way that they could have been responsible for the fire that started. From nothing, the whole rock seem to emit flames within seconds. The flames grew with surprising speed. The noise of wood snapping and fat hissing and sizzling seemed overly loud and filled the whole field—sound that enveloped them like fog. The heat and smoke drove Manoah and his wife back some metres, but the man himself had not moved except to raise himself erect and stand facing them. He seemed quite unaffected by the heat or flames. The noises of the fire were by this time thunderous, or so they were to the ears of Manoah and his wife. Whether real or imagined who could tell? They made speech impossible between them. But the flames were real at any rate and kept growing and spreading until all portions of the goat and the remaining grain had been encompassed. It was the fire of the man's eyes, only now it was unleashed and dancing in wild, unfettered ecstasy, like some kind of elaborate but intense liturgy being performed in front of the great unseen God. The woman was spellbound by the flames. Here, before her eyes was the full extent of what the man's eyes had offered her. Here before her eyes she watched the passion of God himself, on fire with hot and holy zeal for his people, for her, exposed and inviting her to come and be consumed in the dance. She shrank back in mute shame that she had ever doubted; shame that she had never seen that Yahweh's fire and hers shared the common frustration of life lived small, or recognized that his passion too was for the veil to be rent on year after year of senseless existence; shame that she had ever looked with envy at the ritualistic release found in the service of other gods.

The fire on the rock reached higher and higher, and the man, now seen through shimmering liquid air, could be seen rising slowly although not moving. He was ascending through the flames themselves toward their top jagged edges, yet the flames themselves never seemed to come to an end. How high the flames reached they did not know. The heat by this time had set everything in their vision swimming, inanimate objects quivering, rocks pulsating as if breathing. Their senses, already on edge by the mere arrival of the man, were by this time unable to absorb or comprehend what their eyes told them was happening—flames, the man receding upward from their sight, the smell of burnt flesh mixed with the acidic odour of rocks that will not burn but must yield something to the heat, the sensation of noise and wind that invaded the mind so as to make even thought impossible. They pitched headlong on their faces, eyes squeezed tightly shut, waiting for the end.

They lay there for what seemed like hours, exhausted, with their clothes clinging to them from the sweat and grime now accumulated. Manoah spoke first. "We will die, for we have seen God." The sepulchral tone mixed with self-absorbed satisfaction that his death would be noteworthy was enough to bring the woman back to her senses. She smiled. White teeth appeared through a smudged, dark face bordered by disheveled hair that stuck out in disarray. It was the comic reflex grin of a person who has just experienced the most terrifying moment of her life and is foolishly contemplating whether she should be glad to be alive or sad that it is over.

"If Yahweh had meant to kill us, he would have done it before now," she reassured him. The husband nodded slowly as the logic of her argument sunk in. Yahweh had accepted their sacrifice. They had received instructions from God himself. They were to be a part of the deliverance.

And so it was that Samson was conceived and born.

Samson, *Sun's Child,* as it was literally understood, and for the woman, the years following Samson's birth were full of light. Other children followed, something that made Manoah positively glow with pride. The curse on the family had been lifted, and the enthusiasm and energy that are the natural property of children infested both parents, satisfying even the woman's appetite for life lived full out. The birth and growth of the sun child was in most respects not unlike a day itself. All through those early years the woman felt like it was bright early morning, the part of the day when time seems in endless supply, energy is limitless and the anticipation of something good yet to come is palpable. What had before been the stifling routine of daily living now possessed a texture and intricacy that fascinated her, and she threw herself into the myriad details that go with raising a family. Whereas before she had yearned for life on some grand scale, now she abandoned herself to the satisfaction of being able to see and experience life in the smallest of its details. The wonder of life, brought close through the developing flesh of her children, was opening up to her. That this was something common to most mothers was unimportant. Perhaps all mothers are pressed into the service of Yahweh. Enough that it met her needs.

Perhaps the woman simply chose not to see the ways in which Samson remained different. Like the involuntary muscular shiver that horses have— that sudden reflexive spasm sweeping across their coats— Samson would at times seem about to burst apart from internal pressures. She could not quite name these moments when she would find him sitting or standing, quite rigid, trying to manage some vastly superior force within him. It seemed to her that she could see him growing as she watched, the muscles changing shape beneath his blemish-free skin. It was not a metamorphosis exactly, for the new state seemed no less stable than the old. There was always the promise of continuing eruptions. And though for the most part he remained both of lively wit and genial disposition, the woman sensed rather than knew that he was a child of the fire. Sooner or later the flame would erupt. Who would be touched by the flame she did not know. Nor could she worry overly about it. The fire took charge of its own offspring. She had done what was asked of her in bringing Samson into the world. The fulfillment of his nascent prophecy was not her charge.

By his early teens Samson had immense strength, so much that he found himself much in demand for jobs that were impossible for individuals to complete themselves: beams lifted into place during building; wagons lifted while a wheel was taken off and replaced; rocks dislodged from the fields. The ease and speed with which he could perform these feats was like watching poetry in motion. There was an easy-going, good-humoured exuberance that went with all his work, and word of his abilities spread even to the Philistine farmers to the west. Though the two tribes made no secret of their contempt for the other, neither wanted to pursue outright hostility. The farmers of the valley certainly were subject to all the same vagaries of weather, and if the Baal god in charge of weather sent rain to the western end of the valley, Yahweh seemed to give the same in the east. Thus the natural bonds of working the land allowed for some slight cooperation here at the frontier. Samson would often go well down into the valley, working even past Sorek. He seemed to enjoy these forays into "foreign land" and would come back with humourous stories about their peculiar neighbours. There was no common tongue but Samson had some faculty for language and this, combined with the adaptability of youth, enabled him to master enough of the "foreign speech" to converse comfortably.

As the years passed and Samson grew to manhood he would more frequently take to wandering, not always in response to requests for his help. These walks were always solitary. He never offered explanations nor did she question him. He would come back as abruptly as he had left. Into the house he would come, smelling of the field, or of the hunt or of women and she could not help but contemplate the exploits of the night. Though all Zorah was pleased to know him, he had no close friends. His brothers, fiercely loyal, seemed more concerned with fitting in than in joining Samson in his forays into the wider world. This wider world shortly issued an invitation to them all.

"I have seen a young girl from the town of Timnah—a Philistine— and I want her for my wife," Samson announced quietly to his parents one evening. "Get her for me."

If Samson had deliberately set out to destroy all the stability and sanctity of Manoah's world, he could not have done it more swiftly or efficiently. The marriage he proposed embodied all the elements necessary for their ostracization—union with a woman of a tribe beyond the rite of circumcision, whose seed was impure. The prohibitions against marrying foreigners were universally known, if not practised, among the twelve tribes. Add to that the fact that the Timnites would no doubt find some way to use the wedding as a way of further insulting the Danites and reminding them that the balance of power did not rest in their favour. Manoah's position of influence and acceptance within Zorah would cease. The argument lasted for days, but the woman watching in silence knew that from Samson's first request he would win over Manoah. It was not this particular young girl that was being sought. She was simply the fleshly manifestation of the larger world that awaited Samson beyond the Danite borders. She was the emissary enticing Samson to explore further both the world without and the one within. As to the wider world, the woman was now old enough to have concluded that all geography was the same. But she was not so dismissive of the seduction to the inner exploration of one's emotions. Passions of every hue, the sexual, the exuberant, the angry and the ecstatic—these the woman knew intimately—life lived on the very edge of control. It was these that the woman knew were calling her son through this Philistine filly and that he was helpless to resist. It was not just that he was at the age when self discovery was inevitable and which, by definition, had to include rash and impetuous decisions. No. There was in Samson's resolution something that marked him as a victim. He was not pushing as much as he was being pulled. The woman was no great sage but nevertheless had a healthy respect for her own powers of reasoning. But try as she did there seemed no way to logically connect what was happening with the prophecy. The deliverance of Israel being led around by his foreskin!

Manoah in the end walked the four miles to Timnah to make the arrangements. The woman went with him. She was curious to see the girl who had so captivated Samson. What were her features and would she be as beautiful as the woman herself at the same age? It never occurred to the woman that part of her might have wanted Samson for herself or that they shared the same malaise. Besides, Manoah would need help. This was all so new. Samson had gone ahead of them some distance and when they caught up with him just at the town's edge he was breathing heavily, obviously fighting to keep himself under control. There was a sheen of sweat on his skin, though whether from physical exertion or the nervousness of the moment who could say. Samson offered no explanation.

The negotiations were completed. Samson served as interpreter for the two fathers. It wasn't that they were overly complicated but to Manoah the mere necessity of having to ask a Philistine for anything was odious. They would return in one month for the wedding feast. It would not follow the usual form for, truth to tell, the townspeople of Zorah would have nothing to do with the union. They would not permit Philistines within their walls, nor would they appear as guests at a foreign feast. The Philistines might be their rulers; they might even share common interests pertaining to the valley and its cultivation, and even some trade between them was acceptable. But a Philistine was still as slippery as the sea slime from which he had crawled. To sit at meat with one was unthinkable. So the wedding feast was planned for Timnah. The bride's house and courtyard would be the host site for the feast and Samson's companions, the usual complement of half a dozen assistants, normally chosen from the young men of his own tribe, would be supplied from Timnah. Even the chief friend, the one whose formal responsibility it was to look to Samson's interests was to come from the host town. The feast was larger than was either usual or warranted. Manoah realized that this was their way of mocking them without providing a clear point of provocation. Even Samson blushed with shame as he translated the bride's father's words:

"Since this is the first union between our tribes in this valley no doubt you will want the occasion distinctly celebrated in a manner worthy of its importance. Shall we say a feast of seven days' duration instead of the usual three?" Manoah could hardly contain his anger at the effrontery. It was bad enough that none of his own people would benefit from the banquet but that he would have to finance seven days of Philistine gluttony instead of the usual three made the bile come to his throat.

One month later they returned, the feast's provisions having been dispatched in advance. As before, Samson forged on ahead of his parents but met them again just at the edge of the town. His eyes were merry and he had fresh slabs of honeycomb resting on wedges of bark. It dripped onto their hands. They all ate—this last meal of innocence, tinged with some foreboding. The woman saw the tiny globules of honey, each like a small jewel inside the comb giving off a weak but comforting gleam of refracted light. Their meal of fire.

The week seemed like a kind of waking dream for the woman and she could tell it was having a terrible effect on Manoah, whose face was the colour of stone by the end of it. They sat in some prominence at each of the many feasts throughout the week but, whereas they would normally have played their leading roles with grace and movement, here in Timnah they were like statues, rooted and mute while the play swirled around them. Though Samson tried his best to interpret, he was often called away. They would sit for long periods of each feast, assaulted by the cacophony of the language, which grew louder as the wine flowed. Manoah at times was so stern looking as he tried to retain his dignity that it was comical. The woman meanwhile quickly gained her own eccentric identity from her insistence on drinking only water. The water woman and the stone man; lost objects in the middle of a foreign world.

Samson for the most part rose to the occasion brilliantly. There had been some moment of crisis at that first feast but the details were lost to the parents until later. It had started when Samson's male friends were presented, thirty lusty males including the chief friend who would attend him all week and look to his interests. Samson was unprepared for what was a calculated strategy to embarrass him. He had brought gifts enough for eight friends—two above what was the usual number just in case the Philistines might foist on him a larger group than necessary and thus extract more gifts, which were by no means trinkets. But thirty! The number was so large that the intended insult could not be misunderstood. Rising to his feet, he had issued some kind of response that seemed to meet with grudging praise. No gifts were distributed, not even the eight he had brought. But whatever it was that Samson had said sparked an excited conversation. Later that night Samson explained to them.

"I have made this wedding feast one they won't forget for a long time," he said. "They thought to shame me with thirty friends, but I have made a wager with them that lasts the week. I gave them a riddle to solve. If they can guess it correctly I owe them each a linen robe and set of clothes. Thirty in all. If they do not guess the answer by the end of the week they owe me thirty linen garments and matching sets of clothing. A fine wager which they have accepted." Samson's face flushed with pride at what he had managed to do.

The woman saw Manoah's face go pale with fright. Thirty garments! The cost of that much cloth was immense. She knew he doubted whether he had the resources to make the purchase, or even if Zorah's whole supply would be sufficient if it came to making good the bet. The wedding, costly enough as it was had suddenly turned into a high-stakes contest in an effort to blacken the economic eye of the other tribe. Samson repeated the riddle to his parents:

> *Out of the eater, something to eat.*
> *Out of the strong, something sweet.*

It was not one Manoah recognized from their own tribal collection.

"Tell us nothing else," interjected Manoah before Samson could speak again, "lest by our own mouths we are betrayed."

"Yes," his mother joined in. "Tell no one the answer."

The riddle, together with the details of the wager, was known even in Sorek by the second day of the feast. By the fourth, having exhausted their collective wit, a contingency from the band of thirty visited Samson's bride.

"You must get the answer from him," they began.

"And why is that?" she asked. In truth she was more than a little proud to be attached to what looked like the winning side of the contest. The feast was exciting to the point of being intoxicating. Her perception of events up to that moment were quite romantic. Three months earlier she had been simply the older daughter of a commonplace farmer living on the outskirts of their tribe's territory. Suddenly a powerful, well-formed foreign man had appeared in response to their need for a large stone fence to be built. He had stayed, seemingly captivated by her charm. He was magnificent to see and though they had not yet had union she had gone so far as to place her hand on his member, feeling it through the cloth. In exchange she had loosed her upper garments and let him gaze at and fondle her breasts. His eyes had kept looking at her as if consuming her. Sexual desire, on both their parts, once kindled gathered fuel all on its own and would be satisfied with nothing less than the climax of the wedding night, made all the more intense from the delay. Her wedding, which would otherwise have been unworthy of comment, much less seven days of feasting, was now the talk of the entire valley. She did not really mind which way the contest went. Should Samson win, they would start their life with a wealth quite beyond what she was used to. She pictured Samson and herself leaving the village with the heap of goods mounded in a cart. It would be the perfect exit scene in the fantasy.

If on the other hand he lost, then she would play the role of benefactress to her village, whose husband had lavished gifts on all the men just prior to their leave-taking. She did not stop to wonder where Samson or his family would get the payment for the clothing. The public distribution with her standing in the reflected warmth of the gratitude extended Samson for the presents was as far as her young mind could think. The venomous words from the visiting contingency shocked her.

"Do you really think that we will tolerate being robbed by a foreigner, you stupid child? Has the wetness of your thighs left you totally senseless? Do you not remember that you are first and always a Philistine? Were you really so naive as to think that your marriage represented anything more than a chance to have some sport with these newcomers? Do you think we would tolerate giving one of our daughters over to a people whose men mutilate their penises at birth if there was not gain for us? But now the wager is going against us, you dense dog. Hear this. If you do not get the answer to the riddle we will burn you and your father's household to death. If you try to escape with your Danite hero, we will hunt you down like the traitorous bitch you are and drag you through the streets of Timnah before burning you."

The strength of their threat and the manner in which it was delivered had its calculated impact. The girl had no capacity for bearing, much less resolving the irreconcilable enmity between two tribes. All she really knew was that this feast-week fantasy contained a fury that up to then had been quite hidden. Young men with whom she had grown up were suddenly visiting her in secret, promising to burn her family. In the space of four days the dream was taking on the shape of a ghoulish nightmare.

On seeing Samson later she lost the last remains of her self control and unleashed on him all the feelings of the moment.

"You hate me, you hate me, you hate me," she cried, leaping on him, pounding his upper back with her fists while at the same time drenching his chest with tears. She was hysterical and Samson, quite inexperienced, was disadvantaged. Truth told, he was more aware of her body stuck close to his with so little garment separating them than he was of her words. For some reason, the pounding of her fists on his back excited him. To say that she simply out manoeuvred him by alternating between a coy charm and a petulant pout is too simple. More correct is it to say that in her terror she knew only that she must uncover the answer to the riddle, and so went at Samson with a directness and force that carried the day.

It was obvious from her public appearances at the feast that something had disturbed her—great puffy eyes and conspicuous, sudden departures from the table to rush headlong indoors while Samson, to the amusement of all those assembled, would rise and trail after her. They would return together, the composure of the girl only somewhat restored, and tolerate the laughter and leers that clearly intimated what was thought to have transpired between them. The public scenes provided as much entertainment and gossip as did the riddle.

Samson himself was conflicted. The challenge that he did not love her, that he did not trust her stung him deeply. He was aware that at some level this was quite true, or at last partially true. She was so foreign to him still. And part of her attraction lay in the fact that he did not know her completely. And who trusts what they do not know? But the stakes between themselves had grown quite high too. To know her, Samson was being required to trust her first. To hold back any part of himself would prevent him from experiencing the full depth of marital union. That was the club she was using. The carrot was her promise of lavish attention of a kind that made his loins stir.

In the end she won. The morning of the last feast day he told her about having come across and killed a lion with his hands just a short distance from Timnah on the day when he and his parents had visited to make the wedding arrangements. Making the same trip one month later, he had gone to see the carcass, and discovered bees and a honeycomb.

She held him close, but told the riddle's answer to her people just the same.

It was at noon that the thirty men gathered around the doorway of the bride's house, shouting for Samson to appear. The time of day made them the only people outside, and their voices carried distinctly.

"Samson, Samson, come out for something sweet to eat!" they kept chanting. "Samson, Samson, come out for something sweet to eat!"

He appeared at the doorway and his chief friend stepped forward to address him on behalf of the thirty:

What is sweeter than honey
and stronger than a lion?

If Samson was surprised it did not affect the speed of his reply. Perhaps he had been half expecting the meeting.

"Borrowing my heifer to do your plowing," he retorted, "is that how Philistine men stoop to solve a simple Danite riddle? No doubt you will enjoy the last feast tonight now that your brains no longer have to work. See you tonight."

And without further speech he pushed his way through their midst and disappeared from sight.

That last feast was just in progress when Samson burst back into the village. At least people said afterward that it was Samson. The light from the lamps and braziers distorted things with overly exaggerated shadow and only partially revealed people's forms and shapes. But to the assembled, even the unnatural light could not account for the apparition that now walked between the tables. He was taller or bigger somehow. Perhaps it was the huge bundle of clothing and wraps that he carried on the high part of his back when he first strode in. His hair, long to his waist, was now matted with sweat, and clumps of it were sticking together as if from a glue and rife with tangles. His own cloth tunic had rents in it as if he had caught it on some protruding object in haste. It was not that he looked like a wild man as much as he looked like someone who was about to go wild at any moment.

My thirty friends I've brought your garbs
And kept the bet despite your barbs.
Now to your bosoms clutch these clothes
And smell your kin within their folds.

Samson began distributing the contents of the bundle, now laid to the ground. Into the startled face of each of the thirty groomsmen he shoved a wad of clothing. At the chief friend he paused long enough to drape the cloak around his neck from the back so that it looked like a huge scarf.

"My dearest friend, whose job it is to watch my back, pity that the man I took these from didn't have a friend as loyal or I might not have had to get them bloody. If you'd been there you might have sold them to me on his behalf." Samson's voice, hoarse and strong, was not entirely in control. Each man had begun to finger his bundle of cloth uneasily. None was new and all were of Philistine cut and smell. Several showed dark stains. Somewhere in the night lay thirty dead and naked Philistines.

The distribution now complete, Samson arrived back at the head table where his parents were sitting, fixed and mute.

"Come, Mother and Father. It was a feast we'd come to, not a show of finery." And with that he steered them by the arms up off their bench and with one on each side, disappeared back into the shadows. He had never once even so much as glanced at his bride.

In the days following their nighttime journey back to Zorah, the woman watched Samson closely. One would have thought that the whole experience would be enough to put Samson off Philistines for all time. But as the days passed it became clear he still had feelings for his bride of Timnah. It was for the woman like watching a fingerling swimming hopelessly against a current that was sweeping it ever closer to a waterfall. The fingerling, constantly swimming, was never aware that he was in fact going in the opposite direction until the moment it was too late. And besides, thought the woman, even if he knew, what could he do about it? That such a man could be at the same time so totally strong in his body and helpless in his obsessions held a fascination for her. Samson seemed quite unaware of his inability to take charge of his own passions, and watching him spawned a tragic love in the woman that went very much beyond the maternal concern of a mother for her young manchild. That such a man was God's chosen instrument of deliverance amazed her. He seemed as much a creature of the dark earth as of the fiery heavens. It came as no surprise when he announced his intention to make a return visit to his wife. The woman made no effort to dissuade him although Manoah was loud in his arguments. One morning he left. She did not see him again for a long time.

It was inevitable that the conflict with the Philistines would escalate. The sequence of events did not become clear or known to the woman until much later. The one thing she did know was that there had been a terrible fire in the Philistines' harvest fields the week Samson left, and she was sure he was involved. The smoke lay densely around Timnah, just four miles away stretching west into the valley—past even Sorek.

She kept hearing disjointed and conflicting tidbits of news. Wild animals with tails of fire running through the fields and olive groves had lit the dry, standing field of wheat—creatures concocted by the gods and let loose on earth during a conflict in heaven. No, not creatures, but foxes in pairs, with firebrands tied to their tails, running terrified in all directions. Then news of a different kind. There had been a public execution in Timnah—Samson's bride and her father burned! Had they started the fire in the fields then? And there had come news of more killings, done by a roving army some said, attacking quickly various settlements in the valley and even further south. Timnites killed. It was this roving band that had both started the fires and burned the wife of the Danite. No, other stories filtered through to her, giving a different version. Samson's bride and her father had been burned by their own people. Samson had discovered her violation by the chief groomsman the last night of her wedding feast. She had not protested enough. No, the story got worse than that. She was not raped after all but given to the head groomsman at the urging of her father to save face and fob off his daughter, now damaged goods.

Samson, on returning for his bride, was barred from seeing his wife and was offered her sister as a replacement. Samson was on a rampage for this the final public insult—the violation of his wife by the one charged with looking after his interests no less! The foxes were *his* act of retaliation—vengeance with a twist! Confronted with his wife's public adultery engineered by her father, Samson's destruction was justified. Philistine justice concurred. No tribe permits a few to put the welfare of the whole at risk, hence their execution.

Then came sightings of one man, huge, with hair to his waist, attacking anyone he came across, descending on people trying to salvage what they could of the crops, battering them senseless, bludgeoning their skulls and breaking the unconscious bodies like so many dried twigs. It was Samson, of course, as he was the night of the feast, only now without any restraint. The burning of his wife and father-in-law pushed him further into a rage. His ravished wife was still his property. Who were the Philistines to take matters into their own hands? The killings were not the efficient deaths of a military operation, which would try to conserve energy even in the act of conflict. They were the extravagant, wild signature of a man who was now drinking violence like a plant drinks water.

On hearing the story finally with some measure of coherency, the people of Zorah were mixed in their reception of Manoah and his wife. The hardier zealots among them were proud that finally a blow of defiance was being stuck against the Philistine overlords. Those more fainthearted and superstitious whispered that Manoah's wife had conceived a beast-child, that her sterility had ended by copulating with a hill god. The foxes too were somehow offspring of an unholy union. The children of bestiality no less!

The arrival of hundreds of armed men from Judah brought the crisis to a new height. The men had come in search of Samson. A Philistine army was massing at Lehi, the foothill town just at the beginning of the territory occupied by Judah. Because of Samson, brother Dan was now a threat to brother Judah. Samson showed himself finally at Etam, a mountain stronghold high up and to the south west of Bethlehem. Three thousand of the tribe of Judah came up to deliver him to the Philistines. Certain customs are universal among tribes, and retain their common currency in every age. No Danite was going to be permitted to plunge the whole area into ruin and chaos. They would not burn him like his wife. But they would surely deliver him up. Afterward the tribe of Judah claimed to have been in cahoots with Samson all along. They bound him with new ropes with elaborate knots and led him from Etam to Lehi, a distance of more than twenty miles. The journey was orderly but dirge-like, solemn and hugely public. They later claimed that it was all part of a clever ruse to lower the Philistine guard.

The Danite version was less polite. Judah's men, who were only too willing to sacrifice one man, and a Danite at that, for the sake of peace, had every intention of delivering up Samson to the Philistines. The blood of a kinsman would not technically be on their hands so no Danite could seek revenge on them. Peace would prevail among all parties. The blood feuds would end.

But at Lehi, there in front of both Judahite and Philistine, Samson was confirmed and anointed. Some say the spirit of Yahweh came like fire burning off his ropes but not touching his skin. Others say his own body grew brilliant from the inner heat of Yahweh's spirit and caused the ropes to drop away like ashes. Of certain facts all the accounts agreed. A thousand Philistines were killed by Samson, using nothing more than the jawbone of a donkey. His loud battle cry was in verse no less:

With the jaw of a red ass
I have reddened them bright red;
With the jaw of this ass
I have laid them all dead.

And afterward as he lay on the ground spent and parched, the hand of Yahweh himself had opened up the ground and gave the spring of water that revived him.

On these facts, all the stories agreed. Equally clear was that for the next twenty years Samson kept the peace, both within the tribes and between them and their neighbours. It was for Manoah the proudest time of his life—his son was a judge of Israel! He was the leader who would be called upon to settle disputes and track down outlaws living in the hills on stolen livestock.

Samson traveled far and wide. The Philistines became much more circumspect. There were no longer raids on the fields; more than one frontier village was abandoned by them as Judah, under the protection of the Danite Samson, pushed a little further east into the plains. In the absence of conscription Samson was the surrogate standing army and police force.

For the woman it seemed that Samson was still in the dance, still quite unaware of his own possession. What his eye saw, it needed to consume. His sexual appetite was insatiable. Though some tried to explain his exploits as the symbolic act of one tribe publicly making use of another—smearing their seed as it were on the feminine chattels of the other—the woman was not easily accepting of this gloss. There were other ways to remind the Philistines that the tables had turned and they no longer held the winning hand, but she was glad that the blessing of Jacob to her tribe, given as he lay dying in Egypt, was coming to fruition now and that she was the handmaiden of Yahweh's deliverance.

Dan will provide justice for his people,
as one of the tribes of Israel.[2]

But if Samson provided justice, his own personal life denoted no sense of discipline. On the contrary, he seemed as indolent and impulsive

109

as ever. If he appeared to others as the wise judge who brought order and stability to the land, she could not shake the feeling that he was also a bully whose quest for his own gratification was only coincidentally providing leadership to Israel. She was less sure about what the second half of Jacob's blessing was to mean.

> *Dan will be a serpent by the roadside,*
> *a viper along the path,*
> *that bites the horses heels*
> *so that its rider tumbles backwards.*

But she was disturbed by the stories she heard. There was nowhere within the Philistines' land that he seemed unprepared to venture, almost as if the greater the inroads, the greater the proof of his divine protection. Gaza was a city close to the coast and in the south, a major fortified city at least fifty miles from his home, probably twice that when measured by the distance one had to walk. Yet the women were renowed for their pleasures, and Samson indulged himself. On one occasion he rose during the night, carried off the city gates on his back and deposited them on a high hill facing Hebron (Judah territory), not only evading the ambush being planned for dawn but making sport of the city's defenses into the process. That he could seemingly receive the proof of Yahweh's blessing immediately on having just left the bed of a foreign whore disturbed the woman. Her son did not possess any semblance of holiness that one could expect from a Nazarite. His long hair seemed to be the only remaining evidence of his special status—and with it his special strength. How long before that would come off on some whim?

Samson's capture and imprisonment broke the woman's heart. News of it killed Manoah. That a woman's deception had been the cause of his downfall did not surprise the woman. Delilah of the Philistine valley of Sorek was the one hailed as heroine. She was no ignorant farmer's daughter who could be bullied by anyone. And yet Samson's betrayal at her hands differed from the earlier betrayal only in the details. Once again he had succumbed to the enticement: "Tell me your innermost secrets and the ecstasy of our union that will follow will be beyond your dreams and fantasies." A game it was for a while before it grew tiresome. Perhaps Delilah really began to want the year's wages being offered by certain of the Philistine elite for discovering Samson's secret. And was she supposed to forget how her father died twenty years earlier when Samson went on his first rampage in the same area? Then again, how long can one person carry a secret and not finally succumb to the need to blurt it out for someone else to help carry it? And how long can a person carry the guilt of a first wife's death before he screws up his courage to take one more chance to see if the ending might be any different? Samson finally told her the source of his strength. He had already lost his heart to her. His head and finally, of course, his hair followed. The dance had ended. The spirit of Yahweh departed along with his hair, the last of the Nazarite vows.

Samson's mother did not turn out to watch his march from Sorek to Gaza. All through the western plain Samson was led like a great beastly spectacle. His head had been shaved completely. His eyes, burned out, were now just ghoulish empty sockets which combined to give the appearance of something only half human. By the end of the march he had stumbled so often his knees were like the red pulp of some grotesque fruit. In the Gaza prison he was put to work grinding corn, hitched to a long rigid pole, one end fastened to the centre of a large flat stone. He trudged around the fixed perimeter, the grain being slowly crushed beneath the rotating stone. The human ox.

The woman heard little in the intervening years except that Samson had not died or been killed. The Philistines did not rebound overnight from twenty years of systematic reduction, nor did the Israelite tribes immediately revert to cowering. The region lay still but tense, waiting the next development. As time went on and no new leader appeared to take Samson's place, the whole Philistine mood began to grow brighter and bolder. That their collective confidence was leading them to reassert themselves became public when they gathered for a feast to Dagon, their fish god. From their perspective, twenty years of subservience to the tribes of Israel is a long time for the gods to have left them in the hands of their neighbours, and temple feasts had become progressively smaller and more cautious as a result. But with the permanent capture of Samson it would seem that the gods now favoured them and a lavish display of their gratitude not only made good national politics, but made for good insurance against further capricious acts of abandonment. All the leaders and hangers-on went to Gaza for the celebration.

The feast at Gaza in the temple of Dagon was grand beyond any that had happened for twenty years. It was a chance both to see and to be seen, as would-be new leaders jockeyed for public prominence. There were house parties, debauched orgies, public acts of ritual copulation in which the priestesses danced the parts of fertile vessels for the use of Dagon on completing his great victory over their enemy—food for the stomach and for appetites of every kind. It was the rebirth of their national confidence, confidence in themselves, and in their god who had delivered up Samson.

It was inevitable that Samson should play some part in the events. He was sent for spontaneously, led in by a servant boy to stand in the centre of the temple. The temple of Dagon was an unusual affair. Its roof was open to the sky above for most of the area. There was a perimeter rampart that served as a four-sided balcony, with easy access to it by way of several stairs attached to the exterior. From each of the four corners, the balcony extended inward, coming to rest on a circular section supported by two massive pillars. The end effect allowed the roof, together with these four inwardly directed runways, to be a mezzanine from which the rituals could be observed. With the space above and the area below, the temple could accommodate almost four thousand people. Into this centre Samson was led, shuffling. The sight of him caused great excitement. The priestesses began to encircle him and their dancing turned to something decidedly lewd and explicit. The spectacle of such sexual titillation being performed in front of a blind man was exactly the kind of entertainment the crowd needed. It encompassed a cruelty spawned from twenty years of being under the thumb of a rake. The justice seemed superbly appropriate.

Another kind of justice followed without warning, and news of the catastrophe spread quickly. The temple was in ruins, thousands dead. There had been an earthquake. Dagon had been offended by the feast. Egyptians had attacked suddenly. A tidal wave had swept in from the sea. There had been a great fire. There wasn't a centre in the land that did not have a representative at the feast, and the whole coastal plain pressed for facts as if a single village. And then the truth was discovered.

There had been no earthquake or attack. Samson was dead too. His body was found crushed at the centre, arms still touching portions of the central pillars. It was impossible but nevertheless the only explanation that fit. He had pushed the pillars over, causing the roof to collapse. The people above were thrown down, together with the quarried stone of the gallery roof, onto the heads of the people below. An impossible feat of strength! And then the people noticed just how long his hair had been allowed to grow. Yahweh had forgiven him after all and returned to him.

Or had Yahweh ever left him? Perhaps this had been planned from the beginning. Does Yahweh ever leave his people then? The Philistines were as ignorant of Yahweh's ways as the Israelites were of Dagon's. They could but postulate on the nature of Samson's god, who would at the same time kill his servant and dispatch such mayhem on his enemies. If Yahweh could give such strength, why not sight too? That an unseen god could cause such destruction in the very den of Dagon left the Philistines in numb apprehension. What other catastrophe could this Israelite god cause through Samson? This carnage was more than he had caused all his life. Even the body itself was not to be trusted and so a message was sent, and a delegation of his family came to fetch the remains. Such was their fear that the Philistines insisted its final resting place should be outside their territory.

The woman with no name watched as her other sons wrestled the rock away from the entrance of the family tomb, the one into which Manoah had been placed five years back. Samson's body, tightly wrapped and heavily spiced because of the distance it had traveled, lay on a litter, waiting to take its turn to lie among the family fathers. She thought again about Jacob's prophesy of Dan, "*The viper whose bite causes the horseman to tumble.*" She wondered if anyone else cared. Sun's child, set apart for God from birth, whose story would always be full of intense if erratic light and whose ending was like an exploding star followed by blackness. There was not even the usual transition to dusk.

Endnotes:
[1] This story begins in Judges 13ff.
[2] Genesis 49:16

The Bastard Judge

His mother had dropped him in a hut that smelled of old grass. Her hands gripped the top edges of a narrow stall as she squatted, legs splayed wide. Breathe. Push. Breathe. Push. Her hair stuck to the sides of her face. The tunic was wet from sweat and birth fluids. At last he emerged, mucusy and bloody, crying even before the rough grass pricked him. There was nothing pretty about the scene—a teenage prostitute giving birth to an unwanted baby, in solitude. But at least the ordeal was over. Her body was her own once more and in time it would regain its shape. This was important. She had been in the profession just long enough to see other women lose their shape, and in time, their clients. It was a stage of the business she tried not to think about. Just now she had to find a home for the boy and reclaim herself. No prolonged suck for the babe. Her breasts would remain firm for as long as possible. "Besides," she said aloud to herself in a raspy voice tinged with the hysteria of the moment, "my body is never free and if he cannot pay the price, then he shall not have me. No exceptions." Motherhood had lost out to independence.

She named him Jephthah[1]—*God frees the captive*—and her friends wondered to whom it referred.

Finding a home for Jephthah was actually quite easy. His father was Gilead, a name taken from the region that lay east of the Jordan river. He had been a regular visitor and she knew for certain that Jephthah was his offspring. She did not like Gilead much. He would come quietly to her, mouse like, to purchase fantasies of manhood, and afterwards slink out, back to his loud wife, who was wide and heavy set with matching voice. She had already borne seven sons by Gilead, and any female charms she might have had were long since extinguished. The prostitute understood why Gilead came to her, but did not like him any more because of it. Anemic and lacking in any kind of personality, that was Gilead. The other girls in the brothel used to joke that there was only one thing rigid about him and that even it didn't stay that way for long.

And so it was that not long after Jephthah's birth the prostitute walked the few miles' distance outside of the town of Adam to Gilead's house and delivered the boy child. She had taken great care in dressing her part—paint carefully applied to her eyes, and elaborate clothing that concealed her still shrinking body. She wore her best veil, the one with Ashtoreth, the fertility goddess, painted in the centre. There was no mistaking who it was with the exaggerated breasts and pudendum. With the proof of her profession on her face and a flirtatious boldness to match, she swaggered into the compound and deposited her charge on the threshold. She left after a brief but loud exchange with Gilead and his wife, strutting back through the brush fence and out of Jephthah's life forever. The harangue she imagined Gilead was even now receiving from his wife, and which was likely to be the first of many, provided an energy that made her return walk invigorating.

To say that Jephthah's childhood was unhappy would be a callous gloss of those early years. He survived, of course, the way that surviving villagers emerge from hiding after an attack—moving woodenly, cautiously, starting at each noise as if expecting to be attacked again at any instant. He survived the way a warrior survives a fierce engagement and afterward stares vacantly at his own wounds as if peering at someone else's body, wondering if any will be fatal, but still numb from the protective shock of the battle. And if Jephthah lost any limbs at least they were on the inside where it didn't show.

It was a short childhood even by the standards of the day, and ended when Jephthah was turned out by his brothers. Perhaps what triggered its ending was an early burst of growth that, at fourteen, made Jephthah taller than even the eldest brother and that promised a well-muscled physique. That a child still lived within was of no consequence. There were seven legitimate brothers and settled land was too precious an inheritance to divide into eight if it was not necessary.

The law, such as it was, favoured the brothers. In those days the tribes of Israel had no king. The area of Gilead was loosely governed by a council of elders who met sporadically throughout the year according to the needs and to resolve disputes that were larger than the jurisdictional prerogatives of any single town council. A precarious judiciary but it matched the times. Israel's hold over its lands was tenuous. To the north lived the Midianites, to the west the Philistines and to the east the Ammonites. All three were aggressive peoples, seeking to squeeze the newcomers at every opportunity. Boundaries were still fluid.

The council supported the brothers' action. Their verdict was delivered to Gilead's household by Phineas, the religious priest at the shrine of Yahweh and in the inner circle of elders. He had spent some time at Shiloh—the home of the famed ark of promise, fashioned by Moses at Mount Sinai centuries earlier when Israel left Egypt. A priestly stint at Shiloh, located on the west side of the Jordan in Ephraimite territory, gave Phineas a status that he was not above exploiting if necessary. Jephthah had seen him arrive but they had not spoken.

Shortly after Phineas's visit, at a morning meal Jephthah was presented with a small parcel of his personal effects, wrapped for traveling, and informed by his brothers that he was leaving. Where he went or how he would live did not concern them. Gilead's lands and herds (provided they were not lost in a raid) would be inherited by the legitimate sons of Gilead, not his bastard half son. So on that particular morning, Jephthah was allowed to gobble down as much food as he could, and then was escorted to the gate of the compound by the brothers, who remained clustered in the opening until Jephthah disappeared from sight. He was unsure what to do. His natural mother was a dubious destination. It had been fourteen years since she had sashayed out the same gate, and time would finally have stolen anything not already lost to customers. Jephthah turned north instead. In truth what occupied his mind was how lucky he was to have a full stomach and a cloak. It was more than he had expected. Somewhere north he knew there were two cities of refuge established by Joshua for people in trouble: Golan and Ramoth-gilead. He knew nothing else about them but just at that moment they sounded like hospitable destinations. He was in no hurry and insofar as a boy of fourteen is able to think deeply, he contemplated whether his circumstances had improved or worsened. Farms along the way frequently gave him shelter and food, and if it was not readily forthcoming he would steal for his needs without a qualm. His generally pleasant deportment stood by him and often as not he was welcomed.

The cities proved to be considerably east of the Jordan river, in the hill country settled by Bashan and Manasseh. Jephthah found them both eventually. Both were disappointments, full of misfits, squalor and only the thinnest veneer of law and order. Jephthah could not settle in either. It was too much like home—loud and strident. He was disappointed that all the world seemed angry and selfish and continually on the verge of chaos. He was not so naive as to believe that this was universally so, but certainly *his* parts of the world thus far were like that. Peace and quiet seemed like such small things to ask of life but it would seem that these were not for Jephthah.

Jephthah discovered his vocation while he was leaving Ramoth-gilead. He was overtaking a transport caravan of eight energetic burrows and two harried teamsters. Just as he was coming up to them, four rough and determined-looking men emerged from the sides of the path to block their way. A classic roadway robbery if ever there was one and the two teamsters knew it was far better to capitulate quickly and quietly, perhaps escaping with their lives. But Jephthah ran forward from the rear, pushing his way through the animals, and shouted, "No! You will not stop us. Get out of our way and leave us alone!" By this time he had strode right up to the closest bandit, and without thinking, shoved him hard. The man, quite unprepared for an attack from a youth, went down backwards and Jephthah, seizing the chance, followed him down, encircled his neck with both hands, pivoted the head forward and up, then thrust it down hard into the stone path. The man went limp. It all happened very fast. When Jephthah finally stood up there were only the two drivers and himself.

Jephthah became first a caravan guard, and later, captain of a large peacekeeping force. It suited his natural love for sanctuary and his increasing skills at fighting. He settled at Tob, ten miles to the east of Mizpah and seventy miles due south of Damascus. Damascus was a junction point of several trade routes, which had been giving hospitality to travelers since the days of Abraham's visit. Tob lay on the inland trade path connecting Damascus to Rabbah, the capital city of the Ammonites. From there, the trade route continued south through Moabite and Edomite territories and finally into Arabia.

There remained something quite childlike about Jephthah. He was not the first person to make a living from the sale of protection. Indeed the whole north/south corridor of Canaan, which connected the great empires of the Euphrates and Egypt, was awash with petty tyrants, each with his band of followers who lived by extracting "highway taxes" or worse, by outright robbery and murder. But it was clear even from the beginning that what motivated Jephthah was his genuine love of peace, not personal gain. And to his innocent mind, this was an entirely reasonable thing to insist on for himself and to secure for others. Those who opposed peace ought to be killed with as much moral deliberation as one reserves for the killing of wild animals. And Jephthah did just that, without any emotional engagement.

That people actually paid him well for maintaining peace always amused Jephthah and with the proceeds he established a pleasant home base at Tob. It was natural that he attracted others to his service. His lack of unrestrained greed was a magnet. Other unwanted youths, younger brothers pushed off too-small land holdings, ambitious adventurers coming for the sport of frontier combat, or just plain misfits with grit in their sandals joined him at Tob. From there they controlled the road north to Damascus and south to the edges of Ammonite territory. They established regular patrol routes throughout the forests and steppe lands around the Golan hills. The settlers were grateful, and if they appeared overly regular in their spontaneous gifts of sheep, goats, wheat, oil and other foodstuffs, no one spoke of it. The Ammonites, a tribe whose ancestral lands lay south and east, were growing stronger, and the well-organized safety afforded by Jephthah was timely. As a result, Ammonite raiders went west, instead of north, straight into Gilead.

When Jephthah fell in love it was, as might be expected, as innocent as it was powerful. Her father was a farmer from the area of Ashtaroth, a city whose chief activity was the worship of the fertility goddess of a similar name. Jephthah had discovered her while on a tour of the countryside and had been immediately smitten. It was rumoured that she had been destined to be a fertility priestess in the services of Ashtoreth ("temple whore" to put it baldly) before being courted by Jephthah. Certainly it added to the romance that clung to them both. It was not an age in which self reflection was encouraged, and if people noticed any connection between the wife he married and his birth mother they did not comment. "He fell hard," was what his closer friends, more worldly wise, observed with good-natured humour. His love for her was intense, straightforward and uncomplicated. Even the most hardened cynic was softened by Jephthah's obvious happiness. It gave his work new motivation. Home and hearth had taken on flesh.

Their marriage bed produced only one daughter, Seila,[2] and soon all of Tob was caught up in the rearing of Jephthah's daughter. Eden was being reconstructed! Jephthah was determined that she be properly educated. He sent word to Phineas for suitable tutors, insisting that he prevail on his contacts and send back scholars from Shiloh itself. That Phineas responded quickly to the "request" registered even in Jephthah's unreflective mind as to his growing reputation and respect.

Seila was showered with the best of everything. Nothing was denied her. Jephthah loved her without reservation, and without experience. She had no shortage of friends. The townspeople were astute enough to sense Jephthah's resolve that she should never be lonely or isolated. If Jephthah grew obsessed about creating the perfect childhood for his only daughter no one in town was about to object. Besides, the lengths to which he went to educate Seila raised the spirits of the entire little frontier outpost. Jephthah himself would frequently participate as student, learning to read and procuring a library of sorts. He heard the old stories and took them as his own. First there had been Abraham, and Yahweh, the invisible god, had promised that his descendants would be given this very land. Then came Isaac, who had nearly been offered up as a sacrifice in obedience to this new god Yahweh. But Yahweh had intervened and stopped Abraham from killing his son on the altar; so Issac lived and begat Jacob the schemer, who had twelve sons, one of whom was Joseph, whose brothers had sold him into Egyptian slavery. That had been the beginning of four hundred years of bondage in Egypt. Moses had rescued them and commanded the exodus into Canaan.

Jephthah's favourite stories, however, were about Joshua, who actually took possession of the land through five continuous years of brilliant military campaigning. Nothing so delighted him as retelling the mighty battles. He knew all the details of all the battles. With childlike excitement he would talk for hours about what it might have been like to be a commander in Joshua's army. There was the campaign of the north in the very lands that Jephthah knew intimately. Jabin, King of Hazor, led a coalition army of Hittites, Perizzites, Jebusites and Hivites complete with the largest massing of chariots and horses ever seen. Chariots! The Israelites had not seen them since the days of Moses when Pharaoh's army had chased them across the Red Sea. At the ford called Merom Joshua launched a surprise attack after an all-night march. King Hazor and the coalition were annihilated. The chariots were burned and the horses hamstrung.

Then there had been the battle with the five kings of the Amorites, when Yahweh himself participated and hurled down large hailstones from the sky, killing even more than Joshua. It was that same battle where the sun stood still in the sky at Joshua's request so that the fleeing troops could not use the darkness as cover to gain the safety of their fortified cities. The five kings were run to ground and dragged from the cave in which they hid. Joshua gathered together all his commanders and each in turn came forward and placed his foot on the necks of the five Kings. "This is what Yahweh will do to all whom we go out to fight," had shouted Joshua before cutting off the heads of the five and then hanging their bodies in trees for all to gape at. "*There has never been a day like it before or since, when the Lord listened to a man,*" ran the closing line of the ballad which told the tale.[3]

Thirty-one kings[4] in all met defeat at the hand of Joshua and his commanders before he retired, full of years and honour. His last act had been to apportion the lands to the tribes, with some portions still to be conquered. Jephthah drank heavily from the stories of past battles. The Joshua campaign was the golden age of the twelve tribes, when warfare was a holy occupation, and warriors the handservants of Yahweh, driving the barbarians out of the land in fulfillment of the promises made to Abraham. It was a time when he would have found a good fit.

There were other parts of Seila's education that puzzled Jephthah. The worship of Yahweh remained a mystery to him. He was not inclined as others were to be pluralistic in his worship; Joshua's God was his God. If the teaching of the tutors on religious practice seemed to mimic the customs of their neighbours Jephthah did not feel it was his place to probe. His own beliefs were deeply private and like most other aspects of him, straightforward. One was careful in dealing with him. Yahweh kept his word. Yahweh was true. Stern and remote. Jephthah would have welcomed instruction in the area but never could he find the right words to frame his questions and the religious tutors Phineas had sent seemed lacking in their own convictions.

Jephthah presided over the little world of Tob, blissfully untouched by the larger currents of chaos that swirled around him. The roads and hill country around Tob were safe, people and caravans alike were glad to provide for the needs of Jephthah and his troops, and his only child budded into a pubescent virgin whose married womb would deliver namesakes and descendants. It was all falling into place and lasted just long enough for Jephthah to believe it might last forever.

Phineas himself headed the delegation that came to petition Jephthah. Six of them came, four of them weary old men who could not hide their frailties however much they wanted to. They were in the company of two younger men whose carriage reflected defeat and discouragement. They got to the business as soon as it could be decently broached.

"The Ammonites, your enemies, have come out in force against us," said Phineas. "They mean to drive us completely from the land if they can this time. They will push us west back across the Jordan, onto the swords of the Philistines who hold the coast."

Another old man took up the argument. "This past eighteen years you've been gone have been harsh ones for us. The Ammonites raid us regularly. Food and livestock are scarce. It's not just the area of Gilead either. They've crossed the Jordan a few times already in force and now Benjamin, Judah and Ephraim are being harassed."

The third man took up the tale. "It's time for you to come home. Your father's lands are overrun. Some of your brothers are dead. They are polluting our shrines with their detestable idol worship."

One of the younger men concluded. "The men of Gilead will fight, but we need a leader. You are that man!" His voice attempted a dramatic finale to the conversation but instead came off sounding foolish. Jephthah said nothing, knowing the silence was more powerful over them than anything he might eventually say.

"Come home...father's lands...the Ammonites *his* enemies..." What a brazen distortion of reality. Did they think he was languishing in the wilderness awaiting permission to return to the tribe? "Come, fight our battles for us; it's your duty." Jephthah was incredulous at their importunity. And he did not know what to make of their newly recovered piety in Yahweh worship. Ashtoreth and Molech worship, with their bias toward violent sacrifice and fertility orgies, had mingled freely with the Israelite's worship habits for most of Jephthah's life.

Finally he spoke, speaking quietly but intensely, forcing Phineas to meet his gaze. "Are not you the same council that drove me from my father's house? Phineas, was it not you yourself who visited my father just before I was sent away? And now you come to offer me what—to be a temporary commander over an unruly and untrained mob—so that when it's all over I can be sent away once more? Phineas, are you forgetting what a stench I am in your pious nose? What has happened to your scorn of my mother who wore the veil of Ashtoreth? Is your plight so terrible now that you seek help from those you detest? You despised me then. My lineage has not changed. Even if I did find reason to help you, returning good for the evil you did me, will you rewrite history? Will your sons come seeking my daughter in marriage? Look around you, Phineas. Do you see any sign of Ammonites? Were you attacked on your journey here through the territory I control? My home is secure. My family flourishes. See to your own." For Jephthah it was a long speech and he noted that Phineas seemed to shrink under its force.

The other men were now looking at each other the way people do just before they commit to a desperate course of action. One of the young men spoke back: "What you say is true. This is the council that did as you said. Nevertheless we have come to you now with this proposition: Come with us now to fight against the Ammonites and you will rule over all who live in Gilead. You will be made chief judge, the head of all."

It was an awesome offer and spoke volumes about the strength of the Ammonite incursion. It was also the most backhanded of compliments. A bastard Gileadite judge was preferable to an Ammonite overlord, it would seem. Jephthah was unsure as to whether he should be flattered or insulted. He replied at last, choosing his words carefully. Much was at stake for both parties.

"Suppose I do come back with you and suppose Yahweh gives the Ammonites into my hand. What assurance have you brought that I will really be your head?"

Phineas spoke. " We declare our pact with you in truth. May Yahweh himself, the god of Abraham, Isaac, Jacob, Moses and Joshua be the witness to our promises."

"I will give you my answer in the morning," said Jephthah and withdrew. He own commanders would have to be consulted in this adventure before he could make his reply.

Next morning Jephthah appeared, dressed for battle. Around Tob his men were assembling, packhorses were being loaded with equipment and by noon Jephthah, the six men and an impressive honour guard were riding back toward Mizpah. More men would follow in the next few days as they were recalled from various duties, and more supplies would be gathered. But the troops of about three hundred men who accompanied Jephthah would be enough to give the impression of strength at the ceremonies that awaited them. Phineas and Jephthah had come to some practical arrangements. Yahweh might have heard their solemn promises of the night before, but it did no harm to have a hugely public affirmation of Jephthah's installation as commander-in-chief and permanent ruler over Gilead.

The ceremony was solemn and as impressive as it could be made in the middle of the Gilead encampment at Mizpah. Phineas dressed the part of a priest in the service of Yahweh. Promises of fidelity and allegiance were exchanged. Incense was offered up. The name of Yahweh was invoked to witness the pact. And at Jephthah's insistence, the ancient words of Jacob were recited as they were used at the first Mizpah, *the watchtower*, where Jacob and his father-in-law Laban, schemers both, invoked Yahweh as the impartial witness of their bargain:

May the LORD *keep watch between you and me when we are away from each other. Even though no one is with us remember that God is a witness between you and me.*[5]

Next day, to the surprise of everyone, Jephthah sent messengers to the Ammonite king. Out they rode from the camp at Mizpah, well-dressed and unarmed. It did not even occur to Jephthah that they would not be granted safe passage and so they were. Straight to the Ammonite king they went with a question from Jephthah. The tone Jephthah had instructed the messengers to take was conciliatory but not subservient: "What do you have against us that you have attacked our country?" The effort at a negotiated peace was not just a ploy to gain time to organize the volunteer cabal of men, none of whom had battle experience, although it did give him time to send a message to the Ephraimite tribe on the west bank of Jordan. With a little arm twisting, they might send men. Certainly their own security was resting on the outcome of the looming conflict. But the primary reason for sending the messengers was that he truly hoped that there might be some other way than to fight. Why fight a battle if it can be avoided? Jephthah had thought to himself. And if I have been dragged into a dispute in which the Gileadites have transgressed, Phineas and his group would not likely tell me. Better that I ask the enemy what causes him to risk his army in the field.

The Ammonite king sent back a reply: "You occupy lands that are not yours. You took them by force when you came out of Egypt—from the river Jabbok in the north to the river Arnon fifty miles to the south and west as far as the river Jordan. You are the aggressors in this conflict. We seek only what is ours. Now give this land back peaceably. Go live on the west side of Jordan with your brothers the Ephraimites."

Jephthah knew immediately that a battle was inevitable but at least he was satisfied he had not been entrapped in some private blood feud that had flamed into something larger. He decided to send one more message to the other side and in so doing to stiffen the resolve of his own troops as well. Jephthah had observed that men fought better when they felt morally justified in doing so. Besides, there was no harm in invoking the name of Yahweh as their leader. He formulated his reply carefully, reading it aloud to the assembly of men before sending the messengers back to the Ammonite king.

"Israel does not occupy Ammonite land.[6] This land given to us by our god Yahweh was Amorite land. It was they who denied us safe passage into Canaan but instead attacked us and were defeated. This land was never yours. For three hundred years since the campaigns of Moses and Joshua we have occupied this land given to us by Yahweh as an inheritance promised to Abraham our forefather. Be content with the lands allotted you by your god Chemosh as we are with our allotment. Know this, O king, that in this conflict you challenge the power of Yahweh himself. It is you who do us wrong. Let Yahweh himself judge between us." It was an impressive speech linking this conflict with earlier military accomplishments and historical precedent. The messengers left camp on a wave of cheers and yells. The speech had its intended effect on his own men. There would be, however, no reply from the Ammonite king.

Jephthah, alone that night, knew they were unlikely to be victors. It was not just the unequal strength of the armies and the problems inherent in assuming command over men he didn't know and who didn't know him. That was all just part of the calculated risk. No, the problem lay elsewhere and he had said it himself in a burst of public exuberance, *"May Yahweh himself be judge between us."* Jephthah was a serious student of history. Moses and Joshua had been successful because Yahweh had fought on behalf of his people. Supposing Yahweh *did* judge between them and found *the Gileadites* wanting and was going to use this conflict as further punishment? On the evidence of the past eighteen years there was no reason to come to their aid. That was the hard truth; there was no reason for Yahweh to rescue his people. Not even their recent renunciation of all other gods warranted his intervention. Who could ask him to overlook almost two decades of following after the gods of shame? No, on all accounts the Israelites ought to lose. The Ammonites showed more religious fidelity to Chemosh than Israel did to Yahweh.

It was in the midst of this private doubt that the spirit of Yahweh entered Jephthah. His entry, had there been anyone watching, was visible. Jephthah's whole body shook with the force of his possession. His face became ruddy, like a permanent flush or when people have sat too long in front of a fire and their skin starts to glow. There was no part of him that was not invaded by the Spirit and he realized just how intimately God knew him. Jephthah was afraid.

To say that Jephthah now shared the mind of God would be wrong in the way that finitude cannot really grasp infinity, nor time measure eternity. To the Spirit that now possessed Jephthah, time and space were mere playthings. It was more as if Jephthah had crept over some threshold— a doorway created in mid-air—and suddenly found himself inside a great cavernous realm that contained everything that had ever happened, was happening and that ever would happen, and yet all three spheres could be viewed as one composition. Jephthah crouched as it were, sitting so that his whole upper torso clung tight against the door frame, hands encircling the vertical posts and hanging on as if at any moment he could be lifted away by some huge wind. He knew that somewhere in the terrain into which he peered was the whole future of his tribe down to the last drop of rain that might or might not fall. Somewhere in the landscape was himself, was the day of his birth with all its harshness, this day, and the future day when he would face the Ammonites. It all existed already, for what Jephthah now knew was that nothing could happen in *his* world that had not already first happened in *this* world. Whether he lost or won the forthcoming conflict, he lost or won because it pleased Yahweh to order it. And if such purposing required the life of Jephthah to end on the pointed spear of some Ammonite warrior in order for Yahweh's larger schemes to work, then so be it. Sufficient for Jephthah that he had been gifted to see his own life's thread as a part of the larger fabric and that Yahweh sat at the loom.

The mortal Jephthah, however, had no desire to be anything but resoundingly victorious. He wanted to be remembered for having been the instrument of Yahweh's giving his promised land to his people a second time. He wanted his name linked with Joshua, his hero. He wanted gray hairs and grandchildren! He wanted to do something great for the

God he served and who had so powerfully singled him out by this anointing.

Next morning, early, Jephthah sought out Phineas to witness a vow. They stood close together. Jephthah did not kneel but had taken off his helmet and given his sword, unsheathed, to Phineas, who held it now crossways in both hands. Jephthah said aloud:

"O Yahweh, see that my hands are empty. It is you only who can deliver the Ammonites into them. And as it pleases you to do so, O God, whatever comes out of the door of my house to greet me when I return triumphant will be yours and I will sacrifice it as a sweet smelling burnt offering." He put his headgear back on, took the sword from Phineas's unmoving hands, turned on his heel and left. Phineas, through shock or shrewdness, said not a word.

The battle was waged for almost two months and Jephthah's victory was as complete as it was systematic. Choosing to avoid a frontal assault, Jephthah instead focused on the fortified towns, knowing that if these were razed the Ammonite army would have nowhere to go for sanctuary and supplies. It was a campaign of quick over-night marches and surprise assaults—a style of fighting for which Jephthah was ideally suited. Joshua had used the same battle tactics centuries earlier. Not for idle interest alone had Jephthah learned his history. In the end, twenty towns were destroyed. Abel-Keramim was the most northern of them, and just twenty miles from the Ammonite capital city of Rabbah. The Ammonites were pushed back to their historic settlements. Farms and livestock were confiscated along with the usual plunder and booty: clothing, weapons, utensils, young female slaves. Yahweh had given them the promised land a second time!

Jephthah's return "home" was a slow leisurely march back north to Mizpah and then toward Tob. Their last battle had taken place some sixty miles south but further by the roads. Jephthah used the long, leisurely victory parade as an opportunity to inspect the lands over which he was now chief. It did no harm for the common folks' first encounter with their new judge to show him flush with victory, surrounded by troops and able to bestow generous gifts of Ammonite goods as the situation warranted. The whole countryside was aware of the march and quite properly prepared a welcome for him. Jephthah found himself wishing for a chariot in which to ride. The last five miles from Mizpah to Tob would be the sweetest moments of Jephthah's life. People were now staging themselves on both sides of the pathway, shouting and cheering. The Ammonite hand had been heavy for two decades. Twenty towns would not be rebuilt in their lifetime. Freedom! They entered Tob and his troops, in a well executed salute, formed an archway with their swords under which Jephthah strode the last thousand metres to his own house. He heard the sound of tambourines and singing. Rounding the last corner in the town street he watched as Seila leaped through the doorway, rushing headlong toward him to encircle his neck tightly and plant kisses all about his face. And thus Jephthah received the wounds that were to kill him.

His whole body shook and lurched; an aide rushed forward to catch him and Seila dislodged herself from his neck. His face had turned the colour of bleached bones. When he finally spoke it was the voice of someone whose throat is paralyzed from thirst.

"Oh my daughter, you have made me miserable and wretched, because I have made a vow to Yahweh that I cannot break." He told her the details of his vow, unable to meet her eyes. The two sat for a long time on the ground outside their home. The crowd knew only that something had gone terribly, terribly wrong with the homecoming. Later they would know why. Seila was the first to stir. She took Jephthah's hand and led him into their home.

The noise of the night's celebrations could not be kept out of Jephthah's home. He sat at an open window. Smoke from the large fires burning in the town square drifted up, mingled with the distinct aroma of spit roasted meat. It made Jephthah gag. Seila sought him out. She had changed into a plain tunic, and tied her hair back tightly at the base of her neck. She began directly "Father, you cannot break your word. Yahweh has given what you asked for—a great victory over your enemies, and our people freed from their domination. For the first time in my life I can now go wherever I want in Canaan and not worry. Is my life any more sacred than the men who have not returned with you?"

"Daughter, you are my very heart," was all Jephthah said.

"And you are now the heart of Gilead, father. This is no longer a private matter. Will you be the first to break faith with God again?" There was no answer and Seila went on. "I have one request to make of you, father. Give me two months in which to mourn with my friends that I shall never marry. We would not stay here in the town. It would be ... awkward for everyone. If it would be acceptable, we would go up into the hill country where we would not be bothered."

"Go. Of course, go with your friends," Jephthah said. Not much else had registered except that two months' time had been secured. Anything can happen in two months, he kept thinking.

Jephthah quickly became isolated. His wife, who had remained barren after Seila's birth, went home to her parents. His best friend and military aide went on a tour to plan new patrol routes and strongholds. Phineas discovered urgent business in Shiloh. The parents of the girls who accompanied Seila would not speak to him. Everyone was waiting at a safe distance.

The torment of Jephthah was too excruciating to be around, in part because everyone felt implicated. True, it had been his vow but Jephthah had made it for the betterment of the whole community. And had not their elders gone and actively recruited him on their behalf? Yet no one was bold enough to counsel Jephthah to renounce his vow. Who would seriously suggest that he break his word to Yahweh? There were worse things that could happen in Gilead than the death of one girl. Whatever personal price Jephthah was paying, it did not warrant exposing the whole tribe to Yahweh's anger. On the other hand, no one would risk assisting Jephthah carry out his vow. It smacked of the dark rituals required by Molech. What if Yahweh did not want her killed? What if he differed from other gods who looked on child sacrifice as the highest gift? That was the nub of the problem. Who knew for sure God's mind in this matter?

Jephthah, when he could think at all, thought about running away himself, or even better, falling on his own sword. He kept wishing Seila would not return, but knew that this was not really a possibility. His solemn vow, uttered in sincerity, now held him like iron hoops bound around his chest. A proverb that was usually chanted sing-song fashion at prattling children or gossipy women ran through his head over and over again until he thought he would go mad:

Greater is he that keepeth his tongue
than he that taketh the city

Could the keeping of his promise serve the purposes of Yahweh? Surely God had not given Seila to him only to snatch her back in this cruel way. Why should she pay for his indiscretion? Round and round the questions chased each other in a hopeless circle.

The days finally ran out and Seila returned only to leave again with Jephthah. People kept out of sight, but from behind shutters, in the dark recesses of their houses they watched them depart. Seila was beside him and people saw that it was her arm which held his waist. Like Abraham, he was leading a donkey loaded with firewood. Unlike Abraham, he returned alone. Yahweh had not intervened.

— ◆ —

When news of Jephthah's great victory spread to the western tribes, the reaction was not one of relief and celebration over the Ammonites' defeat. Ephraim never had sent troops in support of Jephthah and in so doing had violated the time-honoured custom of inter-tribal military support. Their unwillingness to help the Gileadites was not just a private matter as between two neighbours. The knowledge that all twelve tribes would rally to the defence of one another was a powerful deterrent to their foreign neighbours intent on expansion. Now, after the fact, they felt humiliated and envious. Always quick to remedy the slightest snub, their elders devised a plan to return their tribal pride. Calling out their own men to arms they advanced across the Jordan to attack the Gilead military. Their public stance was that Jephthah had *not allowed* them to participate, choosing to hoard the glory (and the booty) for himself. Such arrogant selfishness was only to be expected from a bastard renegade, but nevertheless could not go unchecked. The sons of Ephraim would teach them a lesson on inter-tribal loyalties. Theirs was a big tribe and put fifty thousand men in the field without difficulty. Jephthah had twenty-five thousand men who were not yet disbanded.

Ephraim sent a small group of emissaries in advance of the armed troops. They were met by Jephthah himself close to the town of Adam. Their question was rhetorical and their threat theatrical: "Why did you go out to fight the Ammonites without us? For that we'll burn your house over your head."

Jephthah, to his credit, replied as if to a serious question: "I did ask you to help, as you well know. But you did not come and the Ammonites could not be placated. It was Yahweh who came to my aid and who gave me this great victory. Who are you to disagree with Yahweh's decisions?" He spoke evenly, without emotion. His words were of no use and he full knew that a fight was inevitable. Privately, he did not much care either way. Would he have made his vow to Yahweh if Ephraim had sent troops to help? He would never know for certain. It was a line of thought, which, if nothing else made the Ephraimites a good whipping post. The meeting ended. Preparation for the fighting continued.

Jephthah's speech to his men was brief. He had only to repeat the Ephraimite slur that all Gileadites were renegade half breeds, not worthy to be called Israelites and he knew he had ignited their blood. Besides, Seila's death was fast becoming holy martyrdom, freely offered as a consequence of their victory. Already there were plans afoot to commemorate her death by way of an annual four-day vigil in the hill country attended by unmarried girls. Who was Ephraim to take issue with their holy war, waged with Yahweh's favour?

Jephthah's battle plan was simple. During the fight a third of his men would break through the Ephraimite lines and take the fords of the Jordan leading back to Ephraim territory. The Ephraimites would be caught between the two forces, and squeezed accordingly. It would be a series of battlefronts happening simultaneously, separated by miles of territory. Jephthah had no doubt about the outcome. He had good commanders capable of independent action and their Ammonite victory more than offset the numeric handicap. Fighting fellow Israelites presented one new problem, however. Both militia were provisional and wore neither insignia nor uniform. Hebrew was the common tongue. The retreating Ephraimites could as easily pass themselves off as Gileadites and thus escape through the blockaded fords.

It was a young outcast in Jephthah's camp who hit on the solution. His cleft was horribly deformed and his speech hard to comprehend, which was, no doubt, the very thing that made him so aware of others' phonetic oddities. The Ephraimites had acquired a fricative defect over time and could not make the *sh* sound. They substituted the sibilant proxy *s* so that words like *Sh*iloh were pronounced *S*iloh. The password *sh*ibboleth was chosen—"ear of corn." Those who rendered it *S*ibboleth would be killed. The black irony of death from a word not spoken sat well with Jephthah.

"Their own mouths will condemn them," said Jephthah when reviewing the plan with his commanders. "There are to be no second chances, and no prisoners." Shibboleth was the password; Seila was the war cry.

The conflict went just as Jephthah predicted. Fifty thousand

Ephraimites crossed over to fight. Eight thousand Ephraimites managed the return trip. This time, however, there would be no victory parade. The Jordan stayed polluted with decaying corpses for months. The downstream tribes received these bloated heralds in disbelief. Jephthah's rule over all of Israel was unquestioned.

Six years later Jephthah died suddenly from an unknown cause. He was found in his bed one morning by his servant. There were no marks on his body and he had not been ill. It was as if he had just decided to stop living. Those who were closest to him made much of his broken heart, which remained unhealed. The widows of Ephraim received the news of his death in stony silence. The Ammonite king, in an unusual gesture, sent a group of professional mourners. In other quarters, however, it was observed that Jephthah had shed more Israelite blood than Ammonite. Phineas, of course, presided over the hugely public burial in Gilead. His was the most effusive of the eulogies; certainly it was the longest. Perhaps it was to detract from the absence of those who usually made these speeches. There were no children to pay tribute. He called Jephthah a great servant of Yahweh, a man of faith, who would be remembered for all time along with the other great leaders of Israel. Phineas always did know what to say at these things. But early next day Phineas hurried west, across the Jordan to Shiloh. A new judge would have to be found.

— ♦ —

Phineas's prediction came true. Centuries later Jephthah would be included in the list of Israel's great men of faith. The list was compiled in a treatise to the Hebrews, in its eleventh chapter.

Endnotes

[1] This story may be found in Judges 10:6-12:7.
[2] The name is supplied. The daughter is never named in the cannonical story.
[3] The story may be found in Joshua 10
[4] Joshua 12:24
[5] Genesis 31:49f
[6] Numbers 21:21-24

The Blessing and the Curse

His lips came together as he sought to repress his anger and rage. Walking back down the hill from the plateau on which his father's tent was pitched, the long shadows of the late afternoon sun only made his dark, swarthy face look all that much blacker. His wife, noting the rigid, tense silhouette and able to read it, knew there had been trouble, and steeled herself for what might come.

"We're moving," was all he said, when he finally reached the entrance of his own tent and entered. Then he withdrew to the isolated comfort of the bench outside.

Ham looked over to where the tents of his two older brothers were, just able to make out their outlines in the evening dusk. Already the fires outside all the tents were beginning to look like beacons in the darkness. But instead of the warm welcoming glow they usually advertised, tonight they only made him more aware of his own isolation—the black night around him holding him tight like a prisoner. He tried to reconstruct the day as best his mind would function. It had been a day of such promise. That morning Noah had declared to all within earshot that the wine was ready at last! They had all gathered in late morning around the shed that stored the clay jars Noah had been supervising these past weeks. Supervising! Obsessing was the more accurate word. But who could seriously blame him. For Noah, vineyards were his life. In the days before the deluge he had owned two whole valleys of vineyards. Only he knew how many different varieties were growing or where some of the more exotic species had come from. His staff was enormous—a permanent indentured group of no less than forty-five men and their families, which could swell to more than two hundred people at harvest times. The grape had been the preoccupation of most of his life, and had made him rich into the bargain. He had also garnered considerable renown and respect for his ability to coax from the vats a wine that surpassed what anyone else could produce. He perfected the technique of storing wine so that it not only lasted season to season, but actually improved with age.

Noah had lived up to his name, given to him by his father Lamech, who said, *"His name shall be Noah: for he will comfort us in the labour and painful toil of our hands caused by the ground God has cursed."* [1] And Noah had done just that. To the end of Lamech's days, just four years before the flood, Noah had provided the comfort of the vine both to his family and to most of those around. What was to most farmers nothing more than one crop among many, was to Noah the ultimate expression of the good earth delivering up her milk for the nurture of her children. Not that Noah was a pantheist, or even took the notion of animism seriously. He followed Elohim, the invisible, all-powerful God who had made the entire world. But for him there was still something mysteriously pure about the whole slow process of converting grapes to wine. For him, the curse of the ground seemed to have been lifted.

Small wonder that today was a day of celebration—Noah's first harvest! That morning the wine had been drawn off and eagerly passed around to the excited chatter and banter that goes with all spontaneous and good-hearted gaiety. Noah blushed as his sons and their wives complimented him. His wife joked about his having hoarded all the jars these months just to make vinegar. Life as they had once known it was slowly taking shape again. They had wine now. The earth had not played them false as the heavens had. By midday the families had returned to their tents—rude shelters, really, of skins, wood, planks from the boat. No one had wanted to be too shut in after the boat. A leisurely afternoon meal had been consumed. Noah had retired to his "tent," his private quarters attached to his main structure but with its own entrance. His wife had stayed with Shem's family, whose wife had been the first to give birth after the flood. Where they had found time, place and inclination within the confines of the boat remained a matter of bemused conjecture. Noah's wife took the usual grandmotherly pride in this offspring and visited at every opportunity. Every family's area was a respectful distance from the others and after a year of living on top of each other, family visits were by invitation. The land was not the only thing that needed healing; family relations among the three sons and their wives had been sorely tested this past year.

It was not until late afternoon that Ham realized that Noah still had not put in an appearance. Ham had spent the afternoon repairing the runners that supported the vines. For his father to have missed his daily tour of inspection was most unusual. Noah was many things but above all he was a man of ordered routines. Curious, Ham decided to investigate, and climbed the hill to where his father's shelter stood. Entering the tent Ham stood quite still, waiting for his eyes to adjust to the interior gloom. He was not sure at first that his eyes were not playing tricks on him. His father lay still on the floor. A clay jar, tipped on its side, had rolled along the sloping earthen floor to lodge against the tent wall. Ham stepped closer. His father lay on his back, breathing loudly, eyes shut and deep in sleep. His father was also completely naked.

The shock of seeing his father uncovered did not dull his absorption of the details. How pale the skin was, with strong demarcations between his sun-weathered neck and the pale, tender skin of his torso. The chest was sunken slightly with loose fleshy skin that was the unmistakable sign of advancing years. The body hair was scant and if there was any grey pubic hair, none showed in the darkness of the tent—only the wisps of white, withered curls that spoke of fatigue. When had his father grown so old while all the rest of them had simply grown tough? Noah was scarcely six hundred years old—advanced but by no means nearing his end by the standards of the day. Methuselah had been his grandfather! The body Ham gazed down at was without question the body of his father, but it had no connection with how Ham knew his father. The tower of strength, the man who had held them all together this past seven years, lay asleep, exposing the proof of his own helplessness to fend off time and decay. The tired vulnerability was embarrassing. It was as if Noah's own body was making the speech that Noah had steadfastly refused to utter himself these long years.

Ham retreated and in the comfort of the sunlight he reached beneath his own robes to feel the tight skin of his chest, the muscles beneath still solid and expansive. It was as if in the act of touching himself he hoped to ward off whatever calamity had befallen his father. His feet took him to his two older brothers, Japheth and Shem. He could see them walking back together from a field. Ham increased his pace so as to intersect them before they reached sight of their huts.

"It's father," he rushed. "The wine must have been stronger than usual, or something, but he's in his tent, asleep. He has no clothes on. He's naked. I looked at...everything...I saw..." Ham's voice trailed off. What had he seen? The brothers had already determined what Ham had seen. Their faces registered their censure mixed with disgust. They began to stride purposefully up the hill toward Noah's tent. Ham trailed along but stopped about one hundred feet from the entrance, leaving his two older brothers to complete the climb. On reaching the entrance they stopped and Ham could see them talking although he did not hear the words. Then Japheth took his cloak off and gave one edge to Shem. They had turned around, their backs now facing the tent entrance, with the cloak held between them. They huddled together, crouching and slowly, letting their feet be their eyes, they shuffled backward and disappeared from Ham's sight. They emerged after what seemed like a very long time. Certainly the sun had shifted visibly. Ham had not moved from his spot. His two brothers wound their way down from the tent and passed him with neither a word nor glance.

And then the explosion. Or in the silence of what was now early twilight that's what Noah's voice sounded like. He stood in the tent entrance with hair and beard tangled, clothing slung around him, hiding his form.

"A curse on you, Ham! A curse to follow you all your life and the life of your children and their children and to the ends of time itself! You'll be slaves to your brothers' descendants. They'll take your territory, occupy your towns, kill your young men and violate your women. The land you go to inhabit you will not keep. Canaan will not be yours, nor will Assyria your empire prevail. A curse on you, Ham, for what you have done! May the black faces of your offspring always be the servants to your fairer brothers."

The outburst echoed and hung in the air between father and son. It was almost as if neither party wanted to accept ownership of the words lest in so doing they would come true. There was a dried white ring of spittle around most of Noah's mouth and the speech had worked up more white paste leaking out the edges. Ham did not reply. There was nothing to say. Noah turned away first, finally, and the tent opening reverted to a black hole. Ham turned and walked down the hill to his own hut. The harsh gravelly voice of Noah, thickened from the after-effects of drink, stayed in Ham's hearing long into the night.

Noah stood in the centre of the tent, his chest heaving at the exertion of such a voluminous outburst, uttered from out of an almost sound sleep. What in God's name had he done? Cursed his youngest son! Where had the words and the rage behind them come from? He cast about, looking for the wine jug, and seeing it empty on its side his mouth immediately became dry and his tongue swelled tenfold. It only added to his rage and he was aware now of how badly his head was pounding. Damnation and damnation—nothing but water around him for what had seemed like forever and here he was seemingly about to die of thirst. Had his misery not been so urgent, he would have smiled even to himself. But the black humour of his predicament at least began to calm his mind and Noah's love of order extended to his inner state, too. He sat finally, collecting himself, trying to piece together the events of the day and ignore the thickness of his mouth. He had cursed his son. Why? He would never know for certain.

The day had started out with such promise. The wine had been ready at last! Noah had not lost his touch and the seedlings and cuttings he had so painstakingly kept alive during the long days in the boat had borne other vines and now fruit. Elohim had not played false with them. The earth was to be trusted. For Noah the day had been a profound relief. Sanity was being restored to creation. Noah was unprepared for the flood of memories this morning's ritual had unleashed; nor did he have any advance warning of their force. Seeing the happy faces of his sons and their wives that morning had made him think of other happy faces he was accustomed to seeing on these days of the first draught. There had been times when he expected to turn round and see his friend, Timori, laughing that big deep chortle as he tipped the vats on edge, pouring them into smaller, more manageable jars. Timori had been there at the last wine tasting. They had stood together, sipping the fruit, both looking out at the acres of vines. In the distance had stood the "shelter," mostly finished except for a bit of roofing and some pitch.

"It's the best vintage ever," said Timori. "You've sold me your two valleys much too cheap." Timori dwarfed Noah by a full two heads. One of the Nephilim, he was the offspring of the sons of the gods and the daughters of men, so it was rumoured. Certainly Timori had never volunteered any information about his father but that did not necessarily mean anything. For the most part these giant beings were fierce and kept to themselves in the higher lands. But Noah and Timori had become friends somehow over the years and it was to him that Noah had gone when the shelter project was first being conceived. Noah knew vineyards and the earth. Timori knew the hills and trees. Besides, his strength was enormous, and Noah was a practical man.

"You're truly a crazy man," Timori had said five years earlier. "A sealed house 489 feet long, 49 feet tall and 160 feet wide, with two inner floors plus a covered superstructure. Pitched with tar inside and out. It would take a decade to build and require the lumber of three valleys off. Why can't this god who has befriended you make more reasonable requests of you? Does he have such a poor opinion of himself that he asks for such a pompous and complex abode as this? Besides, you haven't the wealth or the manpower to do it."

"I need it done in five years, Timori," Noah had said, "And I'm not sure you would believe me if I told you why Elohim wants it done anyway, so what does it matter to you? And I do have the wealth. You're looking at it. I'll give you my vineyards if you'll help."

Timori had never ceased to marvel at Noah's steadfast relationship to his god Elohim, although he was not inclined that way himself. There was no one else that Timori knew who cared two figs for the heavenly residents, much less submitted to their authority. It was a lust-mad world for the most part. Life in all its pleasurable forms was for the taking if you had the power and the inclination. The gods could look after themselves. Certainly if Timori's own rumoured lineage was any indication, they didn't evidence much self control themselves. In fact, Timori had no knowledge of his father; theirs was a clan that did not go in much for history. But Noah had stood out against the turbulence around him and had earned the respect of others. Timori had sometimes wished that Elohim had befriended him. There was a stability to Noah and his family that was quite winsome.

For Noah's part, Timori often reminded him of some great dog who never did know quite where his feet were and was therefore forever tripping over them and being surprised at the ensuing chaos. He was perhaps not the fastest thinker, a trait common to big people. Yes, there was a dark wildness to him that would break out from time to time, but the human race was far from perfect and he had become a good friend to Noah. Timori's clan was large, too, and between them the men served as the bridge that allowed at least some modest understanding between their two peoples.

The building of the "shelter" had taxed Noah's consummate organizational skills. His own brothers and sisters and their families had agreed to help, for payment of course. If Noah wanted this *thing* constructed, then there had to be some good reason for it. Noah might be secretive but he was not stupid. They were not about to help him get any richer from their free labour. Timori too, along with his clan, required payment. In

144

the end they had struck what to Timori seemed a foolish and generous pact. Noah's two valleys of vineyards were to be duly relinquished to Timori on the completion of the shelter. The undertaking was going to bankrupt Noah. That much was obvious. But until then, he was the source of steady employment, regular food and excellent drink. If Noah wanted this structure built and was willing to pay for it, who were others to question the oddity of the undertaking? It was only to Timori that Noah had confided about the instructions and dimensions having come from Elohim himself. So far as the rest of people were concerned, it was a great storage shed whose unusual shape was said to give special assistance to the fermenting process.

Five years of working together, dovetailing the skills and efforts of the two disparate families, had built a friendship between the two men. As the work grew to an end the moods of the two men diverged noticeably, Noah becoming more silent and Timori more ebullient. The project had challenged the carpentry skills of them all and Timori had discovered a certain thrill in the pursuit of craftsmanship, which mingled with the anticipated pleasure of his deferred payment. For Noah, watching Timori so happily rush to complete the prerequisite of his own death was more than he could bear some days.

The two men had stood together sipping the wine, Timori gazing at the vineyards and Noah at the boat, both thinking of the future.

"The valleys will be yours in about a week," said Noah.

"A good thing it's done," said Timori. "You've nothing left to pay out in wages. You know you can always work for me when you finally come to your senses," Timori continued not unkindly.

"We'll see," replied Noah. "For the moment my wife, our sons and their wives are going to live in it. I intend to enclose some livestock in the lower sections. We've victuals and fodder inside to last us for a time. A long time," added Noah to himself.

Noah, if he closed his eyes and listened could still hear the frantic, hoarse screams of Timori outside the boat's walls. At the beginning there had only been the sound of the rains; then later the sounds of rushing water, rivers forming everywhere as the volume of water, some from deep within the earth tried to find some escape. It was through these later sounds that Noah heard Timori's voice.

"Noah! Noah! I helped you build it. Let me in. Let me in Noah. Do you think you're the only one worth saving? Are you that much better than me?" And in the end his voice took on the tone of a frightened child who has been badly betrayed. "Noah, Noah, I thought we were friends." For some reason the cries of his own brothers and sisters together with their families did not affect him as much as the accusing voice of Timori. Perhaps it was because they had sought to exploit him, his own kin no less, and therefore they deserved what they got. Anyway, he did not have to listen to them for as long. Their voices were not as strong as Timori's and they drowned first in the deluge.

And then had come that terrible forty days, with rain making such a thunderous racket that the noise became something physical, like tiny stones trying to beat an entrance into his skull. He could see nothing and would not have seen even if he had been on deck instead of two decks down. The prolonged awareness that the entire world was being utterly destroyed just outside their flimsy shelter of pitch and gopher wood, yet being unable to see it except in his mind, was a torture that threatened to make him go mad at the hands of his own imagination. Elohim was utterly without restraint in his destruction of what he had made. Was humanity that bad to warrant total annihilation? Was it the fault of man that he been made so much in Elohim's image that he even had free will?

Once started, the memories of the flood invaded Noah's mind with an autonomy that could not be controlled. All that afternoon Noah sat in his tent, nursing the jug of wine, a victim of his memories. He and his sons had been saved. All others had been savagely destroyed. Elohim was starting over with just this family. There had been no discussion on this or any other point of Elohim's plan. Elohim had instructed; Noah had obeyed. His own opinions of the justice or even the wisdom of the matter had not been invited.

In the end, a drunken stupor rescued him from further torment. The fact that he had been rudely wakened by his two sons as they clumsily tried to cover him while unable to see him did nothing for his equanimity on waking. And on hearing the details of Ham's earlier visit, Noah at last found an outlet for the rage within him. The empty jug and swollen tongue were also good reasons to get angry. Was a father not entitled to some privacy? Was Noah not entitled to at least one fit of despondency?

The truth was that the flood had changed nothing. Humanity had survived with all its warts in spite of Elohim's outburst. Not that Noah had been under any other illusions, but for a time it had been comforting to indulge in the hope that the flood might have made a difference after all. It would just be a matter of time before the world would be as full of evil men as it was before the flood. God had failed, both in his choice of progeny and his efforts to erase the sins of Adam. Ham, young as he was, might just as well know now as later that the promise of starting over was a fool's promise, that nothing lay ahead for him except violence, apostasy and disillusionment. The jibe about being a slave to his brothers, though, was cruel. Ham's natural deference to them would make him an easy mark for their exploitation. Shem and Japheth would know only too well how to go about it. Had they not watched his father play Timori?" But they would not get off free. Elohim would extend their territory but it was going to include a valley of dry bones. Noah sat in his tent utterly weary. Fresh starts were such a cruel illusion.

Ham sat on the bench well into the night. Cursed in public by his father! His two older brothers blessed. The pronouncement of future servitude. Not bloody likely in his lifetime! For five years he had stood by his father, done the work asked of him, been the loyal son. For five years he had endured the ridicule of the valley, he and his tall, ebony bride who had put off having children so that she could help too. And now this stupid ending. Noah was getting old. His father might be a friend of Elohim, but surely his words in this matter were his own and did not carry the same certitude. Noah walked with Elohim, true; but he was not Elohim.

Ham himself had heard the voice of Elohim—once only, but clear. It had happened at the blessing ritual when the sky had been filled with brilliant bands of colour, a token that the bow of God was permanently hung up to rest. Elohim had made them all a promise. And he had given them all a blessing too. Ham and his wife had stood along with all the rest of them as they stood around the pile of stones. The smoke of the burning flesh had swirled and the fat had sizzled and burned until it made their eyes water. They had been extravagant in their sacrifice of animals and had even eaten their flesh for the first time. What permission! To eat the food of Elohim himself, all but the lifeblood. There were bands of colour spewed across the sky, looking as though they had little diamonds or tears dotted throughout them, but whether from laughter or crying who knew. The earth itself was entering into the thanksgiving rites of having been spared. Being alive at that moment and sharing it with all of creation was a feeling that would stay with Ham all his life. Elohim had smiled and given them a promise:

As long as the earth endures so also will seedtime and harvest
cold and heat
winter and summer
and day and night.
Never again will I destroy the earth in this way
I will hang my bow in the sky that we may both look at it
and I will be reminded of my eternal covenant made this day
with you and all that lives.
Now be fruitful and multiply.
Start over and repopulate the earth.

And that was just what Ham intended to do.

"We'll leave in the morning," was all he said as he turned to his wife later that night. No point in prolonging the inevitable. "Good-bye, Shem; Good-bye, Japheth. I'm taking God's blessing and my father's curse. We'll see which is the stronger."

— ◆ —

Ham's family would spawn many tribes and ethnic groups.[2] Among them would be the Cushites, a black-faced people who finally settled in ancient Ethiopia and other African areas. As well, the Assyrians would claim Ham as their father. They would become a fierce empire and destroy ten of the twelve tribes of Israel. Jonah would visit their capital city, Ninevah, and they would repent. The tribes of Canaan would come from Ham as well. The Israelites never did manage to dislodge all of them.

Footnotes:
[1] Genesis 5:29
[2] Genesis 10:6-20

The Rape of Jacob's Daughter

The invitation came in that first spring after Dinah's monthly flow began and Jacob flatly forbade her to accept it. That in itself was something; it was one of the few times he had ever addressed her directly. It was a harmless enough outing and Dinah was flattered that for once in her life she had been singled out for notice. The young girls of Shechem, a thickly walled town not a mile away from where Jacob now kept his family encampment, had invited Dinah to take the spring spas along with them. Runoff from nearby Mount Ebal, on its way down to meet the Jordan river, pooled in certain rocky depressions, absorbing their minerals and taking on vaguely defined medicinal properties as a consequence, or so the youth of the town kept insisting. The pools never survived the summer heat and so their formation each spring created a buoyant urgency that quite matched the spirits of the season. They were some distance from the town, and elevated into the mountainside —remote enough to be exempt both from prescribed conventions and adults! It had been quite kind of the city girls to think of Dinah, stuck as she was in the family compound, and she resolved to accept no matter how strongly her father objected.

Dinah endured several handicaps within her family of origin: she was the only daughter in a family of eleven brothers; her mother was Leah, Jacob's least favourite wife; she had missed out being the perpetual "baby" of the family by all of six months, a position that attracted at least a little doting; and she was beautiful in a way that could not be hidden. Of all the things that made life most difficult for her this last quality was the worst. The only woman in the family who could be beautiful was Leah's younger sister, Rachel. It was she who had given birth to the youngest child, Joseph. It was she who was the all-consuming object of Jacob's love.

Leah bore her daughter's beauty with more grace. Even before the effects of six children, Leah had never been beautiful. She was solidly rectangular, with feet and hands just overly large enough to be obvious. It was her eyes though that most repulsed Jacob. Leah's eyes reacted badly to light. It was as if they were continually on the move inside their sockets, trying to find shade. When she looked at someone, it was never very directly; her eyes would dart away from the person's face, eyelids fluttering open and shut to a rhythm that was independent of whatever she might be saying, quivering with an agitation that was contagious if the conversation was prolonged. Her sight, however, was unimpaired and, thankfully, the oddity was not passed down to any of her children. There was no explaining it, but she was stigmatized for it just the same. Dinah could not comprehend why this single flaw remained an obsession for both Leah and Jacob. (But then she was beautiful and did not yet understand the shame that is the constant companion of oddity.) It was as if those eyes hovered between Leah and Jacob like furtive chroniclers, building a perpetual memorial out of everything that was wrong between them. To Jacob they were the outward justification for his disaffection. To Leah they were her excuse for not receiving the love of her husband—proof that she was a victim of circumstances beyond her control.

It had all started when Jacob had arrived from the south to stay with his mother's brother, Laban, who was Leah and Rachel's father. Rebekah, Jacob's mother, years earlier had traveled south as a bride for Isaac. Jacob had made the two-hundred-mile return journey in considerably more haste. He had been running from his older brother, Esau, who had promised to murder him the minute father Isaac died, but not, as people took pains to point out, without just cause. Jacob had stolen both Esau's birthright and his blessing, having been coached in the whole thing by his mother Rebekah. This was an important detail of the family history, since it proved, at least, that Laban's own conniving character was not a freak accident, but a trait in common with his sister.

Jacob and Laban had struck a contract: in exchange for seven years' labour, Jacob could marry Rachel, the younger and more beautiful daughter, whom he loved deeply. It was a contract that was not honoured, setting the precedent for a whole string of bargains, schemes, duplicities and deceits that marked most of Laban's relationship with Jacob. The love, however, endured through Jacob and Rachel's entire life together. Dinah, seeing it thirty-two years after it was kindled, regarded it with envy and awe.

Laban had outwitted Jacob. At the wedding celebrations Laban had substituted Leah in Rachel's place. Jacob, who was said to have been falling-down drunk by the time he was escorted to the marriage bed, did not discover the substitution until the morning. Laban, while all the time blustering about the inviolable traditions of marrying eldest daughters first, agreed to give away Rachel exactly one week later—in exchange for another seven years' labour from Jacob. It was a particular part of the family history frequently recited with great hilarity, never, of course, in the hearing of Jacob. But to Dinah's mind, newly awakened to the passions of heart and flesh, the story had some flinty edges to it. To Dinah's mind there was more to this story than just a greedy father forcing a solution to the problem of the unsightly older sister. She could only speculate on how Leah must have felt while Jacob touched her that first night, all the while slurring Rachel's name. And then to endure six more nights of conjugal relations in keeping with the traditional marriage rituals, knowing that it was Rachel he was embracing in his head while thrusting away at Leah.

But Leah must have willingly participated in the scheme from the start, at least that was the only conclusion Dinah could come to. It was something Dinah and Leah never talked about. For certain Laban intended to exploit Jacob's expert animal husbandry for as long as he could, and had taken a shrewd bet that Jacob would agree to the extra term of service out of love for Rachel. Perhaps exploitation was a family trait.

In the early years, after Jacob started his family, there seemed to be a rough equilibrium to the family dynamics. Rachel was the object of Jacob's love but Leah gave him male heirs. Their names were outlandish, and served as editorial comment on the progressive stages in the sisters' lifelong enmity.

Leah became a mother first. When her son was born, Leah, with all the hope of a young bride looking for a brighter future, named him Reuben saying, "*See, a son!*" She always maintained that he was a divine response to her misery, and openly hoped that Jacob would become more affectionate now that she had given him progeny. Reuben would remain a reclusive mystery all his life. One was never sure what he would do or say next. He grew tall and gangly. His forehead was high and flat, eyes set wide apart, with deeply indented sockets and large black pupils. His nose blended flat into his face and his lips tended to sit tightly over his teeth so that one rarely saw them. One got the impression that even he was surprised at what his mouth said sometimes. He was not overly coordinated, having inherited his mother's hands and feet. The overall impression was an anxious timidity, capable at the same time of random outbursts of anger. Under normal circumstances his position as eldest male would have been secure and offered a compensatory ballast in his life. But Jacob's family was anything but normal. His own theft of Esau's birthright and blessing mocked the solemn traditions, and it was not at all certain that Reuben would become the clan chief on Jacob's death. He resented Jacob's cavalier treatment of Leah, yet remained conflicted in wanting to obtain Jacob's approval for himself.

Next was Simeon, so named because "*the Lord has heard that I am still not loved.*" He could not have been more unlike Reuben in both appearance and personality. He would always be short (some said that was what encouraged his vicious temper), thin and wiry with lots of hair like his Uncle Esau, only black and not red. His voice was raspy, as if it was always on the verge of laryngitis, and it added an intensity to anything he said. He and Levi ("*Now at last my husband will respect me*"), next in line, were good friends and organized their duties so that they were always together. They both seemed totally lacking in the art of kindness. Dinah had been a young girl when they had first participated in culling the herds—a periodic event in the cycle of livestock—when the hides of the older or diseased stock were harvested and dried meat was laid up in quantity. She remembered them coming in at evening, their forearms looking like the bottom of a parched riverbed, dried blood caked in crusty clumps. But they had come back from the day as if it had been like any other, as if holding a hundred struggling sheep between their knees, twisting their heads up and to the side with one hand, making a clean swift knife cut across their windpipes with the other, then holding them until enough blood had gushed out that the animal's legs buckled—as if that activity was no more eventful than anything else that they might have done. It was their insensibility that had upset her more than the death of the animals. They loved their mother, but the only evidence was their continual contempt for Jacob, which they made little effort to hide.

Judah was number four son, named after Leah's birth-stool thanksgiving, "*I will praise God,*" presumably for having given her such a productive womb. He would grow up to be strong, raw-boned and some would say decidedly ill featured. He was more level headed than any of the older brothers and remained unmoved by the emotional volatility that possessed all three. There was nothing Judah was afraid of, unlike Reuben, who could be easily cowed by Simeon or Levi's virulence.

Rachel still had not conceived and so Bilhah, her servant girl, in the wake of bitter, bitter words between Rachel and Jacob, was offered as a proxy womb. It was like Abraham and Sarah all over again—when the servant Hagar had been sent in. Rachel claimed both ensuing sons as her own: Dan—*"God has vindicated me"*—and Naphtali—*"I have had a great struggle with my sister and I have won."* She might have won the round, but it proved to be only a temporary advantage. Leah's womb went dormant, and so Zilpah, her servant girl, was sent in to receive Jacob's affections, which resulted in the birth of two more sons, named by Leah: Gad— *"What good fortune I have"*—and Asher—*"How happy I am."*

The competition between the sisters enveloped the children, and each in his own way would find ways to vent his feelings. Reuben once went in search of mandrake plants, a rare aphrodisiac intended as a present for his mother, Leah. But Rachel intercepted them and traded a night with Jacob in order to keep the plants. If Jacob objected to being hired out for an evening, he did not comment. His hands were full during those early years just trying to keep ahead of Laban's continual manoeuvres. Rachel's stratagem did not work anyway. She remained barren despite the plants, while Leah's womb delivered up two final sons: Issachar—*"My reward";* and Zebulun—*"Surely now my husband will show me some honour for I have given him six sons."*

Dinah had been next in birth order to Zebulun but by the time she arrived, Rachel was in the third month of her first pregnancy and no one took much notice of Dinah's arrival. Unlike everyone else in her family, her name carried no significance. Besides, daughters did not count the same as sons.

Rachel was thankful that God had taken away her disgrace but not content with just one, named her boy Joseph, which is to say, *"God, give me another."*

Ten of the brothers, despite the usual infighting and bickering one expects in large families, were united in their disdain for Jacob. It was the birth of Joseph that afforded a common bond. Rachel seized every opportunity to elevate Joseph above all others, shamelessly trading on Jacob's love for her, to gain favoured staus for her son. It went against the traditions of clan leadership, which placed much weight on birth order. That Rachel didn't even attempt subtlety galled everyone. Dinah was never sure the extent to which Jacob divined his sons' feelings about him. She got the impression that Jacob's leadership was tolerated in support of Leah's continued efforts to earn Jacob's love.

And that was the family history, or at least the children's part of it. It seemed to Dinah that the score had not changed one bit from the first volley. Leah may have extracted a putative victory from Jacob's loins but Rachel still ruled his heart. It was never to change.

Dinah had been seven years old when Jacob decided that facing Esau was better than a lifetime of Laban. They started the long journey back to Isaac who still lived in the south of Canaan. Jacob had become immensely rich, and Dinah recalled the journey as a magnificent lark, a country excursion without end. She didn't understand all the intrigue leading up to meeting her uncle Esau. All she remembered was that Jacob had that same look of worried slyness that he got whenever he'd had to deal with grandfather Laban. She watched Jacob separate out substantial herds of sheep, goats, camels and donkeys and was told that these were being sent on ahead as presents to uncle Esau. The whole trip south from Paddan Aram they stayed parallel to Jordan on its east side and stopped at the river Jabbok, a tributary that ran straight east from where it connected with the Jordan.

On the day they met Esau, Jacob was specific in their traveling order: Zilpah and her two sons first, followed by Bilhah, then Leah, and finally Rachel. Each woman traveling with her own progeny was told to keep apart from each other by several hundred yards. Dinah remembered the look on her mother's face as she took her allotted position, but it was not until years later that she divined how they had been strategically positioned as expendable buffers, each group intended to slow Esau's possible assault and give Rachel and Joseph the maximum time to escape. It was the basest, most cold-blooded testimony to Jacob's turpitude, and Dinah received the force of this insult years after its occurrence.

Uncle Esau, as it turned out, had abandoned his grudge years earlier. Dinah remembered him as a huge shaggy apparition, red body hair everywhere, with a voice that made the air shimmer. Dinah had felt it through the soles of her feet. He had rolled over their formations, Jacob trailing in his wake, sweating and unctuous, making the introductions. Dinah remembered Esau chucking her under her chin and promptly forgetting all about her. He hadn't brought any of his three wives, all of them Canaanites, one of them a direct descendent of Ishmael, a side of Abraham's family history that everyone wanted to forget—which was precisely why he had married her. He and his contingent of four hundred armed men had finally left. Esau had wanted Jacob to travel with him, but Jacob, pleading the delicacy of his young children, had promised to follow at a more leisurely pace.

Instead he had promptly turned due west into the lush floodplains of the Jordan's east bank, which afforded ample pasturing for his livestock. In time shelters were built, as were shearing pens, vats for washing wool and racks for drying it, large roofed areas against the harsh rains and even harsher suns, corrals to keep the herds marshaled, and all the usual outbuildings that go with animal husbandry practised on a large scale. It was called Succoth—the place of shelters. The nearest city was Shechem, about twenty miles due west but on the other side of Jordan. "It does no harm to have a river between us and the Hivite clan," Jacob explained. But then Jacob knew all about the use of buffers.

Jacob's group was accepted into the land. He had arrived with so much wealth, it was hard not to accept him. He was astute enough to submit to the necessary protocols required of newcomers prior to acceptance. He was careful not to overtly flaunt his possessions, keeping his livestock to the east of Jordan, out of sight. He did not trade, in part because he could live quite independently of most any town or city, and in part because he was not altogether sure he wanted to display his bargaining prowess just yet. Twenty years in Paddan Aram had taught him patience, among other things; he could wait his chance. In time he even bought a modest plot of land outside the city from Hamor, the chief councilor, paying more than was necessary but letting Hamor know that the price included Jacob's initiation fees into the community.

He now had a small toehold in Canaan, the land his God had promised him, and began to assert himself. He built an altar to his God calling it "Elohe Israel" meaning "*my god is mighty,*" a title that was consistent with his own self-confidence. It was not lost on his neighbours either, that in addition to a mighty God, Jacob had a mighty brother who had visited from the south with a considerable show of strength. On his purchased plot of land, Jacob established his home base, intending it as an eventual convenient locale from which to do trade. All his sons, save Joseph, tended the livestock or supervised those who did, and so spent most of their time near Succoth. Dinah was sequestered. The continual bickering among the four mothers frequently made for ugly scenes in the camp, and Dinah, while she endured them, grew increasingly disgusted with them all. She might have found a sympathetic ally in

Joseph were he not so much the obvious favourite of Jacob and hopelessly conceited as a consequence.

— ◆ —

The Hivites were one of several ethnic groups that populated Shechem and the surrounding area but by far their lineage was the most aristocratic and the most entrenched. They were also the wealthiest and hence occupied almost all the political offices. Hamor was the chief of the ruling council, the senior proctor whose authority extended throughout the region. It was the highest office available but did not carry with it the right to rule absolutely. Public affairs and the ancillary decisions affecting the public weal were settled usually by consensus. It was a system of rule requiring careful alliances between family interests, often solidified through marriage. It required constant private negotiations, carried out discreetly among the council members. Hamor held the respect of all the factions and was passionate in his duties.

Shechem was Hamor's only son, named in the expectation that he would succeed his father as the council chief. Shechem, however, showed no interest in administrative intrigue. He knew he should not be discontented. He was a member of the aristocratic stratum, with a secure future. He was respectful of his father's work but begrudged its intrusion into his own life. Nothing, it seemed, could be undertaken without a regard for its political dimensions. A horse could not be bought or a new cloak ordered without his being deliberate and thoughtful of its consequences. Shechem knew that prudence was the cornerstone of good administration and was not disdainful of the fruit it bore. It just seemed to him that his life had all been laid out neatly before him, lived already in advance of his ever having lived it himself. There was no room for chance or choice. He tried not to think about his future obligations, and chose instead to hunt in the mountains whenever he could.

His particular love was hunting with falcons, and he spent most of his time pursuing this passion. He kept his birds in a special enclosure just beyond the city wall. Two of them he had obtained from Egypt a few years back and they were just now reaching their prime as trained predators. There was nothing Shechem loved as much as riding up into the hills with a bird tied to his elbow-length leather glove, waiting to be released.

Then, from the vantage point of a clearing he would watch the bird hang high in the air, working the warm air currents that shafted upward off the mountain's sides. They would stay that way sometimes for an hour, then, without any advance signal, fold their wings and drop, talons extended, straight down onto the back of some hapless quarry.

He could not have told you why he was drawn to the hunt. Perhaps there was a freedom that was in contrast to the restraints he felt elsewhere in his life. Something grabbed at his heart each time he undid the leather thongs from around the bird's feet, its wings violently beating even before it was free from the forearm perch—an intense, ferocious lunge to freedom. There was a delicate balance between a bird and its falconer. Too harsh a response to the bird's spirited challenges to his authority and the bird didn't hunt well. Too lenient a treatment, and the bird would go wild. Shechem always marveled that his birds ever came back. He sometimes imagined himself in their position and wondered if he would ever return to the outstretched arm and submit to being retied. He often concluded that he would not.

— ◆ —

Dinah left her tent very early. She wasn't sure how soon her absence would be discovered and wanted at all costs to avoid the ignominy of being caught and forcibly escorted back to camp. If her mother heard her stir, she gave no sign. She did not go toward the city but rather climbed to higher ground, to a place from where she could watch the city gates without herself being observed. In time she spied the group emerge and jauntily begin to walk up the mountain's shoulder. The young girls of Shechem were taking the baths, and within the hour Dinah had joined them and been welcomed. They reached the pools by late morning, situated about two thirds up the mountain but on the north face, hidden from town. It was approaching the hottest time of the day and the girls, already hot from the walk, shed their clothes and swam.

A girl named Sakonna took a special interest in Dinah. It had been Sakonna who, on hearing about the new clan's arrival, had sent the invitation to Dinah. She looked to be the oldest in the group and was its natural leader. She had quite regular features; her hair was nondescript brown, straight and long. But her young face already showed a motherly concern for anyone who might need a friend. Her family was not of the highest order but possessed a rugged self confidence that comes of having long and honourable roots in the area. "Solid stock," some said when speaking of them. She had brought her younger sister with her, Effielia, a perpetually smiling seven-year-old whose delight at being included in this "big girls'" excursion was positively infectious. Effielia was learning how to swim and involved everyone in the process, either in the role of loud and enthusiastic spectator, which was what was expected of Dinah, or as rescuers, whose job it was to pull her to safety with great regularity.

Dinah succumbed wholeheartedly to the little girl's self-centered charms. Having experienced only the play of older brothers, she was captivated by the exuberant antics of Effielia. The obvious love that Sakonna had for her little sister—a soft love that had no edges—made Dinah distinctly aware of how different it had all been for her growing up. Her brothers, when they thought of her at all seemed to love her bluntly, abrasively and loudly with crushing hugs that pinned her arms or punches on the arm of the kind they would give each other in play. And they were always prone to interrupt her sentences, gruffly asserting that whatever she happened to be feeling was only a trivial mood, sure to pass quickly. Effielia would have a wonderfully different childhood.

Details of their lives—at least the kind shared at a first meeting—were exchanged. Dinah described her eleven brothers, none yet married, and what it was like to live in tents. She answered all their curious interrogatives as best she could and in turn was told about mud brick houses, market squares, narrow streets and continual noise. By mid afternoon the girls gathered their things and started back. Dinah, who was savouring every minute of this flight into freedom chose to stay for a while longer. It was an easy walk back and there was still lots of daylight. No need either to hasten the inevitable confrontation awaiting her.

Shechem's horse picked its footing carefully along the side of the mountain while Shechem securely hooded his bird and transferred its thongs to a makeshift perch fastened to the back of his saddle. The horse stopped when it reached the pool, and, on looking up to see the reason, Shechem saw the girl sitting on a low rock shelf that jutted out just inches above the top of the water. She sat so that her body was facing him, and she was leaning back on her arms, palms down flat against the rock, taking the weight of her upper body. Her thighs met the water just at the knees and he could see from the ripples across the top that she was swirling her legs lazily back and forth. Her breasts, still not fully mature, hugged her body, the two perfect aureoles, nut brown, contrasting against her lighter skin. He sat and watched her for a long, long time. She was perfection.

His horse broke the scene by snorting loudly and in a flash Dinah was on her feet. Her clothing lay some feet away. She would have run except that the man and horse blocked the easiest path. She watched intently to see his next move. There was always the pond. What Shechem did next was to swing down very slowly off his horse and take short, measured paces toward Dinah until they were no more than a foot or two from each other. They stood for a minute, staring, saying nothing. The abruptness of the meeting had registered in both their bodies, triggering a variety of auto reflexes. Her chest heaved rapidly.

"What is your name?" he finally said.

"Dinah." Her voice was a strangled kind of whisper that she immediately cursed. Before she could move again, his hands had grabbed her arms, just below her shoulders. Shechem was now decidedly in command. She felt the strength of his grip on her upper arms. Though they were both young, his bulk was greater by the weight of a small lamb.

"You are not from the city are you?" he said. His eyes kept shifting rapidly downward to her breasts, then back to her face.

"My father is Jacob," she said flatly. "We live outside the city, not far from here. "

"Ah yes, the sheepherders. Your flocks are very large, and very far away just at present."

She did not respond. Too tough and self possessed to be hysterical, but nontheless shaken by the complete surprise of his arrival, she was acutely aware of her naked vulnerability. She also took note that he was accurately informed on her family's whereabouts. He put his head forward. She drew hers back, trying to keep the distance. Instead, she found herself pulled up against him.

"Let go. You're hurting me," she demanded sharply. She struggled to get her hands in play so as to push him off but without much success. She could feel her breasts slide slightly against his skin, hear his breathing. "I said let go of me, you bastard ass!" she was yelling now quite close to his ear. And quite suddenly he relaxed his grip and restored some distance.

"I'm sorry." He hesitated ever so slightly over the words. "You have such a form. I hardly knew if you were real...and hardly what I expected to see out here. My father said there was a young girl in the shepherd clan but I never dreamed he could have meant you. You are certainly not a girl."

The absurdity of his last comment struck them at the same time and both grinned. It was enough. He let her go.

"And who might your father be?" she asked him while at the same time beginning to move ever so casually toward her clothing.

"My father is Hamor, chief councilor," he answered with just a trace of pomp.

"Ah yes." By this time she had her tunic on and was securing the sash. "My father bought some land from your father and was charged too much."

Shechem was not expecting this kind of reply and kept silent. Finally he said, "You shouldn't be out here alone."

"I've not lived anywhere else but in open spaces," she replied. "I'm not sure how I would feel if I had to live like you, behind those thick walls, all shut in. Still, some of what I've heard sounds interesting. The town girls were here earlier. We talked." A plaintiff note had crept into her voice unawares.

"Would you like to visit my city?" Shechem asked. "My horse can easily take us both. I could still have you back at your own camp before dark."

She shook her head. "My father would never approve."

"Neither would mine," Shechem grinned again. "Maybe that's why I am asking."

Dinah smiled back. "My father says that we have to be careful in our dealing with you prepuce people. You are not to be trusted and are worse than relatives."

"Prepuce people?" Shechem had clearly never heard the term before.

"Prepuce people—people of the foreskin, who don't even know enough to cut a male child's phallus as a submission offering to god. He says that you probably don't even know who the one, all-supreme God is, much less make sacrifice to him."

Shechem was not sure what to make of such a frank conversation but he responded in kind. "My father says that we cannot expect much from people who smell like sheep and who live as nomads. He told me the reason he sold your father the land was because he felt sorry for you all. He also didn't want you moving into the city with us."

"Your father sounds pompous," she said.

"Your father sounds parochial," he shot right back.

"We are probably both right," she responded. Shechem and Dinah welcomed this common problem of parental narrow-mindedness, happy to discover that both families were equally guilty when it came to unsubstantiated, but intractable prejudices.

"I must go." Dinah started to push past him.

"I'd like to see you again."

"That's impossible."

"We could meet back here. Next time the girls invite you."

"Good-bye," was all she said.

The lecture from Jacob was less than she expected, or at least it seemed so to Dinah. She found it hard to focus. Jacob's harangue sounded muted and impotent. She could tell from his gestures that he was intense but his voice was coming from a long way off and failed to penetrate her head. It was too full of other things. Leah said nothing.

Dinah's inner state became total chaos. She was quite unprepared for the release of feelings and urges that were frequently in opposition to her logic—things that would seize her body as if it was thinking thoughts all on its own, private, almost foreign and quite unassailable by her own conscious mind. The pricks of puberty have a language all of their own. Almost any older woman could have helped but there was no existing intimacy within which to have talked, and Dinah would not have known what to say in any case. If her mother noticed anything different, she did not intrude. She would always wonder afterward if it would have made any difference.

Shechem was not in much better condition despite being older by a few years. This unexpected meeting with a nubile, not like anyone else, was just the kind of encounter to cut the claustrophobia he had been feeling. And the image of her as he had first seen her, legs dangling in the pool, would intrude at the most inopportune moments, as if she had some magical power to appear in his mind at will, commanding the most pleasant of physical responses. That he told no one of his meeting was significant. He knew his father would not approve of the liaison and he had not the temperament for a head-on confrontation.

Another invitation came shortly and Dinah went. This time her mother watched her go—evanescent innocence—a slight, lithe figure retreating swiftly and silently into the morning. Whoever he is, I hope he loves you, Leah thought to herself. You deserve that.

— ♦ —

The outing was every bit as delightful as the first one. Dinah had been able to ask casually about the young men of the city and had gleaned some information about Shechem. He was not married and his family was highly regarded. Rumour had it that his wife had already been chosen but nothing had been announced. She too was solicited, casually of course, about the marital status of her brothers, and Joseph in particular. The girls of the city left by early afternoon. Dinah stayed.

Shechem came and raped her.

He took her dignity.

He left her shame.

Dinah did not remember all the details. She remembered that they had swum for a bit. She had gotten out first and was standing, watching him. Then she remembered him standing in front of her, hands grabbing her around her shoulders like the first time. She remembered being pulled down to the ground. He was wearing a short cloth, bound in some fashion around his waist and held up with a broad strap of braided leather thongs. The cloth was entirely wet and where it clung to his body, showed slightly translucent. She would always remember that leather belt with its half dozen braided ends coming together into a fancy knot at the front. He had been able to undo the knot with one hand while never letting go of her with the other.

She was pushed onto her back. Pieces of rock dug into her. As she struggled against his weight, they tore little holes in her skin. Her struggle gave him a kind of pleasure beyond what he obtained from between her thighs. She did not understand it, but felt its humiliation just the same. He pushed himself off of her when he was finished and sat back, hunched, buttocks flat on the ground, with one knee vertical so that it partially hid his face. He was still breathing heavily. She was crying. They were not the wild tears of shock or hysteria. He would have preferred those, and been immune to them. Dinah cried silently, the tears of someone who has been thrust into adulthood with no warning—pierced, literally now, with no possibility of mending the rent. She knew her body was damaged. Her back was hot and she could feel little pieces of gravelly rocks embedded in her skin. Her vagina was on fire and she sensed she might be bleeding but refused to examine herself while he was still staring at her.

Shechem was chagrined but not guilt ridden. He had set in motion a whole chain of circumstances that not even his father would be able to contain. That his was a cowardly form of defiance did not occur to him, and if someone had ever suggested that he was guilty of acting out his hidden hostilities against his father by savaging this stranger, Shechem would have simply stared blankly. He knew one thing for certain though: having started the process, he would not abandon it. He sat watching her. She made no attempt to cover herself or hide her tears, and the continued vulnerability gave her more dignity than the most vitriolic outburst could possibly have done. He did not understand her crying but he found himself quite angry for having been its cause. He was drawn to her in a way not even he was prepared for. If he was deficient in some things, leaving Dinah was not one of his failings.

"Please don't cry," he said. She said nothing, two continuous rivulets trailing down her cheeks. He tried again.

"This wasn't planned. It wasn't supposed to be this way—I imagined it would be...better." He stopped, not knowing where his own words would carry him.

"Was I supposed to agree to it?" she finally asked. It was a taut, iron kind of voice, very much in control.

"I should have waited," was all he replied.

"Yes, you should have waited," she said quietly. "But you did not. And since I have nothing more for you to take, you can go." She heard her own voice, but it was not her speaking the words. It was Leah who sat there, a bruised, unloved girl herself, watching Jacob fasten together his robes after the sixth and final night of their wedding week. How many times had he got up and left to go back to the tent of Rachel—thirty years of being little more than a fertile womb, thirty years of such powerful fecundity on the one hand and yet horrible impotence at engendering Jacob's love. Copulation could be cruel even within marriage. But she didn't want him to go. She, Leah, whoever sat there, did not want to be left to limp back into camp alone and shamed, the object of criticism, harsh interrogation with the clear innuendo that she had been wanting it all along. A damaged chattel was what she had become. Despite her looks, she was her mother's child. She shivered, thinking about how her brothers would react, in loud invective, twisting truth with fallacious fantasy so that even her spoliation would be stolen from her and become theirs.

Dinah was so lost in her own world she did not see the obvious affection with which Shechem watched her.

"I cannot leave you. That would only add to what has already happened." It was the closest thing to an apology she was going to get.

"And so what are you suggesting?" she asked, "that you take and keep me like one more of your silky brown birds to be released for sport when you are in the mood?" Dinah was beginning to get angry.

"I am suggesting that I marry you," he said abruptly, covering the strength of his feelings by getting to his feet and retying his clothing. He stood now, over her but with a hand stretched down offering her help to stand.

"Dinah, come to the city with me. I don't want to be without you."

She could not trust herself to speak. His hand was tenderness. They rode into the city just before the gates closed for the night. She sat in front of him, leaning into him slightly, claiming his protection.

Supper in the home of Hamor the Hivite, chief of the ruling council, was a silent affair. Dinah had been placed in the care of Shechem's mother who arranged a bath, ointment for her back, and new clothing. Even before they sat down, the state of Dinah's back had been relayed to Hamor, who, with his wife, correctly deduced what had transpired. Dinah's deportment did her credit. She allowed herself to be received as a special visitor, the daughter of a wealthy foreigner, and made not the slightest reference to her unorthodox entrance. The subject of her return home never arose; she was shown to a private room and retired for the night. Shechem's mother left Shechem and Hamor alone after supper. She sent a servant to discreetly seek out Leah and tell her that Dinah was safe. Let Leah say whatever served her purposes after that.

"What do you propose we tell her father?" Hamor began. "That you rescued her from rogues but unfortunately not quite soon enough?"

Shechem looked straight at his father. "I want her as my wife. Make the necessary negotiations."

"Shechem, your gallantry is duly noted; and I appreciate that you feel obliged to render some emolument for what you've done. But to marry her is foolishness itself. Some kind of payment, yes, but marriage—she's a foreigner! You must have some idea of who we'd hoped you would marry."

"And now you know who it is that I hope to marry," Shechem replied. His tone was measured and respectful, his gaze direct. "Providing Jacob, her father, agrees, I intend for Dinah to be my wife. If you are not prepared to talk to him, then I will go myself. In fact, under the circumstances it would be best if I did my own arrangements. He may as well see what manner of son-in-law he is getting."

"Jacob agree?" The thought of any family refusing the chance for such an alliance was preposterous to Hamor and his blustering left Shechem in no doubt. "Jacob will be giving orders for a feast the minute he sees us ride into camp. He wants in, Shechem. His kind sticks out like bad meat at the butcher's stall. He's got everything except the one thing he really wants—respectability. Has he ever once been invited into the city? Did you ever stop to think why he hasn't invited anyone out there for a meal? It's because he's afraid, and doesn't want the shame of a refusal. Refuse the marriage? Jacob will fawn over us so that it will make you retch." Hamor was becoming quite worked up but for once Shechem ignored the signals and engaged in kind.

"Don't be too sure of yourself, father. Do you see him dependent on our markets for anything? I know better than you the size of his flocks at Succoth. There isn't a fortified city in the whole of Canaan who wouldn't go out en mass to secure an alliance with such wealth. We would do very well by having them as in-laws, father, once you and Jacob quit competing for the upper hand. The truth is, father, that for once you've met a family who is beyond your control. You've not got the leverage you're used to, and the truth is that it's you who is afraid of rejection. That's what this is really all about, isn't it?"

There was a long, tired silence and then Shechem added: "Father, all my life I've watched you make deals, broker power and keep the peace. I look up to you for it. It takes a special talent and by all the household gods we keep, I'll try to do the same when it's my turn. But please, father, just once, help me follow my heart."

So Shechem convinced Hamor to go and talk with Jacob, and Shechem, because the outcome of the talks was now the most important thing in his entire life, and because he had some suspicion that his father might blunder, accompanied him.

— ◆ —

Leah told Jacob the message she had received. Jacob instructed her to tell no one else and withdrew to himself. The brothers were all scattered around Succoth and beyond. It would be the better part of two days before they would come. Jacob sent word for their return with a cryptic message about needing to consult on dealings with the city. He never did discover who communicated the truth but from the white fury with which they arrived, someone had got to them. He wondered if it might have been Joseph, but just then it wasn't important. He went out to the altar he had built and stood in front of the mound of rocks. A large flat one capped the mound on which he offered up the occasional animal sacrifice. It was his third such altar.

The first was in Bethel. That one had marked the amazing dream he'd been given the first night he had fled from Esau—angel warriors from heaven marching down stairs that began from beyond where he could see, and ended just above his stone pillow. There had been one warrior above the rest, features hidden by a bronze radiance; Jacob had sensed more than actually seen that this one was in charge of all the others. It was Abraham's God visiting him, unannounced, confirming that Jacob would not be abandoned, that he would inherit the land he walked on; that he would be the father of a great nation; that his children would be like the dust, too thick to count. He had wakened and turned his stone pillow upright, pouring out all the oil he had with him, rubbing the top of the rock until it shone. A meagre affair, but it only reinforced that the promises had been unilateral and unconditional. It was a side of God that Jacob didn't understand very well.

The second altar had been called Mizpah, erected in concert with Laban at the point of their final separation—stone for stone, animal for animal, *"and may God be the witness if ever the two men tried any more tricks."* Neither would go beyond the marker. How different these two talismans were.

He had wanted to build another, at Peniel, where he had wrestled with the god figure all night, just before meeting Esau. But then, in the early light he had been too exhausted and his hip hurt from where the wrestler had touched it. It had been all he could manage just to cling to the stranger's waist, while kneeling on the ground. Jacob knew he had been beaten but could not break off, taking a certain comfort in the one-sided embrace. The stranger had not cast him aside, even if he did not hug him, childlike, as Jacob had wanted just then. He had felt a huge relief in no longer being in charge or responsible for what would come next. Jacob felt again the man's hands on his head, pressing his face close into his rough tunic, not shirking the sweat and grime that encased him. Indeed, the man's tunic was not much cleaner than Jacob's face. The man's hands now cradled his cheek and brought his chin upward so that, had the light been stronger, Jacob could have seen his face.

"Jacob, you have struggled with God and with man, and you have overcome. For that your name is now Israel, '*He who struggles with God*'." Jacob had sobbed. He cried the tears of twenty years' intrigue and watchfulness. He had cried the tears of lonely fatigue that had been impossible to acknowledge, the tears of tension from always looking over his shoulder, poised for flight. He had cried the tears of a lifetime of struggle from which he could not disengage, because there was no place where it did not follow.

"Tell me your name," Jacob had pleaded. "Just tell me your name and I will be satisfied. Give it to me as my mantra to carry with me."

"And once you have the power of my name what would you do with it, I wonder?" said the man. "No, you shall not have my name, but I will keep yours forever on my lips." And with that Jacob had felt the hands move again, this time to his forehead, parting the tangled hair to press their fingers into Jacob's forehead, feeling the etched crease lines that were now deep furrows, gently touching them in a departing caress. Enduring unction. Jacob had called the place Peniel, "*For I saw God's face yet he did not kill me.*" Not even Isaac had ever touched him like this man had. Isaac, for all his strengths had been a fearful man all his life and his embraces took as much they gave. But the wrestler's hands had taken nothing, and Jacob hadn't even built an altar to mark the most important encounter of his life. Instead he had limped into the cold water of the Jabbok to rejoin his family and trudge painfully through the grey light toward his brother.

Now Jacob stared moodily at the pile of rock in front of him. The base stones had been dragged from close by, field stones whose edges were weathered and rounded. The top rock had been carted from the Jabbok river bed, flattened and smoothed from the water. Judah had overseen the transport of it although no one knew why Jacob had asked for it. He was utterly weary just at that moment and wasn't sure that the return of his eleven sons from the field would do much to alter his mood. They had the beginnings of a home, here, near Shechem. The grazing lands were good, the camp at Succoth represented several years' investment in labour. He did not want to move again. This was Canaan, the land he had been promised. From here his sons could spread out comfortably in any number of directions; there was ample water in the Jordan delta. His daughter, of all people, now threatened to topple his whole enterprise. Jacob did not think he had it in him to pull up the clan and move. The Dinah episode would be contained. He would find a way.

— ♦ —

Hamor rode into the clearing. Shechem, on his own horse, hung back while Hamor approached and got off. He and Jacob stared at each other.

"You've come," said Jacob. "My daughter is not with you I see."

"Your daughter remains an honoured guest in our home," replied Hamor, "under our protection."

"Word has already reached me," said Jacob. "You have a peculiar understanding of these terms, Hamor."

"If it matters to you, Jacob, our present circumstances are not as I would want them," replied Hamor. "But we are neither served by dwelling on yesterday's events."

"What do you propose?"

"My son, Shechem, seeks your permission to marry your daughter, Dinah, and has sent me to plead his case."

Jacob could not have been more surprised but his face showed nothing. They would not have to move after all! It was beyond anything he had hoped for. Hamor continued.

"Jacob, let the two marry. Form the bonds of kin with us. The land is big enough for all of us. Settle here. Let this be the first of many marriages between our peoples. Trade with us, and, through us, with others who live closer to the coast. Buy more land. Inhabit it. There is an honourable place here for you Jacob, a seat on our council. Make this your home."

Jacob received the words like oil on his head. It was the warm hands of the wrestler on his head once more, now fulfilling the promises.

But custom, not to mention his natural shrewdness, required at least some reluctance to accept the offer. Negotiations that concluded too quickly were a loss of face to both sides.

"My sons will return from the fields by tomorrow," said Jacob. "Return here at the same time. We will assemble and hear your offer together. It is as much their decision as mine. Until then, Hamor, you are standing on my land, fairly bought." Jacob's voice was rising and threatened to become shrill. "I suggest you leave and take your son. He is an offense to my nose!" His voice had ended loudly; Shechem had been meant to hear.

Hamor bowed, and retreated on foot, not remounting until he had reached where his son stood. He would allow Jacob the insult. A father was entitled to one fit of temper under the circumstances, especially when it was aimed at his future son-in-law. Truth to tell, he would have said worse.

The brothers, in fact, arrived that night. Jacob was glad he had promised nothing to Hamor. He reported his conversation in as much detail as possible, concluding by saying that there would be another meeting the next day with all of them present. He said nothing about his own feelings in the matter. It made no difference. They were in such a state of rage that any reasoned discussion was impossible. The draughts of raisin drink, a fortified wine consumed in quantity long into the night, did nothing to assuage their mood. By morning the brothers' mood resembled a sky before a storm—black oily clouds boiling across a horizon, breaking occasionally to show a bilious, green-grey sky behind. Jacob inwardly braced himself for the meeting.

Hamor and his son returned. This time they tied their horses at a tree some distance away from the altar and approached on foot. Hamor, following an ancient custom, drew a short sword from his belt and laid it on the ground. It was a gesture of concession, and in making it, he had gained an advantage by pulling the sting of their accusations before they were ever made. Whether sincerely meant or not, it was a brilliant opening tactic for which the brothers were quite unprepared. Hamor told of his conversation with Jacob and of his son's desire to marry Dinah. He said that Jacob had sent him and his son away until the brothers could be assembled and give a reply for the clan. He did not dwell on this point, which made the flattery seem all the more effective to the watching Shechem.

While he spoke, Hamor was careful never to once look at his son, and had not given Jacob more than a nod at the beginning. He played to the sons, watching their faces, looking for the leaders, gauging the opposition. He spoke of their strength—of their unity, of their knowledge of the tribes beyond Paddan Aram, of the toughness that is the trait of tent dwellers, in contrast to the soft hands of those who lived in cities. But he also spoke of traditions of great bravery and valour on both sides, of the security afforded by thick walls and stout gates, of the determination that was required to have built such a city, and how a union of the clans with their complementary strengths would create an alliance without equal. Shechem was as captivated and convinced as seemed the brothers. He had never seen his father deliver such a stellar performance and he ached with the pride of watching. At the end of the speech there was a silence. Shechem stepped forward.

"My father has offered an alliance. There are benefits for us both if it is accepted. It is not for me to persuade my elders in that regard. I ask only for your daughter in the name of love. Set whatever bride price you like. There is no price above what your daughter is worth to me. Tell me and I shall pay it at once. Dinah is everything to me."

The silence returned, louder than before. Simeon finally spoke. His raspy voice was an unpleasant contrast to Hamor's rich timbre.

"We cannot agree to the marriage. It is an offense that one of ours should be given to a prepuce person—given to someone who has not honoured our God in this way. It is this sign that sets us apart from all other tribes, a ritual instructed by God to our great grandfather Abraham, which we continue in our bodies as a testimony to the solemn promises he has made to us. Submit to this rite and we can agree to this marriage, and all other unions between us. Refuse to become like us, and we will take our sister and go. The mark of God is above negotiation. No other price is required. But anything less than the circumcision of all the males of your city, and we will leave."

"We cannot promise on behalf of the city," responded Hamor, "but I will organize a meeting at once. It seems a small thing to give up, this piece of skin, in exchange for an alliance. My son and I will both support your request."

— ◆ —

The evening meal was a somber affair despite the size of the gathering. Normally with all his sons around him, Jacob would have presided over a boisterous, lively repast. It was Joseph who finally voiced the question everyone else was thinking. "Father, do you think they'll agree to the circumcision rite?"

"I do not know. Shechem is obviously sincere in his affections for your sister."

"My half sister," interrupted Joseph.

"Your sister," continued Jacob, evenly. "He reminds me a bit of myself when I first saw your mother. At one point I wondered if he wasn't going to mutilate himself right there in front of us all, so anxious is he to complete the marriage union. Hamor gives less away. I think he will do everything he can for the sake of his son. And he is clever enough to find some way to carry the argument to the others, if he genuinely wants to. That's the real question: does he *want* to be joined to us?"

— ◆ —

The men of the city gathered that night in the open area just inside the gates. News of the earlier meeting with Jacob's family was throughout the city and everyone was caught up in the unfolding drama. Hamor addressed them.

"Men, you have honoured me with the office of chief of the council, and I have sought only the good of our city. If any of you dispute this, let him now speak."

There was no reply. Hamor had confirmed his position and motives. Hamor's personal gain in the proposal, once it became apparent, could not now be used against him nearly as effectively. He continued.

"The family of Jacob is not just another band of nomads as we see from time to time. His father-in-law is Laban, son of Bethuel the Aramean, whose father was Nahor, brother to the noble prince Abraham who lies buried on Hittite land to our south. Jacob's brother is Esau, in Edom, also to the south of us, and commands a large number of men. They have visited here once before. Jacob and his family have been friendly toward us. And they are rich! They are very rich!" Hamor paused to let the words sink in so that no one could miss the force of his next point. "I have proposed that my son Shechem, who enjoys your favour, take Dinah, Jacob's only daughter, as a wife—to be the first of many marriages between our people. There is land enough for all, and there is wealth enough for all, especially their wealth. Their chattels will follow their children and we can absorb this clan together with their possessions. Who among you can propose an easier way to increase our comfort and ease?" It was obvious that Hamor's words were being well received. Hamor pressed on while the momentum was in his favour.

"They have made one stipulation of us, however. They follow the practice of male circumcision as an act of devotion to their god. And," Hamor paused here for just a fraction to change his stance and tone, "I have it from a reliable source that it enhances the pleasure as well." He stopped to receive the laughter he had anticipated and just as quickly changed his tone again, this time deadly serious. "But we would do well to consider this mark of servitude for other reasons, my friends. Who can say what power their god possesses. I have seen the altar Jacob has already built to this god. Rumours have reached me that this god bestows magical fertility on their herds—it is obvious they have been blessed. Surely a small piece of skin is a small thing to give up in order to secure the protection and blessing of such a god. And if we do not, who knows what harm he could inflict on us for having refused the rite of adoption into his family?" It was a speech every bit as effective as the one delivered earlier. Hamor's ability to package the facts, binding them together with just the right amounts of greed and fear, was legendary. It was persuasive, potent, and Hamor drank of it deeply himself, believing every word.

— ◆ —

It was early the next morning. A lone horseman rode into the centre of Jacob's tents. He shouted, "A gift from the men of Shechem!" and flung a bundle on the ground. He was gone before the first brother had reached the bundle and untied it. It was full of foreskins. The messenger himself made it back only by wrapping his arms around his horse's neck, cursing every jolt, trusting that the horse would find the stable. He passed through the city gates and slid off, moving ever so gingerly to his pallet in the guard house. He did not even bother to secure the gates behind him. Hamor's speech had not mentioned anything about pain! The men of the city would be immobilized for several days.

— ◆ —

Simeon and Levi met at noon out by the altar, a time when most everyone rested.

"How many foreskins?" asked Levi.

"One hundred and fifty-seven; fewer than I expected," replied Simeon.

"Just make sure you keep strict count when we go," replied Levi.

"Have you warned the others to be ready?" asked Simeon.

"Not yet," answered Levi. " I want to give them no more than a few hours' notice—the less time for talk, and the better the chance for a complete surprise. Tonight, just before sleep I'm going to speak to Reuben and Judah and ask them to organize the others so that they're ready at first light to meet us."

"And if they won't cooperate?"

"By then they won't have any choice. They'll know we've left."

"Will Joseph be included?"

"I'm asking Reuben to be responsible for Joseph. They get along the best. Joseph will be the last to know anything. And yes, he'll come. I don't think even he would want to risk meeting us in the fields if he didn't."

The predawn grey never did last very long in that region. Night seemed to stay soot black until suddenly the upper lip of the sun would protrude, swollen red, over the horizon and within a third of an hour the entire globe would be visible, beginning its daily march across the sky. But between the black and the bright, there was a little time when a candle was not required to find your way. Simeon and Levi walked carefully around the outer perimeter of the wall from where they had left the protection of the bush line, toward the gate. They moved through a cluster of coops, and as they did so a bird, sitting tied to its perch, murmured uneasily. Its head was covered with some kind of hood so that it could not see, but only sense the presence of humans moving close by. Simeon reached out his hand quickly, too quickly for the bird. The feathers were very soft in his hand and the bird's breast was much warmer than he had expected— a pleasant contrast to the still chilly air. He rubbed the bird across his chest before stooping to place it silently on the ground. Breaking its neck had felt good. There was total silence once more. Time to get to work.

— ◆ —

Shechem stirred on his couch. Two days' experimentation had confirmed that there was no position that alleviated the pain for long. That knowledge, however, could not stop his body from incessantly trying. Some had chosen to stay as drunk as possible but this remedy had its own excruciating repercussions. "What goes in must come out," he had heard one woman mutter as she supported her man while he endured the agony

175

of voiding. For himself, he had decided to simply lie as quietly as he could, a thin strip of ointment-soaked shroud wrapped loosely around his cut.

Of everyone affected, he was happiest, and distracted his mind with thoughts of Dinah, who, he imagined, would be in her quarters, suitably awed by the entire city's actions. No question but that it would remain the most unusual bride price ever paid. She would be famous throughout the region, and that perhaps would be the best present of all. It would make up for the rough beginning.

He thought he heard a noise on the stone floor and began turning from the wall in order to see. In so doing the coverlet collided with his member, and even so light a weight resulted in a pain that blurred his vision and made his head pound. He brought his knees up reflexively and continued to shift his weight around until his feet connected with the floor. He sat, thus, on the edge of the sleeping berth, doubled over, his upper body supported by his bent arms, hands locked onto his thighs just above the knee caps. He noticed his breathing was heavy from the effort. He raised his body slowly, allowing his head to straighten so that he could focus out into the room. The point of Simeon's sword caught him just below the walnut sized knob in his throat, where there is a small opening before the breastbone starts. The force of Simeon's thrust carried Shechem backward so that very little of his blood ever dirtied the floor. When he needed to be, Simeon could be extremely neat.

Hamor was sleeping very lightly on the outer edge of his couch. His wife had flattened herself against the inside wall, leaving her husband as much room as possible to be comfortable. The last two nights he had been continually thrashing around trying to find a comfort that did not exist. He bore the condition with his usual stoicism. He was actually awake when Levi entered the room, and found his short sword was in his hand instantly.

"Treachery!" he roared, or at least tried to. But his voice was still thick with sleep and his voice chords could not resonate without some coaxing each morning. It came out more as a muffled croak that could have meant anything at all. Levi had come close. Hamor had gotten to his feet but not much else.

"Bastard," was the next word he tried, and swung his sword.

"Fool!" was the last word he heard. Levi thrust his longer weapon past the blade into the loose, folded skin of Hamor's belly. Hamor dropped his sword and gasped. One hand now reached back for support on the couch; the other fumbled at his stomach, his eyes registering the shock ahead of his body. Levi delivered a second thrust, this time pointed upward so that the lungs were certain to be penetrated, perhaps at least one other organ as well. Hamor fell heavily back onto the couch. His wife tried to soften the impact of his body but it didn't do any good. Levi was gone before the body had settled.

Levi and Simeon met back at the gates, not more than an hour after they had entered. Both were sweating and panting. Simeon had a small cut on his left arm but it bled very slowly. Their clothing was a mess, deeply stained from where they had continually wiped their hands, trying to keep a dry grip on their sword hilts.

"How many?" said Levi.

"Sixty-one." panted Simeon.

"Seventy-three," offered Levi

"We've missed twenty-three," said Simeon after a few seconds furious thinking. Make sure our brothers know. Go get them. They'll be at the edge of the bush line directly opposite the gate. I'll stay here and look." There was a movement from the door of the guard house, a figure was leaning on the door post for support. Simeon whirled around and charged. The figure fell.

"Twenty-two, twenty-two! Twenty-two more skins to do!" Simeon was quite beyond control. Blood-lust lunacy had taken over. He disappeared into a narrow alley. Levi wondered if the killing was going to stop at just the men. With Simeon, you could never be sure. He seemed to like it. Levi ran out the gate to find the other nine brothers. They had been watching and ran out to meet him. The brothers were not alone. Reuben and Judah had organized about thirty men servants as well. Levi was pleased at this spontaneous improvisation of his original plans. Well done, Reuben, he thought to himself. I didn't think you had it in you. He continued aloud:

"We've killed all but twenty-two of their men. Simeon is going back through the houses but keep a sharp eye. Their goods are ours—take everything. Dinah will be avenged!" The company followed Levi back to the gates, the shouting increasing each second. Heaps of clothing started to appear haphazardly in the streets as the tightly packed houses were searched. Women, young girls, female children and servants were hustled through the streets like so much livestock, which, for the moment was precisely what they were. Someone had found the stable and had hitched up a half dozen carts of various sizes, which now stood just outside the city gates, themselves now wide open. Sacks of housewares, bags of dried fruits, grains and other foodstuffs, bundles of clothing and now the women were flung into the wagons. The older women tried to shield the young girls from the worst of the abuse. There were other horses, saddled, to which some of the girls had been dragged, hands trussed together and bound to the saddle pommel. None were well dressed, most having been dragged from sleeping couches—barefoot mostly, which made them wince as each foot connected with sharp stones.

It was Simeon who found Dinah, awake from the noise and sitting on the edge of her couch.

"We've come for you, sister!" he cried. "Thank the gods you are safe." Dinah did not reply as he seized her arm and hustled her down into the street, manhandling her toward the gate area, which by this time was chaotic bedlam.

"I've found her. I've found her. She is unharmed. It's time to go." The first of the carts lurched into motion. Others started up. Men were still rushing up from the various alleyways, some carrying booty, some pushing females ahead of them, using their swords as prodding sticks. There seemed to be a last-minute frenzy of clutching and grabbing onto anything as the looters vacillated between their greed for more, and fear of being left behind. Dinah had been unceremoniously shoved atop a horse from which hung several panniers. She looked across the scene to see Sarkonna, hands tied together and raised over head, trying to keep pace with the horse to whose saddle she was tied while at the same time avoiding his hooves. She couldn't see who was leading the horse ,and only hoped that it wasn't Levi. Whoever it was, she did not want to think about what would inevitably happen. She would not have wished her own experience on anyone. Dinah was rudely brought back to the scene at hand with Simeon hoisting a screaming child off his shoulder, throwing her across the horse in front of Dinah.

"Look after this one—caught her escaping off a cart," was all he said. Dinah looked down at the matted tangles of hair.

"What's happening? What's happening?" It was Effielia, but Dinah had no answer.

I'm being rescued whether I want it or not, she thought. All of this will be justified in my name. She braced herself for the moment when Effielia would turn and recognize her. Betrayal clung to her like a bad smell. She felt dirty beyond words.

By midday things were remarkably sorted out. Household chattels, clothing, weapons and tools were allocated through all the families in Jacob's entourage. What flocks were close at hand were rounded up and dispatched to Succoth where they would be merged with the larger herds. The women of all ages were spread among the families. That division had been more contentious. Leah, Bilhah and Zilpah each took a young girl; Effielia was not among them to Dinah's relief. Rachel declined with great hauteur, saying she would not have her tents soiled with foreign refuse. Joseph elected not to take a wife, and showed no interest in exploiting the economic windfall of escaping the usual heavy bride payments. The women, including the children, were incredibly valuable, as Jacob's own years of servitude to Laban testified. The newcomers learned quickly that it did not pay to protest. The few who were defiant were summarily beaten. Not a single male had been brought from the city. Assimilation, though it would take time, was a certainty.

It was late in the afternoon when Jacob finally located Simeon and Levi to confront them. It was significant in itself that he had gone to them. As it was, he had to stand in the open, peering into the gloom of the cloth awning that served as an open porch.

"Have you no shame for this trouble you have brought on me?" Jacob was wasting no time on opening greetings. "Will you never learn to think further ahead than a sunrise? Whose blood will be sought when what you have done becomes known? Simeon and Levi—who knows these names? No, it is the man Jacob who will be sought. It is the man Jacob who can go neither north to Laban, nor south to Esau. It is Jacob's head they will seek to hang as an ornament on some city wall. You have made me a stench in the noses of the Perizzites and the Canaanites who also dwell in this land, and they will get rid of my odour quickly enough. What kind of chance do you think we stand against a combined attack on us? You stupid bloody fools! The men you face next time won't be groaning on their beds, unarmed and unsuspecting!" Jacob was in a towering rage by the time he was finished. "Why can you not think about someone else's welfare for once in your lives?"

The brothers were brusquely indifferent and, flush with the immediate thrill of their accomplishments, were not about to submit to a self-righteous diatribe from Jacob, however intense it sounded.

"We did think of someone other than ourselves," Levi replied. "We thought of Dinah. Are we to think that you condone Shechem's treatment of our sister? He took her as one takes a prostitute; and you—all you managed to do was talk to him. Is that how you regard the purity of our family, that any Canaanite dog is free to smear his seed at will? Or is it just Leah's children who can be violated with impunity?"

Jacob withdrew in the face of their questions. In truth, he did not have answers to what they were asking. He was glad he had not confronted them on their duplicity, too aware of his own deficiencies in that area. But he knew the family was vulnerable. And for that, he was frightened. The real betrayal Jacob felt was at the hands of his god— the warrior angel who had played him false. Shechem was not a solution; it had been a snare. The soothing hands of the wrestler had been a mock embrace. Once again Jacob was on the run, except now more weary, and more endangered. By nightfall, that first night after the raid, a rigid silence had settled over the camp. It was quite in contrast to the expected revelry. The sharp exchange between father and sons was public knowledge. Jacob, leader of the clan, had pronounced the day a day of shame, and Simeon and Levi's minority opinion could not lift the mood. Jacob had retreated outside. Not even Rachel was solace. Her own smugness at seeing two of Leah's sons the target of Jacob's angry words only irritated Jacob. Just once, why could his family not see beyond their noses? When the attack came, nobody was going to be spared. He thought of Rachel, still beautiful, being mauled by some boorish lout, half drunk. She would not do well as a captured serf.

He was outside, resting his back against the altar, trying to collect his thoughts and plan the next move when he realized he'd been joined by someone or something. A voice spoke.

"Israel." But whether it was truly audible or simply an imagined sound within his own head, he could not tell.

"I'm here," he said, or thought he said it. His own voice did not quite enter his ear, at least not as he was used to—more as if it was coming out of his ears, creating speech quite independent of his mouth. There was a film of something, a numinous cloak between the camp and where he stood—not a wall, more a thickening of the air so that no sound was likely to pass between them. He was still self-aware enough to know that the strain of the day, the darkness, and his own mental agitation were enough to make any of his senses unreliable, and though he did not have the words for it, he knew the strength of suggestion and hallucination.

But he knew beyond doubt whose voice had called to him—the wrestler was close by.

A part of Jacob reacted savagely to the voice, wanting to heap the blame for what had already happened and for the fugitive future that was now inevitable. The anger, spawned from a misplaced confidence, was invigorating. Oh, did Jacob have questions to hurl at the wrestler this time! Would that he would show himself. It had all been one elaborate enticement right from the time he had left Laban—the band of warrior angels that had reappeared to herald his entry into Canaan; the clarion promises of sovereign protection by the supreme God. He waited in the darkness, tense, listening for the voice to speak.

"Israel, this land and all that's in it is mine to give to you. And I will give it to you, and to your descendants. But Israel, it is mine to give, not yours to take. Why do you still live as one called Jacob?"

"What do you want from me?"

"I want you to choose."

"Choose between what?"

"I want you to choose." The voice did not continue. And it contained no hint of threat or persuasion but simply hung in the air somewhere as a calm, detached intrusion. There was a long pause, or at least it seemed long to Jacob but he was not sure of time any more. The voice hung out there, not in any kind of hurry, and it infuriated Jacob that he was having a conversation with someone who refused to show himself. "Choose, choose, choose." It was like the phrase of a song that had gotten stuck inside his head and could not leave. He finally spoke again.

"What should I do?"

"Leave this place." The voice was as close as ever, still level in tone. "I want you to leave this place and go back to Bethel, to where I first met you. Leave what you have built here. Shechem was never the way I intended you to inhabit the land. Leave your buildings at Succoth; leave this purchased plot; and especially leave this altar. Build me one at Bethel where I met you first. Go."

"Is that what I am to choose between?"

"You decide."

Next morning Jacob ordered the entire encampment to assemble. They stood round him, irregularly thronged amid the tents. Some could not see; some could see only his back. He did not care. In the light he looked visibly older.

"Yesterday you witnessed a great lesson," he began. "The people in this land cannot claim the protection of our God simply through the rite of circumcision. My sons are right. You all heard them." The force of this admission riveted everyone. Jacob plodded on: "Purity *is* essential. The protection promised us by the God who has been with me wherever I have gone is not to be bartered as if at a bazaar. It is not ours to trade.

"But now listen to *me* carefully. We can no more be like the people of Shechem than they can be like us. And today, you will follow me in practising the truth of this. Today, you will go to your tents and bring out all your household gods, all the foreign spirits that are sprinkled through our camp like head lice. You will go and get them and bring them here and put them at my feet. And you will not stop there. You will change your clothes, you will go through the ritual of purification and make yourselves clean. And you will do one last thing. You will take your earrings off and put them with the god images. We will no longer look like the people who live in this land. When you have finished, I will bury these gods and your ornaments here at Shechem. Only then will we leave. It is to Bethel that we are going. And when the pilgrimage is completed, I will build an altar there to the God who has kept us safe, who has answered me in the day of my distress, and who will go before us even now."

Jacob's long speech ended, and no one said a word. Little by little people broke away, walking back to their tents, keeping their eyes carefully averted so that they could not be engaged. Little by little people started to return, uncomfortably holding assorted statues, amulets and medallions. They would slink up to where Jacob had remained standing after his speech and deposit whatever they had with embarrassment, disclaiming ownership as quickly as possible. Even Rachel came forward with the household gods she'd stolen from Laban years earlier.

No one offered to help Jacob bury the heap of objects that he finally tied up in a large cloth. He put it over one shoulder and walked, alone, out of camp.

The Rape of Jacob's Daughter

— ◆ —

Scripture records this conclusion:

And they journeyed to Bethel:
and the terror of God fell upon the cities
that were round about them,
so that they did not pursue after the sons of Jacob.
                                                          (Gen. 35:5)

The story of Dinah is recorded in Genesis 34.

The Marriage

Shall I tell you my story? The official records leave much unsaid. What does the story of one man's misery count for anyway? The chroniclers, those eunuchs of the court, sitting on the sidelines of time, seem to get their only pleasure from watching and recording. And yet, for all their purported wisdom, the facts they have included seem almost to have been random. Even I do not understand how they were chosen, and of course I was never consulted. Objectivity is the exclusive preserve of the historians. As if I could possibly know the truth about my own life.

And never a word about the good times. Were they embarrassed by them, or did they just assume that I shared their disgust for her? I did not even know them, but the chroniclers have won, and a few fragments of my life remain—just enough to keep the pain fresh—for all who chance to read them.

My name is Hosea—*Yahweh has saved!* Beeri was my father, a proud misfit if ever there lived one. He stood not more than five feet, and nothing about him was very handsome. But his high forehead and wide face could not hide deceit of any kind, and for his honesty he was well liked. We were farmers, living near the city of Shechem. Funny thing about names. You can spend your whole life living in their shadow, as if it's not enough just to get through life, without also having to carry the burden of your parent's expectations along with you. But at least my father was honest. A stubborn little man who clung to the old ways, believed the old stories and looked with those wide-set, round eyes of his for Yahweh to save the whole bunch of us.

I say we were farmers; it's a big enough occupation to receive us. Beeri had been an only son and so inherited the whole of his father's lands intact. I have brothers. Our lands lay north of the city just where the foothills of Mount Ebal begin. It was a bit out of the way. The better grazing lands, much better than our area, all lie to the east of Shechem and closer to the Jordan river. But they are much more vulnerable to the vagaries of chance.

We did a bit of everything: some olive trees, a modest vineyard, a few of the slopes planted in grains, and the rest for our two herds of goats and

187

sheep. It was enough. Beeri never did become ambitious about enlarging our holdings. Perhaps it was this flaw that protected us.

Our holdings had a faded, tired look about them. There were always a few rails of the livestock pens that teetered visibly on the brink of falling down; the thatch on the barn roof showed a hole, now so aged that the edges sagged inward. The open space leading up to the house was always jumbled: piles of brush dragged from one area, now cluttering up another; posts for the repair of the stock pens, never used; a hodgepodge of fire wood. Our house lay about halfway up the side of a small hill. The path up to it meandered on a gentle slope, forming a long, lazy arc as it found its way to the barn. A cart, an ugly two-wheeled thing, lay with its axle broken just where the path started up toward the house. Beeri had made it himself, a fact that could be seen in its every awkward detail. It was one of those repair projects that he always meant to do, but which had now lain there for so long that our yard would have looked nude without it.

In the end I think it was my father's measure of untidiness that saved us. Our farm always looked like it had already been looted, so escaped the worst of the incursions. But I digress.

It was not that our family was slothful, more that we could be easily distracted. Visitors always received Beeri's undivided and sincere attention. Growing up, it seemed to me that we were always being visited. Usually they would come alone, men who never seemed to look quite normal, though I could never precisely identify the oddity. Perhaps it was something furtive in the eyes, clothing that didn't sit right, as if they had put on someone else's and hadn't noticed. If we had been at war, they might have been spies. But Jeroboam, the second king of Israel by that name, had been king since sixteen years before I was born, and would stay on the throne until I was twenty-four. Their talk was never secret, far from it. Beeri and they would talk non-stop, sitting outside on benches, leaning their backs against the house wall, or hunched close together, their bodies bent deeply at the waist, heads together as they read from the same parchment. I was always welcome to listen, and as I grew older, to join in. Often I would be asked to make copies of the writings—oracles for the most part—that some of the visitors brought with them. They were usually dark pronouncements of forthcoming doom and chaos about to be meted out on our people. The words always seemed as eccentric as the men who brought them, black angry lines of energy, looking foolish in the bright light of a rural day. Bloody retribution at the hand of Yahweh, that ancient god of Israel, was the constant theme. To my young mind, as I sat carefully transcribing the oracles, I could never take them very seriously. The seedy farm with all its tatters always reached up to impose its comic homeliness, like a large gangly dog that intrudes into its owner's serious conversation. But copy them I would, and in the process underwent a slow initiation into a fringe protest group of *Yahwists* who stayed loosely connected throughout Israel and Judah.

Our farm was a convenient place to stay. It lay about six miles from Shechem and about thirty from our capital, Samaria. Beeri was an enthusiastic member of a scattered community, bound together by an uneasy conviction that Yahweh was about to deal harshly with this chosen people, in short, to mete out a punishment so savage and brutal that Israel would not recover from it. In the beginning, their premonition seemed absurd, the words of fantastical naysayers, who, having been shut out by the religious professionals, gave their lives meaning by hurling insults from outside. But in the end, they were right, and wished they had been wrong.

If my father was a casual farmer, he was passionate about the Yahweh traditions. Since the land was kind to us and our wants were simple, he had the time to focus on the religious landscape of our age. You might think that the Yahweh traditions were self-evident, things that everyone knew about and either did or did not practise. After all, the books of Moses were stuffed full of instructions and sacrifices for every category of wrongdoing: guilt offerings, sin offerings, even an offering for the unintentional sin. Then there was the list of thanksgiving offerings— the savoury scents of burnt flesh flowing heavenward to waft in the nose of Yahweh. The feast days had been laid down too. There was the Day of Atonement; there was the feast of Weeks, the feast of the Trumpets and the feast of the Booths. There were the daily rituals, the weekly Sabbath, and the monthly New Moon observance. There were also the half dozen annual high feast days. And if that wasn't enough, there was even a whole year set aside to be specially celebrated every fifty years.

It wasn't that nobody agreed on what Moses had originally said. The problem was that ours was an age of innovation! The feast schedules were always being adjusted to the whim of the court or to synchronize to the celebrations around planting and harvest. Substitutions were made to the sacrificial meat chart, depending on the general level of wealth and the vagaries of agriculture.

Local shrines lay strewn through the land, especially in our northern kingdom, which had lost access to Jerusalem. Our kingdom, Israel, had two religious centres: Bethel, lying almost on the edge of our southern border; and Dan, one hundred miles to the north. The first King Jeroboam, Solomon's chief minister of public works before he staged a revolution, had erected two huge golden bull images in these cities. They were magnificent sculptures, done in gold, just slightly larger than life size. It had been the first of a whole history of making Yahweh worship more convenient, and, I think, optional. In this case, it eliminated the need for his subjects to make the pilgrimage to Jerusalem, which was now in the kingdom of Judah. Political loyalty should never be assumed, as Jeroboam's own rise to power demonstrated. Who knew what wild ideas might be incubated during a trek to Jerusalem?

"These are the gods who brought you up out of Egypt," he had proclaimed. As a political strategy it was shrewd move. As a piece of religious leadership, my father said that it guaranteed the destruction of us northern tribes. Nobody rejected Yahweh with impunity. I never knew what to make of Beeri's view of the past, but in the end, of course, he was right.

I say that Beeri was Yahwist, as if the only other choices were to be followers of Baal or Asherah or Molech or Chemosh or any of the twenty or so Phoenician gods that had small followings within our borders. It wasn't that simple. Religion never is. Lots of people were followers of Yahweh, but not many people were followers of *just* Yahweh. From Beeri and his friends' perspective, this was nothing short of idolatry. "Idolatry" was an intolerant word. Nobody paid much attention. Life was a varied experience. Why not religion too?

Over time, our house collected quite a number of Yahweh writings. We never had the money to commission a scroll of the words of Moses. We had a few of King David's poems and I could recite a dozen or so without effort. Even after two hundred and fifty years, his was still the voice that dominated our music. I had read parts of Job's treatise, brought by a visitor and carried with great care. Not even the visitor knew precisely how old his copy was, but by the style of certain cuneiform it could have come from the days of Solomon.

But the more recent oracles, I think, commanded more interest and study than the ancients. Certainly they were the ones that my father and his friends debated hotly. The oracles of a man named Joel,[1] just recently dead, were now circulating in written form. He had been a prophet of Yahweh and, judging from his work, given to visions. He wrote about huge locusts coming to strip the land bare, marching in straight-line formation, never breaking ranks, yielding to nothing.

> *They do not jostle each other;*
> *each marches straight ahead.*
> *They plunge through defenses*
> *without breaking ranks.*
> *They rush along the city.*
> *They rush along the wall.*

But what did it mean? There had been one disastrous year when locusts had come, veering off their usual eastern migration and had infested our lands just at the second harvest. For Joel, that event had been nothing more than a handy metaphor.

> *Rend your hearts and not your garments*
> *Return to Yahweh as your one God.*

His appeals for a return to the old ways of Yahweh worship were touching. But the prospects of anybody responding, I thought, were remote. I couldn't even imagine anyone tearing a cloak, unless it was one they didn't want. It just wasn't *done* that way anymore. Religious enthusiasms, well, there was a certain style that should be followed, that was all. The sacrifices and all the rituals required nothing excessive of the participants. Extremism was left to the lunatic fringe, the fanatics—people, I realized eventually, like my father and his friends.

Joel had another pronouncement, though, that did intrigue me. He had written of a day when –

> *I, Yahweh will pour out my spirit on all people.*
> *Your sons and daughters will prophesy*
> *Your old men will dream dreams;*
> *Your young men will see visions.*

To a young lad growing up on the edge of what seemed to be a special, clandestine sect, the prospect of being drenched with the Spirit of Yahweh sent shivers through me. For all I often wished our family was less extreme, and that we fit in more, the intrigue of such an eventuality kept alive in me a healthy interest in what my father and his friends talked about. In the end, it was men like Joel and Jonah, and later Amos, who became my heroes. True, none of them was honoured at large, though most people knew of them—the way most people keep track of contrarians. And despite their abrasive styles, their refusal to submit to the protocols of any of the prophetic academies, they all obviously spoke from an experience or from a perspective that was larger than themselves. Even their critics, who publicly pilloried them and privately plotted their exile, could not penetrate their mantle of authenticity.

We were not stumbling country peasants. We had our brilliant wits who delivered protest literature of the highest order, which could shake the land like a cat shakes a dead mouse. Jonah,[2] a modest, some said shy, man living in Gath-Heper, had written his story just ten years before I was born. We had our own copy of that of course. Our Jeroboam had banned it from the court, which promptly meant that everyone simply *had* to read it.

It was a tactical error on the court's part, or so Beeri informed me. Jonah had correctly prophesied Jeroboam's military successes and the king had made much of this implied endorsement from Yahweh's barû. So by the time his story circulated, the author's status as prophet could not be questioned. A few traveling entertainers added it to their repertoire of entertainments—the comic scenes of Jonah being thrown overboard by "the sailors," who in some versions wore the colours of the court, and then meeting the great fish were made for marketplace drama. Even better were the scenes of the old, bedraggled Jewish prophet wandering around Ninevah, capital city of Assyria, making a veritable hash of their language, telling them they were all going to die a horrible death of judgment. The subtle jibes were exquisitely served up in a sauce of high wit. But the message, for those who bothered to think about it, was unsettling.

Nobody knew for sure whether Jonah had ever really gone to Ninevah. The city was more than five hundred miles away, closer to six hundred and fifty miles by the trade routes. It wasn't that it couldn't have happened. Stranger things have happened to our nation's holy men than being swallowed by a fish. Truth was I never found that part of the story very relevant or interesting anyway. I almost missed the force of his book, and would have, if I hadn't seen it performed. A troupe from up country, near Dan, performed it at a New Moon celebration in Shechem. It was never in the repertoire when they went to the capital, Samaria. Even doing it in Shechem was a chancy thing; you never knew who was in your audience and Jeroboam, the second one, had not stayed on the throne this long by being stupid. The Assyrians, of course, were the buffoons—not much better than animals and a whole lot more stupid. Those who played their roles always managed to look like gaping idiots—faces painted white with black circles around the eyes and childish trinkets braided in their beards. When it came their turn, they would sit in a circle, the Jonah actor usually shuffling round and round them yelling out his apodiectic doom chant. Then they would start in to wail and moan in "foreign" gibberish, throwing fine white flour on their heads, ripping the rag costumes they wore for sackcloth. I laughed along with everyone else. That wasn't how repentance was done! The very idea of any Assyrian comprehending an oracle of Yahweh much less responding to it in genuine repentance! It was pure farce.

The Assyrians *were* a savage warrior race. Their men, with their short, massive necks, wore their hair plaited into tight braids. Their beards were the same, only sometimes they would have interwoven small white human bones, making portable necropolises of their faces by way of decoration. They looked barely human. Mine was the generation that watched them come and strip our land clean. Oh yes, they knew how to use women, too. On that fact I had considerable evidence. My wife slept with a lot of them.

When I was seventeen, my father took me to Bethel to celebrate the New Year festival in the middle of the eighth month. Until then I had no idea just how sheltered my own upbringing had been. It's one thing to be told that Yahweh worship was just one style among several but quite another to see it. I was young. I have never forgotten that visit.

The golden bull was still there, installed on a raised knoll in the centre of the town. The wide circle of space around formed a small grassy field defined by the town buildings on all sides. The setting for the sculpture bespoke a masterful understanding of both context and light. The wide circle of space around it allowed the sun to rest on it for most of the day. He was perpetually alive with light. The bull had been cast in the act of trotting, right front leg stretched out, neck slightly extended but head poised high. Watchful. Alert. His two horns thinned into two sharp, curved weapons. I shall never forget the first time I saw him. The sun's lustre accentuated the muscular curves of the sculpture. The relucent strength that the beast radiated went into me. My knees felt as though they would give out. From the distance, the smoke from a sacrifice burning in a small square altar firebox that lay recessed behind his shoulders could well have been the beast's own breath, snorting a declaration of his power. He was a thing you simply had to touch.

I went forward slowly, by no means alone, yet quite unaware of anyone else. There were numerous attendants. Possibly because I was young and, by my gaping mouth, obviously from out of town, they let me touch him. Perhaps I was amusing, gawking so openly at something they so casually acknowledged. I put my hand gingerly on a haunch. The whole beast was warm. I took my hand back, peering carefully at my upturned palm, half expecting to see some mark. Afterward I felt shame that a metal artifact could have so easily influenced me. But I could not deny my own intrigue. There is a thrill that goes with the illicit, and there I was touching the backside of a pagan art form as it stood belching smoke. For all I followed my father's ways, I would have easily followed the way of the bull at that moment.

We were in town for just over a week, staying with father's friends. Bethel's primary occupation was as a religious franchise. For particularly important festivals such as this one, the population would swell five-fold as pilgrims and sightseers would collect. And there was such a cornucopia of oblations from which to choose. A ministration for every persuasion and purse—that was Bethel. Syncretism in all its glittering montage. For those who held to the ways of blood sacrifices, obviously the golden bull was the chief attraction. One brought or bought the designated animal and received the mediated blessing or absolution from the god via his staff of earthly attendants. For the most part they lived in houses built from the king's treasury, ate the proceeds from the offerings presented and bridged the gap by way of modest payments obtained at the time of sacrifice. It was the business of religion, modulated through custom.

There were all manner of lesser, or perhaps I should say alternative, attractions. There was a temple for Baal, an ancient god with deeply rooted claims on the people of Canaan. There was an earthiness to his shrine. His was a story of crops and rain and harvests, and afterward of dying only to be enticed back out of his grave at the next seedtime. The weather was his element, his to control. It was a story that fit so much of what we were about and was respectful of the rhythms of the year and the yearnings of our hearts. Harvests such as the ones we were experiencing of late were never certain. Every generation had first-hand memory of drought or disease. There was so much that lay beyond our control, a little libation poured out at the feet of Baal's image seemed only prudent. Besides, the public rites in his honour were always such happy, exuberant, and inclusive affairs—the fruits of the earth consumed or quaffed with much revelry in gratitude to Baal's fecundity.

Asherah, that patroness of fertility and consort to Baal was also represented in the town. Her shrine was modest, but everything about it advertised the sleek sensuality that characterized her followers. The main building was open on all sides, supported only by columns spaced about every twenty feet. The result was an airy, covered portico that could be entered from any direction. It was a brilliant architectural interpretation of the essence of her cult: entrance was easy. Though smaller than the buildings of Samaria and even some in Shechem, it had an artistic intelligence of expression that was formidable. In the centre was a large stela, rough-hewn rock on one side and brilliantly painted on the other. It was Asherah, standing naked with a shameless smile, receiving favours from two lesser gods. Her feet were on the back of Mot, Baal's eternal foe who fought with drought and disease but was, in this picture, subjugated. Overhead, Baal arched as a kind of heavenly canopy. There was an eroticism to her pose that was only accentuated by the soft indirect light that wavered between the pillars. Her breasts were round and turned upward just ever enough to dispel any hint of the maternal and confirm her public concupiscence. In my innocent embarrassment I imagined her smile to be a smirkish awareness of the desires of my body. And somewhere on her face was the invitation to enter her through any of the scores of attendants, of either sex, whose job it was to be her phallic envoys. The postulants of Baal and Asherah commingled freely as befitted the relationship of god and concubine. There was an aura of sybaritic ease that clung to the festivities, permeating the whole town.

Like Baal, Asherah found us where we lived. It wasn't just the legitimizing of casual sexual encounters, as if that wasn't enough to ensure a following. The need to perpetuate was such a mainstay of our lives. Progeny, lineage, the promulgation of our family names—Asherah was the patroness of everything that we honoured, mingled with permission to act out all the bestial biases that come when sex is loosed from responsibility. The union of the darkness with desire.

I spent one whole afternoon wandering the bazaar that had expanded into every corner of the city. For the artisans, religious feast days marked a harvest of an entirely different order. The array of religious iconography was limited only by the skills and imagination of the craftsmen. No good pilgrim would dare be caught without some talisman of his or her god, however humble. It was a captive market. Clay figurines, used to burn incense, were hawked at every corner and came in all sorts of shapes and imagery. There were small fertility dolls, I think they called them "obees," with huge, exaggerated breasts spilling over the figure's folded arms; medallions; charms; embroidered pictograms that caught the gods in various earthly forms. The more skilled artisans, especially the metal smiths, had perfected the detailing of eroticism.

One in particular captivated me. It was a small pendant, copper I think, not at all expensive. The artist had fashioned it for a young girl's neck. It was the shape of a flattened arrowhead, with a small roll of metal where the shaft would have started and through which one threaded the thong. The whole face of it was a delicate etching of Asherah, thin, tall and with none of her usual head adornments. Her breasts, however, had been pushed out from the back so that they were raised toward me. A similar texturing of her pudenda made the pendant both pleasing to the eye, and hand. But out of her navel sprouted a small, young tree, a sapling in leaf. It was the most delicate of an outline, fragile thin lines, a clever rendering of the two images, one feeding from the other but in a way that avoided the cloy of maternity. But that was the lure of the fertility cult. In the end I did not buy it. In fact, I spent so long gazing at this one small trinket that the merchant finally chased me away. But afterwards, I realized I had carried it home just the same.

Another day my father's friend, Omani, was my guide. He took me to a smaller square where members of various prophetic guilds could be consulted, or just listened to as a kind of entertainment. Ever since the days of Elijah and Elisha, our people had made room for these holy men. They spoke for Yahweh, or claimed they did. Some were seers, able to look into the future, who made a lively business in proffering personal direction. I always thought of them as a kind of raspy voice that cut across the honeyed tones of the priests, or the court for that matter: a kind of institutionalized conscience, to the extent that conscience can ever be contained. "Thus says Yahweh;" "Thus says the LORD of Hosts;" "Thus says El, the supreme God;" "Hear my words given to me by the Sovereign LORD"—these were the preambles that characterized the prophets' speech.

Omani, who, it turned out, had a delightful sense of humour, told me that in his view a prophet was a little like finding a cactus during a desert trek: it could be counted on for water, but you'd never hug one to show your gratitude. He was a wonderful guide to the various activities of "prophets' square," and I warmed to his lyrical cynicism and appreciation for the absurd as the day went on. I learned afterward that he had spent three years apprenticing in a guild before abandoning the vocation. He was obviously well known and, I think, liked for the open amusement he showed for the proceedings. The last great guild of prophets, Omani said, had been Elisha's academy, now seventy years past.

"Now that would have been a guild worth joining," explained Omani. "These men here," he said, pointing to a small group that sat in semicircle around their obvious leader, "couldn't hear the voice of Yahweh if he was standing right beside them shouting in their ear. Oh, their delivery is superb I grant you. And they are pleasant enough people. I count many among my friends. They know history, they are well read. Some are even fine poets."

"What makes them frauds then?" I asked.

"Frauds? Did I use that word?" chuckled Omani. "Everything is not so black and white as Beeri would want you to believe, Hosea." He continued, "This is a complex state of affairs and people have sophisticated expectations. The prophetic guilds exercise an exclusive monopoly on Yahweh's voice. They don't offer sacrifices and the priests don't sell oracles. But they have to earn their keep like everyone else. And above all, they will say nothing to upset the way things are. They can't. There is no audience for bad news, much less a patronage." I was not ready to let the matter drop.

"But if they twist the visions of Yahweh, or worse, invent them, why are they not frauds?" I wanted to know.

"A fraud," replied Omani, " is someone who knows he's cheating his client and does it anyway. He may do it out of spite, out of malice, or because he doesn't have anything genuine to sell but needs to survive just the same. He might even do it because the client won't leave him alone but keeps hounding him for a personal assurance that Yahweh still smiles on him or her. But regardless of the reason why, a fraud still knows what he's doing, and does it anyway. He's one of the more honest people in the world."

"And so what of these men?" I asked.

Omani looked at me strangely for a minute and then said, "I think these men sincerely believe they hear the voice of Yahweh. And for that I hold them in both great pity, and great fear."

"What do these people do all day?" I asked finally. There seemed to be a great number of conversations going on around us.

"Why they offer you a holy word of comfort or advice. They will tell you the mind of Yahweh on practically any subject you care to suggest." He turned suddenly to confront me squarely. His eyes became slightly crossed and he began tugging at his beard. "Oh Matron Elphicath, how good to see you again. You look so well. Your husband is with you this year? Oh, that's sad. Well, no matter. A special word has come to me concerning your next child...and I suppose now, your next husband, too." I started to laugh but Omani was only just warming up. In an instant his face had changed again and when he spoke it was in somber tones. "Salutations and blessings on you, O Mellameezi. Your herd of goats has pastured in my dreams ever since you last were here. You have sold them, you say? Then who is it, pray, that owes me for having tended them so carefully this past year?"

A commotion was building in one corner of the square. Loud voices, one in particular, began to dominate, causing even Omani to break off his comic show. Heads were turning all around us, ours included. Somebody in the centre of a tight crowd was holding forth in a voice that eventually triumphed over the whole square. Omani listened intently for a moment and then turned, grabbed my hand and began to pull me toward the crowd.

"Come," he said. "You'll find this interesting." If he knew what I was about to observe, he gave none of it away. With him as a wedge, we shoved our way through to where at last I could see the man of the voice.

"Look at these hands and tell me you can't see the dirt that's under their nails." He was waving his arms above his head. "Tell me you can't see the stains from pinching sycamore fruit. These are not the hands of a prophet, soft and manicured, trained to write poems and count coins. Smell me! Go on. Stick your noses close and tell me I haven't tended sheep for a living. Come closer and take a good whiff. You can return to your lavender sachets concealed in your robes soon enough. I appall you! I embarrass you! Yet you crowd round about like jackals to a carcass. Why?"

There was dramatic pause. I watched Omani standing quietly, looking at the crowd more than the man. He did not seem to be listening overly. I was beginning to appreciate the technique of dramatic presentation. This man had it. He continued, "You can't possibly be afraid of me, one lone crazed barû come up from Judah. But we can't both be right, can we now? Our same Yahweh, the God who led our forefathers up out of Egypt, he isn't a God of contradictory messages is he? And that's what's bothering you. Somewhere in behind those wax-filled ears of yours, you're afraid my words from Yahweh might be the genuine oracle. You're both afraid and attracted at the same time.

"Why do you long for the day of Yahweh to come among you? That day will be darkness, not light, for thus says Yahweh..." It was the formal signal to indicate the import of what would come next.

"I hate, I despise your religious feasts. I cannot stand your festivals. Even though you bring me the burnt offerings and the grain offerings, I will not accept them. Though you bring me the choice fellowship offerings, I will have no regard for them. Away with the noise of your songs! I will not listen to the music of your harps. But let justice roll on like a river, righteousness like a never-failing stream!

"Thus says Yahweh to his people at Bethel!" The man had changed his tone again. He was no longer interested in the people around him. I wondered if he had ceased to be aware of us even. He was shouting over our heads.

"Thus says Yahweh to you women—you who are like fat cows lying on beds inlaid with ivory. You oppress the poor and crush the needy and urge your husbands on saying 'Bring us more drinks.' You drink wine by the bowlful and use the finest lotions. The time will come when you will be led out of your country by fishhooks. By your nose will you be led into exile beyond Damascus. But until then, go to Bethel and sin. Go to Gilgal and sin yet more. Bring me your sacrifices, and your tithes every three years. Brag about your freewill offerings. Boast about them, you Israelites, for this is what you love to do."

It was too intense. Someone started to laugh. Others joined in, quick to seize this release from an impossible message. A young man made a loud sound of a cow, and with that the crowd rocked. A voice called out: "I pass on the drink, but bring us more lavender!" The show was over, and people started to break up and disperse. But I could not help but think that silence now stalked the square, clothed in much noise. Omani had remained quite unaffected through it all. I wanted to leave but did not know where to go. Most of all I did not want to talk with this strange man who smelled of sheep. Omani finally spoke in a mild, even voice and it was to the man that he spoke.

"They will never listen to you my friend, no matter how often you visit our city."

The man found Omani's face and seemed to recognize it, perhaps from an earlier visit. It became less agitated but also more worn, I noticed. His speech had required much energy.

"It doesn't matter anymore. Amaziah, the presiding priest, has obtained a royal order that banishes me from Israel. I have been ordered out, accused of raising a conspiracy and spreading treasonous advice."

"May Yahweh's face be ever on you," said Omani, reciting an ancient benediction. We started to move off, leaving the man standing where he was. I turned back once, aware that somehow I was still connected to the scene I had just left. We walked for a time through the streets in silence. Then finally Omani asked, "What are you thinking?"

"Not thinking," I replied. "Feeling."

"And so what are you feeling, then?" His voice was that of a teacher to a student being examined, not unkindly.

"He gets no pleasure from those speeches. His own words cut him off from the rest of us. And for that I feel sad."

Omani spoke very softly. "You have perceived rightly young man. Often the cost of being a true barû of Yahweh is great loneliness. It is one of the signs."

"You seemed to know the man," I ventured, changing the subject.

"Yes, I do," said Omani. "His name is Amos.[3] He has come to our town now five times."

"Are all his oracles so confrontational?" I asked.

"Yes, most of them, except one that I recall. I have it on parchment at home. You are welcome to read it."

And so that night I read another oracle of Amos:

The days are coming, declares the Sovereign LORD
when I will send a famine through the land—not a famine of
food or a thirst for water,
but a famine of hearing the words of the LORD.
Men will stagger from sea to sea
and wander from north to east
searching for the word of the LORD but they will not find it.

The dreams started soon after we returned from Bethel. It was a long time before I told my father about them and not until their persistence began to frighten me. What young man would willingly approach his father to tell him that his nights were filled with visions of a dancing woman? In the beginning the dreams were quixotically erotic. Bethel had been an orgy of images and no doubt they were the foundations for these nocturnal assaults. Dreams are such vague things, too. Not that they aren't compellingly real when you have them. I would start awake, lying rigid under my covering, the woman and her dancing still visible to my eye. Her poise, my physical response, even at times the noise of her tambourine, all the intricate detailing of each scene would confront me like an erotic portrait. But the pictures would not stay. It was as if the strength of the sun eroded the pigments and all I had was a faded collage of disassembled colour, formless evidence that something intense had transpired. By the time I had pulled myself up from the sleeping couch and begun the morning rituals of chores, all the strength of the dream was gone, retreating against the regularity of daily living. At least that was the way it was in the beginning.

If my dreams had stayed that way, nothing would have happened I am sure. They would have remained the commonplace events of male adolescence. Gradually, things changed. The dreams grew stronger, more frequent, and more consistent. The skeptics, I am sure, would have a half dozen explanations as to why the dreams occurred, including that they were the obvious byproduct of an impressionable, highly active, fantasy life. But to be fair, by the time I mentioned them to Beeri, I told him the truth. I told him that a recurring dream had visited me with such regularity that I could now recall the main image at will—a young girl, beautiful, dancing before a gold bull. Did this dream carry some special significance?

What I did not tell Beeri was that the girl's every feature was now so known to me I could draw her. She would dance facing the bull. A short kind of jacket, held together by only one clasp, covered her breasts. The front hung open and had been cut away to show her smooth flesh and decorated navel. Her curved, bare waist undulated in a dance rhythm I had never seen performed before. She never stopped moving as she danced for the bull. I could see his eyes, drinking in her form, inwardly consuming her. He, too, was in motion—a slow swaying back and forth. His horns would sweep in a vicious arc, the dancer's breasts sometimes just inches away from the thin tips. But she never drew away, as if daring the beast to gore her, confident in the strength of her charm. It was bestial and beautiful all at once. I told Beeri none of these details. If he guessed at them, he never said.

He did not give me an answer right away. I think he consulted some of his friends. This surprised me, as did his answer. What he suggested was that this was an image sent from Yahweh—a picture of his people bowing down at the graven image of Baal. It had been given to me as a warning of Yahweh's anger, and I should write down this picture, and others I might receive. In short, what he suggested was that this was an inaugural event signaling my vocation as a barû of Yahweh. I wanted none of it. What had happened to me was that I had had a dream, clearly erotic, and it had become engraved in my memory. That was all, and it was all I wanted to consider.

I first saw the dance woman about two months after that. I had known of her, but never actually seen her. Gomer. That was her name. She lived by herself in a large but simple hovel about a mile outside of Shechem. She was still young, unusually young to be on her own. But her family was poor. Diblaim, her father, was an indifferent farmer on a small and miserly patch of land. She had left to offer "hospitality" to travelers. Beside her hut was a pen for animals. For a fee, travelers could secure food and shelter for their beasts, a hot meal and a willing wench, all in one stop. They didn't even have to enter the city. In short, she was a prostitute.

I came across her house on a walk. As it happened I approached from the high side. From the elevation I watched as she poured water into a trough for two mules. Their riders, obviously foreigners from the north, stood by. Even from my distance I could see the invitation extended through her moves, and the deliberate appraisal of her body in the fixed postures of the two men. They would both have her before morning, of that I was sure.

Just before she went into the house, she turned to look at me, and smiled. I felt a fool. My face was on fire as I ran back up the hill out of sight. But I knew I would be back, and I was, a month later. One of our goats had got out and I volunteered to go look for it. I walked toward her hut steadily enough but my mind was in chaos. What if someone saw me? But I had to talk to her. She was the woman who had visited me at night this past half year. I was not making that part up nor was it some kind of youthful, desire-driven wish fulfillment.

It was the first of many meetings. She did not make fun of me. For my part I did not leer, although I must have been self-conscious. There was a wholesomeness to her that belied her primary occupation. We must have been close to the same age, although in almost all respects she was my superior in knowing the world. I don't think either one of us expected to get along. I was a curious neighbour coming for a closer look under the pretense of a lost goat. She was a seductress who had no morals, and therefore, it was assumed, no standards at all. But instead, what we found in each other was two young adults trying to find their way in life. I discovered more excuses to visit.

Her knowledge of conditions outside our borders was refreshing. Up to now, my only news had been by way of my father's friends. Always their news was heavily draped in Yahwehism. In contrast, she knew a world that was full of trade goods, intricately woven fabrics emanating from Egypt, rumours of palace coups in far off Assyria, ships landing at Tyre, having returned from the edge of the world, their goods now starting the long journey inland by way of pack horses. Hers was a world that begged to be investigated, ravaged, in the best sense of that word. She never made apology for what she did. I arrived once to find her occupied with a guest, and was introduced to the trader, a Hittite from the north on his way to buy papyrus in Egypt. We were polite. I made some lame pretense that I had come to warn her of rogue wolves recently sighted in the area, and then could have kicked myself at the unintended allusion. I left quickly and we did not speak of it at our next meeting.

The dreams started to change after I met her. Her dance was no

203

longer a solitary performance. Instead, I kept seeing happy crowds, and at their centre, a couple. She was a bride, with all the happy energy of youth. Of the bull, nothing was to be seen, and Gomer's movements were never more than the joyful exuberance and spontaneity one would expect from a bride on her wedding day. But now I was in the dream, too. It was me who had hold of Gomer's shawl fringe and it was me dancing with her as we moved in the centre of the crowd of well-wishers. I was her husband. We were receiving the good wishes of the town as we walked from the town square to the feasting. Where the old dream was full of alluring sharp edges, this one radiated pure, innocent light. The dream made me hopeful. I knew by now, and was coming to accept, my capacity to receive dreams that were portents of some kind to others. Beeri and his friends were sensitive enough to the workings of Yahweh to conclude that I was being singled out. Their inclusion of me as a full but younger member of their academy was without reservation and they were diligent in teaching me to the limits of their own knowledge. I think, looking back, it was more because of the certainty of my father that I surrendered to this strange yoke. And because I respected my father, I allowed a little room in my own mind that he might be right.

Again he helped me. I was to marry Gomer. That was the message of this dream! I was to marry Gomer—a covenant bond between Yahweh's young barû and a fallen girl. This was, after all, the metaphor of our age. My visit to Bethel confirmed that, to crudely condense it, Israel slept with many gods. Yahweh, formerly their exclusive patron, was now sharing his consort with others, and that against his will. I was to be part of a real life dramatization of the spiritual whoredom that was eating the soul out of our nation. God was not prepared to relinquish his covenant made with Moses; nor would he tolerate the religious polygamy that he was now party to. The dream, in that context, *was* a dream of hope. Yahweh was active again. The harlot was to be redeemed. The covenant was to be restored. But I admit that I embraced this new word from Yahweh with a secret smugness and illicit anticipation.

At a practical level the prospect of actually living with Gomer was captivating. There were days when I could think of nothing else. I was not so ignorant as to miss the fact that her past sexual experiences were certain to enhance my own union with her. The dream, from my perspective, was a permission to live, as it were, in the pleasures of her past but in the safety of divine approval. Yahweh once more declaring his fidelity.

The Marriage

That my marriage would not be a happy one did not once cross my mind. To have one's union be not just blessed but actually instructed by Yahweh was a marital surety not found in our history since the days when Yahweh hand picked the wives of Abraham, Isaac and Jacob.

And so we were married. Beeri and Diblaim made speedy and easy terms. For her part, Gomer seemed happy to leave her hut, with all its notoriety, and live with me at my father's house. The courtship itself was short, self-conscious and truncated. I, of course, had no idea of the necessary ingredients for an appropriate preparation for married life. I felt terribly conspicuous, as if Yahweh was always with us like some kind of hovering stage director, or worse yet, a chaperone. When I tried to tell Gomer of my dreams of her, somehow the words sounded wooden and even I had trouble believing them as I listened to myself. Looking back with all the bitter accuracy that memory affords, I think she probably found me arrogant and presumptuous, as if my divine vision had relieved me of the tedious obligation of winning her heart and tenderly persuading her of the great adventure that beckoned to us if only we journeyed together. For my part, I know I fixated on her past profession, not seeing past it to her person.

The wedding was a modest affair but genuinely happy. Diblaim, his wife, and their relations showed a sincere appreciation that Gomer was being given this fresh start—that is, after they stopped being suspicious that our family wasn't making sport of them. In the local pecking order, our family was several levels above Diblaim. It wasn't just the accidental wealth that our lands bestowed. Beeri's reputation in Shechem was solid. His friends, though possibly odd, could be counted on. It was a family heritage that was sterling enough to absorb one spotted lamb into its fold and confer on her a new community status that placed her past life beyond gossip. I did not realize until much later that even I contributed in a small way. The claim that Yahweh had on my life was becoming publicly recognized. Our union too had some measure of public consequence. The symbolism it entailed gradually became known. For those who paid attention to the Yahwists, it augured hope that Yahweh would show blessing to his people, and in short, that, just like Gomer, they would be restored to a former and more glorious status.

Sometimes, in certain years a hot, moist wind comes in from the great sea just at harvest time. Particularly in the high country, the sharp cold mornings of the pre-dawn are stayed. It is a soothing extension of the summer and it is easy to be deluded by the gentleness of the wind. But it is a fool's delight to be taken in so. For, once the temperature cools, those same winds loose the rains they have kept hidden. Those are the years that the Jordan floods, that the mountain streams engorge and rush brown with sediment. The losses among the herds of sheep are always highest in those years and always there will be at least one farmer who postponed some of his harvest, hoping for a few extra weeks, now to see it ruined. That was our marriage.

Those first years were, I believe, happy for us both. Certainly they were for me, and Gomer never said anything if she wasn't. And I *did* love her. Slowly, even in my nascent self-awareness, I came to see how she complemented me. She had such an easy, open way of embracing each day, not questioning every detail of life. Perhaps it was because she was much more experienced at the range of men's moods that she could accommodate my own predilection toward introspection. She was such good company for me, drawing me back from the morose, into the good humour of the every day. She asked only to be able to whole-heartedly enter into whatever joys our life encountered, consuming them as they came and as they were, resplendent reality in all its variety. It was a needed balance against my own tendency to see everything in terms of the great mythic metaphor, which, while possessing a certain kind of grandeur, provided no sustenance. Our marriage couch was where I learned about pleasure for the sake of pleasure, and it was such a different world to my own, which had largely been written in the language of duty and devotion. She had this happy way of never asking from life anything more than what it was capable of giving, nor holding a grudge whenever the fare was meagre or mundane.

I pursued my proclivity toward intuiting the thoughts of Yahweh toward his people. Beeri encouraged me in this. It wasn't just a matter of strong dreams coming to me. Certainly as my knowledge of our people's history increased I became sensitive to the hand of Yahweh in our affairs. In parts of our story, his intrusion into our presence was massively obvious. How else could our deliverance out of Egypt be explained? But elsewhere, it took a discerning eye to see the faint traces of his presence, especially in the more recent times since Solomon.

Did I ever actually hear Yahweh speak to me? Did he himself ever appear to my eyes? Those questions do no good. If I tell you yes, you will accuse me of delusions. If I tell you no, then you will accuse me of being a pretentious opportunist, or worse, some kind of insurrectionist. Either way, you will have already closed your mind to my words. And to be frank, your skepticism cannot upset me. Once Yahweh invades your life, all your concerns get rearranged. But I will answer your question sincerely anyway. The best I can explain it is that I have lived my life in some kind of dialogue. Always there would be some prod within me, shaping my own observations and then raising up some new idea in response. It was as if I was always in conversation with someone inside my head. At first I thought it was just myself, caught up in some kind of projection—a re-bounding image, like a beam of light that bounces back at you off of water. But new ideas would come to me that could not possibly have been self-generated. They were either too obscure, or so contrary to what I thought to be the true perspective, that they had to come from beyond me. And so I practised the habit of listening for this second voice within me. In time I grew to see a person who stood behind the voice, never totally, but enough of an outline to give his words a certain inflection, a certain tone that often carried more message than the words themselves.

Our first child came within the year. At Yahweh's prodding I named him *Jezreel*, after the place about fifty miles to the north. The naming was an act of provocation, a reminder that we were not going to escape the fruits of our past. But that had been the message from Yahweh. The name was a subtle reference to a part of our history that nobody wanted to remember.

Seventy years before I was born, Jehu, a senior commander in the King's army took the throne by force away from Joram, the son of the old reprobate swine, King Ahab. In this way Jehu became our tenth king after Solomon. Jehu's subsequent eradication of Ahab's entire household amounted to a holy war carried out on the instructions of Yahweh, deliv-ered by none other than the prophet Elisha. But it had gone beyond the necessary brutality to protect himself from vengeance. The killing had gone beyond what was even prudent. The king of Judah, one Amaziah, happened to have been at Jezreel just at the time when Jehu staged his coup. It had been a friendly visit between two neighbouring regencies. Amaziah had taken an arrow in his back while trying to flee the conflict in which he had no interest. The wound proved fatal and his servants took him home to Jerusalem amid much public lament and anti-Israel senti-ment. Whether Jehu had reason to think that the king of Judah would challenge his rule and seek to reunite the kingdoms by force (Amaziah had, after all, married one of Ahab's daughters) or whether he just got caught up in the blood lust logic of the moment, it was never clear. But either way the shameful deed would ensure generations of suspicion and enmity between our two kingdoms.

There was a whole series of bloody confrontations, all of them some-how autographed with Jehu's penchant for the grotesque. From Jezreel, Jehu had written to the city elders of Samaria, the royal city and home to Ahab's seventy sons. The letter was a masterful stroke of public insolence.

"Since I have now killed Joram, son of Ahab," he had written, "choose the best and most worthy from among the seventy remaining sons and establish him on his father's throne. Then come and fight me for your master's house."

The city elders did nothing of the kind. Instead they wrote back in the most conciliatory of tones, asking how best they should demon-strate their newly discovered loyalty to Jehu, the rightful king of Israel. So he wrote them a second letter saying, "Come then and visit me at Jezreel bringing with you the seventy heads of the princes who hide in your city." And when the heads arrived, Jehu had them dumped from their baskets and arranged in two piles. Standing between them, he had confirmed his singular responsibility in the revolution. Whenever I read that particular part of the chronicle, I always imagined that he was in fact taking part of the credit, sorry only that he could not have hacked the heads off personally.

But the killing had not stopped there. Relatives of King Amaziah were discovered innocently traveling to visit their king, whom they thought still to be alive. They were summarily slaughtered, forty-two in all. Next Jehu rode back to Samaria and executed anyone who had even the remot-est link to Ahab's family. It was holy punishment, begun in the name of Yahweh but extended well beyond his intentions.

The priests of Baal were exterminated entirely. They had been rounded up at a single public ritual, presided over by Jehu, staged as a kind of inaugural ceremony at which he had promised to entrench the prerogatives of all Baal's priests. Any priest in the land who wished to have their services, and therefore their pay, confirmed were invited to attend at the temple in Samaria. It was deception on a grand scale and no sooner had the sacrifices started than Jehu had the doors sealed and his troops began the orderly butchering of the unarmed priests. The bodies were hauled away, the Baal stone was dragged out and smashed, and the temple demolished. Jehu had a crude taste in humour. What he ordered to be built instead was a public latrine. It is still in use. Like the killing of Amaziah, it was never clear whether he genuinely hated the Baal cult, or simply feared it as a potential conduit for political intrigue.

But for all that Jehu publicly hated the Baal cult, he did not relinquish the bull statues. For the murderer of Judah's king, temple worship in Jerusalem was not an option. And so Jehu left the two statues intact, and Yahweh worship remained a syncretistic mudpack of rituals. Yahweh did not overlook this. He had promised Jehu a kingly dynasty for having eradicated the wickedness of Ahab, but it would be limited to only four generations. The royal standard would be wrested from his great grandson's hands. That was the oracle. *"Thus says the LORD."*

The year our son, Jezreel, was born Jeroboam, the grandson of Jehu, was in his thirty-fifth year of rule, and getting old. It would not be too many more years before one of his sons, probably Zechariah would be proclaimed king. I could imagine that for those who followed the predictions of Yahweh's barûs the installation of Zechariah would coincide with a collective inhalation, as people held their breath, waiting to see how the royal banner would depart from Jehu's household. The skulls of Ahab's seventy sons watched in eagerness from the dust around Jezreel.

And so my oldest son got caught up in the metaphor, too. His was a modest part, requiring him only to carry a large sign saying, "Remember Jehu's butchery. Remember that he did not forsake the golden bulls. Remember Jezreel! Punishment is just one generation away, and Jeroboam is getting old." Like me, he was not asked how he felt about the assignment, but you can see now why some people accuse me of palace intrigue. But I tell you true. Yahweh told me to name him so.

The names of my other two children were similarly designated by *Him*. Gomer conceived easily, and a year after Jezreel was birthed we had a daughter. Her I named Lo-Ruhamah, and it meant *Not loved*. What other response could Yahweh have to his people who persisted in ignoring him? Did they think there could be no consequences to their continued casual indifference? Instead, Judah, our southern brothers, would become his favoured ones. *"Thus saith the LORD."*

Our third child, a boy, followed quickly after Lo-Ruhamah was weaned. This time the name Yahweh put in my head was Lo-Ammi, meaning *Not my people*. It was the final condition—abandonment. And so the naming of my children became a prediction of the fate that awaited my people. There would be punishment. There would be retribution. There would be rejection. There would be repudiation. Yahweh would renounce them. It was a brilliantly lucid pantomime that my family performed. *"Thus saith the LORD."*

The names of my children made me uneasy. They were in such contradiction to the personal hopes I harboured for our family. I did not want these children of chaos to be simply object lessons in my proclamations. I preferred to dwell on Gomer's having forsaken her past. Surely this was a more telling, more authoritative bit of the drama, the dominant scene that would still be intact at the finale.

Three years later Jeroboam died and his son Zechariah ascended the throne. In all, Jeroboam had ruled forty-one years and died full of years and honours. Our oldest son, Jezreel, was by now eight years old. Lo-Ruhamah was seven, Lo-Ammi, six. We were a busy household. Beeri was now where he needed help with some of the routines of daily living. I did some of the farming but I was never really good at it and I confess never liked it. One brother who had not yet married lived with us. Zechariah lasted six months as king before he was cut down by Shallum ben Jabesh during a public appearance. I could never settle on which was the greater proof of the deep decay that seemed to haunt our monarchies. Was it the murder of our monarch or the crowning of the murderer? Zechariah seemed to have been so ineffective a king that somehow within six months he had alienated the palace administration. A public assassination at which no one lifts a finger to interfere! It was an ignominious way for the household of Jehu to whimper into oblivion.

I speak of the murder of Zechariah as if we lived at court and it affected us. Strictly speaking, that wasn't true, of course. Oh, news of the event reached us quickly enough. But it didn't really change anything for us. Beeri, frail and forgetful, still needed care; our three children continued to ask for more hours than were in our days; the farm needed attending. Gomer and I coped. She had been beautiful when we married. Three children seemed not to have left their signature on her body. She did not complain. We did not talk deeply in those days. There wasn't the energy. There wasn't the time. And I believed that Gomer was not interested in my vocation and my emerging skill at interpreting our times. If there was trouble in Samaria, it would get sorted out, and in the meantime there was a farm to run, children to raise—the stuff of our lives.

A month later, Shallum was murdered. Menahem ben Gadi, until then a minor rogue whose home base was the town of Tirzah, now wore the crown. And suddenly, our lives turned ugly. We got the story of this latest palace coup from refugees, people on the run out of the way of Menahem's brutal assault on Samaria. Tirzah is about ten miles north and east of Shechem, but Mount Ebal lies between and Tirzah is pocketed away in the folds of the Wadi Earah. It is not hard to hide troops in the hundreds of gullies and ravines that form the base of Mount Ebal. Obviously that was what Menahem had done, and from there, Samaria is only fifteen miles due west. They advanced on Samaria with no warning or fanfare. There was no public support for Menahem's campaign. Why should there have been? Shallum hadn't been in place long enough to estrange or endear himself to anyone.

Menahem killed more of his own people traveling to Samaria than he did in the capital itself. The walled town of Tappuah made the mistake of not opening up its gate quickly enough. Menahem didn't even need to go there—it was not on the way. Maybe he wanted to soften up the countryside a bit, or give his troops some sport to increase the momentum of their campaign. True, a docile countryside was a prudent safeguard to have at one's back before the main assault. It ensured that Shallum had fewer places of refuge in the event that he slipped through their siege. But there was a ghoulish savagery to Menahem's sacking of Tappuah that none of us was prepared for. In he marched through the broken gates. In he marched and proceeded to gut the bellies of any pregnant woman he could find like they were just so many dead fish.

Like a blow to the face that diffuses to the whole body, news of what happened went out, and we shuddered physically. The action made sense only when I learned afterward that the core of his men was a troop of Assyrian mercenaries—huge brutes, whose own version of this same kind of bloodletting was to toss infants high into the air and then jostle each other to catch them on their spear points. I say we received the news physically. That was not a metaphor. Shocked, damaged people suddenly would show up at our door, looking for food and somewhere safe to stay. They had had no time to prepare for flight. They had no possessions; some were not even dressed for travel. For some, I think, it had still not sunk in that they were now dispossessed people. Theirs was not a coherent story. Perhaps it is a blessing that no one person had to endure the total carnage.

That was the first of my waking dreams. I was in the barn when the first account of the barbarity Menahem had visited on those pregnant women was told to me. I listened but I was no longer in a barn. I was up in the hills, at a point where a mountain stream drops thirty vertical feet in a cold, steady cascade. I was standing under this natural water shower, except suddenly it was no longer water but hot, sticky blood that kept coming, and coming, clogging my hair and my mouth so that my chest spasmed. I kept stepping out of the stream, jumping and leaping, but no matter where I moved the stream of blood would follow me, pouring down my head, off my shoulders, soaking my tunic, forming a slippery thick goo between the soles of my feet and my sandals.

The problem with being a barû is that you are allowed to feel more accurately. A melancholy rested on me like a heavy, damp suit of clothes. I found myself looking at Gomer's stomach more frequently after that, even inventing some reason to brush by her and quickly touch it as if by accident.

The people of the land must bear their guilt because they have rebelled against their God. They will fall by the sword; their little ones will be dashed to the ground; their pregnant women ripped open."

I wish I could say that as news of this atrocity spread there was a popular uprising, that people found the courage to respond in force to this repugnant slaughter, that Menahem was resisted and routed out like the garbage he was. But it was Shallum who was killed, and not a word of protest was heard anywhere. Shallum, king *for* a month. Shallum, king *of* the month. Loyalty to a highborn household was a high-stakes proposition.

It was about that time that Gomer started to spend unusual amounts of time in town. At first there was an array of clever excuses: people who had detained her, purchases that had required considerably more dickering to conclude, friends who were ill and shouldn't be left, family obligations. Off she would go toward Shechem for any reason or whim, and I was never sure when I would see her next. My worst times were that last half-hour before sunset. The sun drops quickly off our land. The transition between light and dark takes no more than half an hour. There was a knoll just above the house, a kind of promontory that jutted out. From

212

it I could look a fair piece down the broad mountain apron that shaped the distance between our farm and Shechem. The path, while there was still light, was distinct. A hundred years of feet and hooves had formed a deep and permanent scar on the land. From the knoll I could see the spot where the path disappeared, about a twenty-minute walk from our door. I knew that if Gomer did not show at that particular place before sunset she would not come at all before morning.

On the days she was away I would gravitate to that knoll, standing and staring fixedly at the distant point, willing her to appear. The usual end to this torture, though, was that the path would become a shiftless murk of shadows, and I would shuffle down off the knoll back to the house. I would cobble together a meal for the children and make some kind of excuse for their mother's absence, and we would eat mostly in silence. Then late into the night I would sit and brood on what was happening.

It was my blackest pain. It was also some of my best poetry. Later she stopped even the excuses.

We never knew when she would leave, or return. I tried to talk to her. But it was only then that I realized how little practice we had had. She had this smile that I could not penetrate, a look of amused interest at my consternation, that told me nothing of what she thought. To be fair, I cannot say that she now looked at me differently than before. But I had misunderstood this smile of hers. It was the smile of our wedding night, coquettish, coy, and yes, a bit brazen. But I had wanted it to be joyously intimate and fresh, full of energy and a new start. I had not looked at it critically then.

She did not deny that her body was no longer mine alone. Perhaps the cruelest thing about it was the casual way she still offered herself to me, as if I was the one who was behaving strangely, and her conspicuous absences were quite within the boundaries of any ordinary marriage couch. Such was her impenetrable composure that at times I wondered myself who it was that had really slipped the traces of normalcy. And yes, in case you want to know, I wanted her, sometimes with a desperation and urgency so strong that I could forget that smile. But in the morning, there was always that private smile that relegated me to just one more pleasant diversion.

Only once did I see that rigid composure soften. She had returned much earlier than usual. In the predawn light I heard her come into the house. She must have left Shechem while it was still dark for her to have arrived home at this light. I got up and went to her. There was a red diagonal welt that ran up from the corner of her mouth, ending in an ugly dark bruise high on her cheek. It had been more than one blow that had caused it. I found water and a rag, and the bottle of salve we keep. Gently I washed her face, brushing the hair back off her forehead with my hands, trying to straighten the worst of the tangles with my fingers as best I could. I touched her gently, feeling her for other hurts. Below her waist was a wet stain on her tunic, and without words I pushed her down so that I could assess the damage. She had been badly used, most likely by more than one man. She was torn but how badly I could not tell. I made a pliable kind of poultice, ripping a rag and smearing it with the salve, then folding it over so that it became a kind of bandage that could be wedged into her folds. I handed it to her and turned away as if to busy myself rearranging our bowls that sat on the table. Just at that moment dignity was the medicine she needed most. She did not need any more intrusions. When I looked back up, the rag was gone from sight.

But a month after that, she left entirely.

Then began the busy years: children to raise on my own, a father to care for and finally bury, and all the time the voice of Yahweh getting louder and louder inside my head. Those were the cruel years, the years I would lie awake at night and curse the day I had married her, curse the children of unfaithfulness in all their helpless plight, curse the fact that I was an unwilling barû living with a voice I could not dislodge. But most of all I cursed the woman I had once loved and had once been foolish enough to believe was grateful for having been saved from whoredom. What a fool I was, a sad little pitiable, misguided barû who never saw that he too had been part of the great metaphor, one with a vicious ending. Where once I had been so proud and yes, I shall admit it, smug, about the role of rebuke my children had been called to play, now I saw only three little children who did not understand why their mother had abandoned them. I had no answer for them. Mother had left and, "No, I wasn't sure when she would come home. Yes, I missed her too."

Their mother has been unfaithful and has conceived them in disgrace. She said "I will go after my lovers, who give me my food and my water, my wool, my oil and my drink."

The Marriage

But it was I who gave her the grain, the new wine and oil,
who lavished on her the silver and gold.
She decked herself with rings and jewelry and went after her lovers.

Why did she leave? Do you think that question didn't stand in front of me like some accusing inquisitor? Do you think I have not relived every moment of our marriage, looking for clues to her discontent, for things I might have done, or not done? You can live with someone for a long, long time and come to believe that you know the person as you know yourself. And then one day something happens and you wonder just who it was that shared your bed all those years. It's like looking at a face you've seen every day for your whole life and then you catch it in some unusual light, or perhaps up too close, or you stare at it for too long, and the familiar features that your eye has registered only as a whole, break into component parts, each of which is foreign.

Was it boredom? Was it some craving for some peculiar sexual activity of which I was unaware? Was it just for more money to buy certain luxuries I could not afford to give her? True, we were not wealthy, but neither were we destitute. I do not know why she left me and she never said. That was the worse torment of it all, not knowing—like suddenly being confronted by the city elders and sentenced to an indefinite term of isolation, yet never being told what you had done to deserve the punishment. But I did not stay hurt indefinitely. Eventually, I got angry. Very angry.

Our country was falling apart in front of me. Even from my relative shelter, the signs were everywhere. Markets were more boisterous and less safe. When I went, I kept my purse out of sight. Ruffians were more in evidence. It was a time when the good of the land kept their heads buried in their cloaks, letting the bias toward prurience have its natural expression. Prostitutes were more numerous, merchants less honest; the elders of the town who kept the peace were rarely seen. I started to hoard certain foodstuffs in the gullies above our house. More Assyrian soldiers were seen passing through the land without any challenge. And why should there have been? They were our masters as it turned out. Menahem kept his throne, and probably his head, by paying tribute to their king, Tiglath-pileser. It was raised by way of a poll tax—fifty shekels from each able-bodied male of fighting age. In all, sixty thousand of us were called on to make this annual contribution for the "maintenance of peace" in the land. I paid it once, and the next year, since I did not have it, took my children and hid in the hills above our house when the collector arrived.

How to describe it all to you? There is an old joke that says dementia is strictly a matter of majority sentiment. There was no self-restraint left in the land anywhere. And now we did not even have the strong hand of a king, good or bad, on the bridle. We were a horse that had spit out the bit and would not be subjected again. The only rule was that one could do what one wanted, provided that no one stronger interfered. Yahweh worship was not something to be debated, as if through public persuasion people could be brought back to the traditions that had safeguarded us in the past. Yahweh worship was simply not to be found. We had journeyed from a religious mosaic to a mess of offal. And the real tragedy was that we did not know how bad we smelled.

> When they go with their flocks and herds
> They will not find him, he has
> withdrawn himself from them.

When I wrote such things, there was no audience who cared to read. And always in my head there was this voice telling me that it was everyone else who walked crookedly, that my vision was still unclouded, that the energy with which sexual behaviors of every description were given a varnish of religious respectability was only self-delusion played out on a grand scale. There were times I thought I would go mad from the gap between the voice I heard and the noises of my world.

> Hear the words of Yahweh
> because He has a charge to bring against you who live in the land.
> There is no faithfulness,
> no love,
> no acknowledgment of God in the land.
> There is only cursing,
> lying and murder,
> stealing and adultery;
> they break all bounds, and bloodshed follows bloodshed.

The Marriage

But no one was listening to the words of Yahweh anymore. Amos had never returned to Bethel, even after Jeroboam died. A younger man called Micah[4] seemed to have received his mantle. He had a home base in Meresheth, about seventeen miles from where Amos lived. Like Amos, his pronouncements were mostly about our impending doom and I think part of his popularity was because he delivered a rousing good promise of punishment that was about to be meted out to us, his northern cousins. Throwing stones at your neighbours has a long and popular tradition, especially if you believe that Yahweh has supplied you with the ammunition. He took accurate aim with his oracles. Some came my way, of course. And even though I was on his side, so to speak, they stung nonetheless. Yes, I was Yahweh's barû, but that did not mean I could not be embarrassed for our nation. And I could not help but wonder what he thought of me. Did he think my marriage was just one more evidence of the depths to which the office of the prophet had been brought? Or worse, did he think I somehow profited from her profession, that I was her agent? Certainly I could not blame him if that was what he saw from a distance and concluded that there was mud on my cloak. I was never able to speak with him. The thought that I had been lumped in along with all the others was a cruel wound to carry.

I will make Samaria a heap of rubble.
I will pour her stones into the valley.
Since she has gathered her gifts from the wages of prostitutes,
as the wages of prostitutes they will again be used.
Israel's leaders judge for a bribe,
her priests teach for a price, and
her prophets tell fortunes for money.
If a liar or deceiver comes and says "I will prophesy for you plenty
of wine and beer,"
he would be just the prophet for this people!
The seers will be ashamed and the diviners disgraced.
They will cover their faces because there is no answer from
God.

How did I cope in those years? My children learned to be self-sufficient more quickly than most. Lo-Ruhamah, the middle one, had the worst of it. I was not equipped to guide a girl through the agonies of puberty, and she suffered for it. The boys fared better but not much. My public appearances were infrequent. Shechem was not receptive to marketplace oracles and Bethel was too far for me to go. The voice in my head became marks on parchment and little by little these began to circulate. I wondered if somewhere there wasn't a small boy who had been given the job of making a copy of my oracles, and if so, what he thought of them. It was my anger at Gomer's desertion that saved me. It was like food. It was the anodyne that kept me from bleeding to death on the inside. It was a force strong enough to counteract my humiliation. To be angry at her was a prism that caught the more diffused lament of the voice within, and concentrated it into potent protest. It was, I think, what gave my writings a certain raw edge—a bite that otherwise would have eluded me. The result was a kind of literary brilliance that drew attention not otherwise afforded to Yahweh oracles. There were, I think, those who read them just for their literary lustre. But it was a brilliance that came from splashing acid on dull copper, leaving the surfaces bright but the metal itself brittle as the core eroded under the strength of the acid. There is something unique about the drug of anger. Even though you know that something inside of you is hardening, receding under the strength of acidic bitterness, you don't care. You can't care. All you can think about is how your rage is justified, how, if given the chance, you would have your wife publicly whipped and then shorn for having violated the marriage bed so shamelessly. I drank deep from the draught of anger. That was how I survived.

Rebuke you mother.
Rebuke her for she is not my wife,
and I am not her husband.
Let her remove the adulterous look from her face
and the unfaithfulness from between her breasts.
Otherwise I will strip her naked and
make her as bare as the day she was born.

Our nation continued to rot away with a speed I would not have believed possible. Menahem died peacefully, and for that I was sorry. His son, Pekahiah, was not as smart or as lucky. Within two years he had been murdered in another coup, led by Pekah ben Remaliah, a palace official who had bided his time patiently until the Assyrian power behind the throne was distracted by its own internal problems enough to reduce its military presence in the area. That was when Pekah staged the coup, leading the populace into an orgy of nationalistic zeal. The poll tax was stopped. Tribute to Assyria was withheld. "Divinely sanctioned self rule" became the new mantra, and no one bothered to point out that the term was an oxymoron. Pekah joined us to an international conspiracy—the *Grand Coalition* it was called—that was absolute madness. There was trouble of some kind on the eastern borders of Assyria, six hundred miles away. Tiglath-pileser had withdrawn the bulk of his garrisons, which were strategically scattered through the area, so that he could use them closer to home. Rumour was that he faced superior forces—a propitious moment for us to escape his yoke if ever there was one.

We had gone beyond mere idolatry. Even our foreign neighbours evidenced a discipline and fidelity to their own gods that showed us to be the religious thrill seekers we were. And somehow our perversions had slopped over into our public affairs. When it came to international relations, we were hopelessly outclassed. Why Pekah ever thought he could outwit the Assyrian empire and regain a semblance of sovereignty I will never know. But clearly that was the political ambition he had used to garner support for his insurrection, so he could not have been alone in sharing this fantasy.

How to describe it? It was like watching an old whore gyrating her body in public, trying to catch the attention of some customer. You could not help but stop and stare; it was pathetic to watch. And because you could not cry, you laughed. Her breasts were stretched, fat hung around her waist, her haunches were large and jiggled, and you could see the blotches of broken blood vessels beneath her skin. Yet she would usually be so besotted she would mistake your laugh to mean arousal, so she would dance all the more obscenely in your direction, thinking she was close to catching a customer. It was a scene that made you retch both at her ugliness and at the illusion through which she observed her world.

Even I could not find it in me to tell this vision. Yet it was the one that stayed with me most consistently all through those years. The setting would change, as would certain details. Sometimes she would have the face of Gomer, but sometimes her face would be so disfigured I could not be sure who she was. Always in my mind I would see an aging prostitute, growing ever more grotesque as she became more frantic. In the end I chose a different metaphor to describe the debacle into which

Pekah was leading our country.

*Israel is like a dove, easily deceived and senseless—now calling to Egypt,
now turning to Assyria.
He makes a treaty with Assyria yet sends olive oil to Egypt.
Foreigners sap his strength but he does not realize it.
His hair is sprinkled with gray but he does not notice.
His arrogance testifies against him.
He is swallowed up among the nations like a worthless thing.
For they have gone up to Assyria like a wild donkey wandering alone.
But despite this he does not return to the* LORD *his God.*

It was my first act of mercy, this softening of what was in my mind. In retrospect, it was also my salvation.

But there was a sense in which our land itself took on life. Everywhere there were troops of militia, small cadres going to join the larger encampments, scouting parties, foreign divisions sent down from Syria, our northern neighbour. To people like us, it didn't much matter what regimental ensignia was in evidence. All soldiers stole; it was just a question of what they did to you after that. Farming necessarily became more haphazard. The number of our animals was reduced; we kept them in clusters hidden in makeshift enclosures in the ravines above our house. Foodstuffs were cached all over. We spread the risk of discovery across as wide an area as we could. As best I could make out, the coalition army was massing on our own southern border. There was no sign yet of an Assyrian force, which would come from the north when it came. Instead, Judah had refused to join the coalition, and for that he was to be punished.

Life somehow seemed to me to be lived out on two levels. Nationally, there was this feeling of confidence, the strutting of a yearling cock not yet blooded. Pekah rode the euphoria of independence that worked through the land like yeast in the dough.

*They are all adulterers, burning like an oven
   whose fire the baker need not stir
from the kneading of the dough till it rises.
On the day of the festival the princes
   become inflamed with wine
and the king joins hands with the mockers.*

220

Superficially at least, we looked to be masters of our own future. But for those of us not fabulously wealthy or powerful, the land was constantly shifting under our feet. Our own army was mostly provisional, and not overly disciplined. There is a special kind of lawlessness that accompanies the large-scale movement of troops back and forth through a countryside. The demarcation between donations of foodstuffs for the national cause of independence and extortion grew indistinct. The land shimmered with the metallic gleam of armour but the voice within said it was more like the shiny scales of an unclean reptile. Trust in one another had fled like a refugee. I kept a shelter in the hills. The children and I slept there more frequently.

Now, Ahaz, king of Judah, was not a follower of Yahweh. In fact, he followed most anything else except Yahweh. His penchant for the religiously grotesque was well known and did not stop even at child sacrifices. But he retained a singularly brilliant barû at his court. I never met the man named Isaiah but I would have given a decade from my life to sit at his table. Even at this early stage of his public office his oracles had an energy and punch that made mine feel like the rantings of feeble mind. I ferreted out as many of his oracles as I could.

I think it was the unassailable evidence of Isaiah's brilliance that kept Ahaz from doing him harm, not that he ever listened to any of the advice. Despite Ahaz's personal apostasy, Isaiah had promised that Yahweh's protection would intervene against the coalition armies. Isaiah had gone out of his way to assure the king, who was barely past twenty years old, that Yahweh would not abandon him. In fact he had gone so far as to tell Ahaz to ask for any kind of sign of assurance that he cared to choose, and Yahweh would grant it. Anything! If ever there was a chance to put the power of Yahweh to the test, surely there could not have been a better time. Nothing to lose, everything to gain. But Ahaz would have nothing to do with it! Instead he turned his head to the wall and obstinately declared that he was not going to ask anything from Yahweh, not now, not ever.

It was one of the most bizarre displays of pig-headedness ever recorded. That Yahweh would stoop to be a dancing bear for an arrogant king, and to have his offer rejected out of hand! Isaiah, so I was told, was beyond speech, such was his anger at the boy king. He gave him a portent anyway and promised that the proof of Yahweh's having saved Judah from the coalition was that a virgin from the house of David would some day give birth to a son and that his name would be called Immanuel—*God with us*. A strange and obscure utterance if ever there was one.

Jerusalem did not fall to the forces of Israel and Syria. There was a battle at Geba, fifteen miles south of Bethel, and Ahaz lost badly. I don't know exactly what the body count was. Some say it was as high as one hundred and twenty thousand men. Afterward, our troops marched back to Samaria, ecstatic at the victory. News of it swept ahead of the army like smoke blows ahead of a brush fire.

One of my brothers had gone with the army, and Jezreel had gone as his attendant. I needed to know if they were safe. Their safety however, was not the first thing that came to my mind when I heard of our success. My first thought was that now perhaps the troops would leave us alone, that they would have looted sufficient spoils to slake their appetite, and the meagre foods we had we could now keep. It was only later I realized that the food I hoped resided in the baggage animals of the returning army would have been forcibly seized from fellow Jews. I decided to travel to Samaria as part of the welcoming throng of curious people.

I did not go all the way into the city. The city was preparing a victory celebration that would cater to every debauched whim imaginable. My not entering the city had nothing to do with being a barû. The truth was I could not bear the thought of coming suddenly, by surprise, face to face with Gomer. I knew that if I entered the city I would search every face, strain at every woman's voice of sexual invitation. I did not want to meet her. I could not meet her. For both our sakes, I hoped she had not drifted to the capital, or worse, become a camp follower that I would see in the returning processional along with other trollops.

On its return to Samaria, the provisional army was met by a Yahwist holy man. Oded was his name, old by this time. I remember him as a friend of Beeri, although how he had managed to stay alive all these years living in the capital, I do not know. Old perhaps, but totally fearless, and with a voice of protest still strong and skillful enough to stop the returning militia in their tracks.

It is a commanding spectacle to observe a grand master of public speech confront and convert a popular mood. Like some great mountain bear with his fur tipped with silver, Oded stood in the centre of the highway and roared out his warning: If the returning troops did not release their prisoners and relinquish their stores of loot, then Yahweh would visit them with a punishment far worse than what they had just meted out themselves.

"Did you think you were allowed to make war on your brothers except as allowed by Yahweh?" shouted Oded. "Ahaz has violated the very house of God and shut its doors. For that Yahweh was angry and gave Judah into your hands as punishment." The marching troops, already in a leisurely formation, surrounded by their personal baggage and loot, looked more like a parade of nomads on their way to market than a returning army. I watched as the procession was parted in two by the unmoving figure of Oded as he stood like a rooted tree in the centre of the broad road that formed the approach to Samaria. As the companies marched by, they would slow, step aside and spread out so as to hear the conclusion of the man's address. Barûs know the power of words. Invisible though they are, when the words are true words, shaped on the anvil of deep conviction and loosed without fear, they are like a shower of arrows that find their way into people's hearts. Perhaps that is one of the marks of a true barû—he carries his sword in his mouth.

Oded pressed his warning.

"Do you think Yahweh's anger cannot rest on you as well? Because the LORD, the God of your fathers, was angry with Judah, he gave them into your hands. But you—you have slaughtered them with a rage that reaches the heavens. And if your excessive slaughter in battle was not enough, you now intend to make slaves of their wives and children. Send these prisoners back if you want to escape the vengeance of Yahweh. Clothe them with the cloth that comes from their own looms. Give them back their rings. Mount them on the asses you took from their barns and load them up with the seed corn that was in their storehouses."

It was not the homecoming welcome speech the victors had expected. Neither was the unexpected show of support that Oded received from a number of clan leaders. Azariah, Berekiah, Jehizkiah, and Amasa were four residents of the court who had never spoken out against Pekah, much less worked in unison. But they let it be known that they agreed with Oded. Furthermore, they let it be known they had sent word back to their family clans not to harbour the war prisoners or allow them any occupancy. Pekah bowed to this popular sentimentalism and did nothing. The homecoming turned into a sombre, almost sheepish affair. The usual drunken roughness to which prisoners were subjected, especially the females, instead became almost solicitous care for their comfort. Comic absurdity gripped the entire city. Samaria's streets would normally have hosted a more or less continuous, ribald party. Instead the streets became full of orderly soldiers, still in battle dress but now tending to the wounds of the very people they had force-marched back from Judah for the express purpose of enslavement. They emptied their supply sacks of food and drink. They returned stolen clothing, built shelters for the weak, and distributed healing salve. After a few days the prisoners were gathered and escorted under protective guard to the outskirts of Jericho, which lies just inside Judah's border but thirty miles from the centre of the battle.

When I heard the news, hope stirred in me. It had been so long that I thought the capacity for hope had forsaken me. But the story sounded as though it had sprung from the seeds of repentance. Yahweh's barû had been heeded, and a corporate act of mercy had been accomplished. I thought of Isaiah and Micah, of Oded and Amos and others in the land. I wished that my father were still alive. Perhaps the wave of idolatry they had stood against was finally spent, and this unprecedented relinquishment of battle wages was the signal for a new national sentiment, one of sober contrition. And yes, I did also think to myself, Gomer will return to me. Would Yahweh change the hearts of the many and ignore the one?

But my hope was premature. It was the only act of decency my nation would undertake in the rest of its existence. And shortly after Pekah's return from the southern campaign, the Assyrian beast, having swatted whatever insect had been bothering it at home, descended on the coalition with bloody-minded vengeance that was systematically brutal. The main force entered our lands along the coast, driving deep south, stopping only at the brook of Egypt, which was the natural edge of the Sinai wilderness. The Philistine coastal cities fell. Gaza, the seat of the original insurrection, was made to fall very hard. Damascus, capital city of our Syrian neighbours and home to King Rezin, was taken. Rezin was publicly killed and the bulk of the city's people deported to other jurisdictions. We were not exempt, of course. I think it was just the freakish fortunes of war that made us last in line to receive Assyrian retribution. We braced ourselves as best we could for the punishment we were about to receive.

What saved us was that Pekah was murdered in yet another palace intrigue. This time it was a group who had seen what had happened to our neighbours and had no wish for the same treatment. Hoshea ben Elah was the insurgent snake this time. He assassinated Pekah, had himself declared sovereign king over all of Israel, then promptly sent a formal surrender and vassal pledge to Tiglath-pileser. Assyrian troops did not in the end destroy Samaria, at least not then, although by the time all the new boundaries were decreed and four new Assyrian provinces were established, our King Hoshea, sovereign ruler over all of Israel, was left with a territory not much more than twenty by twenty miles square. In reality he was not much more than a collector of tribute, and this time the poll tax beggared us.

But we were not going to be left even this small patch of pseudo independence. Tiglath-pileser died and Hoshea, proving that he could be just as big a fool as his predecessor, withheld tribute. Instead, he sent an envoy to Egypt seeking military support against Assyria. Egypt promised everything and delivered nothing. So Assyrian troops marched against our capital, built siegeworks and settled into the slow but inevitable leveling of the city. The siege lasted two years. The surrounding countryside surrendered immediately on occupation, not that it protected them overly much. Assyrians did pretty much what they wanted to do. It was like a prolonged rape. And in the end, nothing remained of us as a nation. Extinguished.

I remember the beginning of the siege clearly because it was marked by a visit from Oded. He had fled in time and was on his way south to Judah. He stopped for a while with us, sharing news. The last night he was with us he did something most unusual. It was at our evening meal. Taking a small vial of oil from his purse, he went to my two younger children and touched their foreheads with his fingers. Then, with a hand on each, he turned and said: "Blessed be the God of Abram to whom he gave the name Abraham, and blessed be the God of Jacob to whom he gave the name Israel. And now, blessed be the God of you, Lo-Ruhamah, to whom he gives the name Ruhamah, meaning *Beloved*. And blessed be the God of you, Lo-Ammi, to whom he gives the name Ammi, meaning *My People*. From this day forward these are your names, for Yahweh desires you both for his own." He made no further comment and my children did not respond. Indeed, it was carried out so matter-of-factly that had Oded not carefully called them by their new names several times that evening, I might not have been sure he was serious.

He did not refer to it when we were alone later that night. Instead he asked about Gomer and if I ever thought of her.

I don't remember if he said anything else that night. What I do remember is the hours and hours that I talked to him about Gomer. How I hated her, the ridicule I had been subjected to, the capricious and abrupt departure, the loneliness, the humiliation at having been spurned by a prostitute. I read him some of the poetry I had written. It spoke of her blindness, of her pitiable self-deception, except that I did not pity her. I have never been listened to so attentively as that night that Oded received the harvest of my years alone.

It was not until we were saying good-bye the next morning that he quietly said to me, "I happen to know that Gomer lives now as an indentured menial in Tirzah. It's unlikely that I will be back this way again, Hosea. I feel this is a piece of knowledge that I should not take with me." He left me standing as one who had been turned to stone. The wounds I thought were now just jagged lines of scar tissue were as inflamed as if she had left yesterday.

My days and nights started to run together after that. There was no peace and no escape from the voice within. As long as I had not known her whereabouts, I had been exempt from having to make any attempt to restore us. The pose of abandoned, cuckolded husband nursing his justifiable anger had been seven years in its formation. I now wore the image with ease. By then Gomer had faded to a kind of shadowy image, a useful object to be used as an illustration. It was only by depersonalizing her, blunting her talons, that I had survived. And in one brief sentence, Oded had pierced my defenses. Gomer was still my wife. It was no longer a question of whether she wanted to return. She could not, having sold herself into lifelong servitude. The decision to act or not act had been neatly returned to me, and it never let up its torment. Could I leave her in the wretched circumstances to which she had succumbed? If I did, who then had really broken the marriage covenant? Did she even want to return to me?

The voice within said that Gomer's state of mind was irrelevant. The voice said the only thing that mattered was my own actions. The degree of Gomer's gratitude, should I decide to rescue her this second time could neither be calculated in advance, or insisted on afterward. The probability was that even if Gomer did welcome my re-entry into her life, it would be a temporary sentiment.

No, the only thing within my control was whether I still loved her enough to redeem her. The voice never wavered asking me this essential question. Try as I did to reframe the facts, shift the focus from me to her, the voice would not let me sidestep this. Yahweh was not angry in his asking. But he was unswerving. In time it occurred to me that it was not my question only. Abraham's children had betrayed the trust placed in them. It seemed that Yahweh, too, in the end could control only his own actions. I thought about Samaria, and the siege that had begun. Had Yahweh decided to answer the question? Did I still love Gomer? Did Yahweh still love us?

A true barû spends most of his life wishing he were anything except what he is. It is a life filled mostly with rejection or at best, misunderstanding. Occasionally though, there are moments of such intimate communication with the God we serve that the years of harsh service are forgotten. Yahweh's voice slowly became muted, but it was not that he was removing himself, like the voice of someone leaving the room. It was the words themselves I had trouble hearing, as if he had shifted dialects, the syllables of which were muffled and indistinct. Because I could not recognize the words, I started instead to listen to the tone. It was the sound of a man trying to talk but who has started to cry and whose voice is now so husky and broken that what he says is washed away in his tears. In all the years the voice and I kept company, I had never wondered who there was to comfort God, and where he turned when he cried. To see a suffering God, and cry along with him: That was my life's work.

So I took what coin money I still had, fifteen shekels of silver, and a pannier full of barley. Since I had no horse, I fastened strips of leather to the pannier so that I could carry it on my back. My forehead bore some weight as well from a flat thong that rested just below my head covering. It took me three days to get to Tirzah, all of thirty miles away. But by this time the land was filled either with Assyrian troops or refugees. In my vulnerability I could take no chances of losing my barley. It was all I had with which to buy back Gomer.

I found the household to which she had sold herself. In a strained and painful conversation with the master I gave him all I had brought with me. Who knows what he thought about me. Certainly from my uncertain speech and obvious discomfiture he knew I was no merchant. The price of a slave among our people is thirty shekels and has been that price since first established by Moses. I wasn't exactly certain what my barley was worth. I had supposed there would be some kind of premium charged me for not being able to pay the entire price in coins. But on the other hand, foods of all kinds were more highly valued during war times. In normal times my barley alone was worth thirty shekels. I had thought perhaps to leave again with either my coins, or half my grain. But the master of the house demanded both, and would not let me even see Gomer until I had been relieved of everything I had brought. He was my master too when it came to trade. I scarcely recall our conversation. He must have seen that I would not leave without Gomer. Did I pay too much for her, a badly used whore, now past her prime, good only for menial work? If you have to ask the question, you have understood nothing of my story.

She was summoned from the back of the house and I checked myself just in time from gasping aloud. The years had not just been hard on her—they had been cruel.

We left and spoke hardly at all. She seemed a little unclear about where she was and where I was taking her. I wondered if she even knew who I was. But she allowed me to lead her readily enough and we made it home. Home. By the time we arrived, she had begun to shiver. She kept working her tongue over her lips. There was sweat on her forehead. The cause of her suffering I could only guess at but I had a premonition that the path back would be full of pain. In the end, I decided not to take her to the house. What purpose would it serve for the children to see her in this condition? Besides, I did not entirely trust her mind; it, too, seemed damaged in some way. Instead I made a place for her in our barn, and when I left to gather things from the house, I locked the door.

I cared for her insofar I could. In the days that followed it seemed she got worse. The cloth over the pallet of straw was always damp from her sweat whenever I checked. Often the meals I brought would not have been touched. Instead I would find her curled on her pallet, legs tightly folded up into her chest, deep in some kind of delirium. Despite all the wraps, she always seemed cold. Another time, she tried to rush past me to the door, and when I blocked her path she leaped on me, trying to bite free of the hand that held her. I gave her the things I thought would do her most good—breads, stews, warm milk from goats, a little cheese. But no wine or strong drink.

Once when I came at midday to check on her she was awake, hunched over on her knees, leaning against the barn wall. I paused just inside the door, uncertain what to do.

"What are you staring at?" she finally said. "Come to inspect your merchandise and see if you got your money's worth?" The voice was mean and tinged with hysteria.

I did not answer her immediately. In truth I wanted to hit her. I wanted to take her shoulders and shake her so violently that her head would whip back and forth like the head of young piglet when you've broken its neck. I wanted to shout at her, "Why, why, why? Why did you run off and leave me? Am I not worthy even of a reason?" But I said only, "I've come to see if you need anything."

"You've come to see if I am grateful. You've come to see if I have come to my senses and will ask a thousand pardons for the terrible way I have abused you. You've come to get the proof you so desperately want that will make this whole thing my fault. It's not me that needs anything, it's you." She was worked up. Her eyes were bright but whether from a fever or fit, I had no idea. At that moment I did not care.

"I've come to see if you need anything," I repeated myself, aware of how stupid it must sound. And then finally, "And yes, since you seem to have the strength to talk about things, it would be nice to know what it was that drove you away seven years ago."

She sprang to her feet and for a moment I wondered if she was going to charge me. Instead she tore the front of her tunic downward exposing one breast. "All right, you want to know and I will tell you. See this? Take a good look, Hosea. You are disgusted with what you see. My breasts have stretched and are flat. My vulva is splayed wide from entry by a thousand different men who differed only in their degree of roughness. Do you think I wanted to live this way? Have you no understanding of the word compulsion? Do you know what it is like to have desires that you are helpless against?

"I thought you happy at the thought of leaving..." I had started the sentence wrong and was now in terribly precipitous territory. I started again. "I thought you were happy to become my wife. You seemed so at home here. You visited me in my dreams. Yahweh approved of us."

"Yahweh approved of us!" She was now yelling at me with all her strength. "That was the first thing that was wrong. Did you ever stop to think how I might feel about being singled out to become some kind of object lesson for you and the rest of your holy freaks to gape at? Was I destitute when you found me? Did I ask for your disparaging notoriety? I was content just to live life the way I was. But you couldn't leave me alone. You want to know what bothered me most all those years? It was having to endure the knowledge that all through the land people were huddling over your little scraps of parchment, clucking their tongues at the naughty things I had done. I could not even hold my head up high in front of my children—children of adultery—that's what you called them once. That, and those freakish names that they had to wear like the marks of Cain. Oh yes, I am not so illiterate as you assumed all these years." She had come close, close enough for flecks of her spittle to light on my beard but she kept yelling at me.

"You want a simple answer. But you have no idea what agony it was to live with you. All the time, when you weren't giddy with the affirmation that Beeri and his visitors heaped on your work, you were off in some kind of mysterious communication with your voice. There were days when your self-righteousness stunk worse than this barn. And if you were righteous, did you ever once bother to think how big a gulch was being dug between us? I never despised you for what you did. But I despaired finally of ever crossing over. But you wouldn't understand what it's like to live without the freedom to choose. You don't know what it's like to be in the dark, groping for the door. You don't understand what it's like to be driven. You don't understand what it's like to be willing to walk ten miles just for the chance to drink enough raisin wine to forget your torment, if only for an hour. You don't understand what it's like to be so crazed for any kind of touch that recognizes you for who you really are, that you would take the hands of a customer regardless of what he paid you. But you Hosea, you never wanted to believe that I was as bad off as I really was. We could never start from where I was, only from where you were. You don't understand. You don't understand."

She had come close enough to finally be touching me, pushing her hands into my chest as she finished, crying, flailing and finally sagging her body into mine. I held her up with my arms around her as she kept sobbing and choking into the circle of my arms and chest. I found myself crying with her. We stood like that together, each crying, in the darkness of a broken-down barn in the middle of a broken-down land. I wished with all my heart that someone would come. Someone who could explain it all to us both—that Oded would return, that another barû, older than I, would suddenly appear. But there was only the two of us. I could not respond to what she had said. How much of her hardship could have been avoided if I had been a better husband? It was a road I could not go down. Instead, I blurted out the single thought that had taken over my entire mind.

"Gomer, Gomer, I've been lonely without you. I've hurt so bad while you were gone."

The fourth morning I noticed a change. She was still asleep when I entered and I stood in the gloom. Slivers of light trickled through the many breaches of the wall and caught the dust bits that hung in the air. Across her body two shafts of light fell, and in the light of them, I saw her chest moving in a steady rhythm. Above her in the light, the dust moved lazily as it was pushed and swirled by little gusts of air. It was a slow and peaceful dance. My eyes started to link the swirls together and I made believe I was seeing the antics of angels come to watch over my wife. Whatever illness had possessed her body these last three days had left. I went back to the house and returned with a bucket of water, rags, a washing stone, ointment, comb and a new tunic. These I left by her pallet and withdrew. Later in the day her children visited her and by afternoon, leaning on their arms, she took a halting walk in the yard. Life was starting over.

> When Israel was a child I loved him,
> and out of Egypt I called my son.
> But the more I called Israel,
> the further they went from me.
> They sacrificed to the Baals and they burned incense to images.
> It was I who taught Ephraim to walk,
> taking them by the arms;
> but they did not realize it was I who healed them.
> I led them with cords of human kindness,
> with ties of love;
> I lifted the yoke from their neck
> and bent down to feed them.

Two years later Samaria was taken. In their rage at having been

defied by such a small impudent nation, the Assyrians smashed the walls. King Hoshea, who had gone himself to petition for the saving of his city, was summarily taken captive, and some twenty-seven thousand people were sent overland to Assyria. It was the end of us as a people. Judah was now all that remained of the twelve tribes that had come from Egypt to occupy this "promised" land.

We hid in the hills during those last months. Life was too precarious and the Assyrians followed a policy of mass deportation with rigour. Gomer and I spoke infrequently but comfortably, and never about her time away. I pursued my oracle writing and she took the daily responsibilities of our fugitive life. Her health improved. A measure of serenity entered her. We were now more impoverished than before, yet I confess to a happiness that was given me from beyond. This was the period of my greatest hope, though I had no clear picture of how Yahweh intended to redeem his people. Foreign groups from elsewhere in the Assyrian empire would shortly resettle here. In very little time we would lose our tribal distinctives and dissolve into a dubious lineage.

I was content to live in the quiet of the metaphor once more. For if Yahweh had changed the heart of one, how could he ignore the condition of the many? It was enough. I would wait.

Therefore I am now going to allure her;
I will lead her into the desert
and speak tenderly to her.
There I will give her back her vineyards,
and will make the place of Jezreel a place of hope.
There she will sing as in the days of her youth,
as in the day she came up out of Egypt.
In that day, declares the LORD,
you will call me "my husband;"
you will no longer call me "my master."
I will remove the names of the Baals from her lips;
I will betroth you to me forever;
I will betroth you in righteousness and justice,
in love and compassion.
I will betroth you in faithfulness,
and you will acknowledge the LORD.

Endnotes:
[1] Joel's writings can be found in the Old Testament.
[2] II Kings 14:25
[3] The writings of Amos can be found in the Old Testament, immediately following the writings of Hosea.
[4] Micah's writings can be found in the Old Testament

About the Author

Rob Alloway spent fifteen years as a printing executive and holds an MBA from the University of Western Ontario. At the same time he has maintained a lively interest in biblical studies, having graduated from Regent College in 1980. Since leaving the printing industry to pursue writing, he has taught Old Testament at a small Bible college in Toronto, and remains active in a variety of non-profit organizations.

Printed in the United States
2786

9 781573 831413